ABOVE AND BEYOND

THE AVIATION MEDALS OF HONOR

BARRETT TILLMAN

FOREWORD BY JOE FOSS

SMITHSONIAN INSTITUTION PRESS
WASHINGTON · LONDON

Lord, guard and guide the men who fly
through the great spaces of the sky.
Be with them always in the air
in dark'ning storm or sunlight fair.
Oh hear us when we lift our prayer
for those in peril in the air.
—*The Navy Hymn*

Copy editor: Jack Kirshbaum
Production editor: Ruth G. Thomson
Designer: Jody Billert

Library of Congress Cataloging-in-Publication Data
Tillman, Barrett.
Above and beyond : the aviation Medals of Honor / Barrett Tillman ; foreword by Joe Foss.
p. cm.
Includes bibliographical references and index.
ISBN 1-58834-056-2 (alk. paper)
1. Medal of Honor. 2. United States—Armed Forces—Medals, badges, decorations, etc. 3. Aeronautics, Military—United States—History. 4. Air pilots, Military—United States—Biography. I. Title.
UG977.T54 2002
358.4.11342—dc21 2002023038

British Library Cataloging-in-Publication available

Manufactured in the United States of America
09 08 07 06 05 04 03 02 5 4 3 2 1

∞ The paper used in this publication meets the minimum requirements of the American National Standard for Information Sciences—Permanence of Paper for Printed Library Materials ANSI Z39.48-1984.

CONTENTS

FOREWORD

Those of us who survive war represent those who don't. That's why I have such great appreciation of our veterans, regardless of their branch of service, because they're all part of the team that defends our nation from foreign enemies. Whatever you do in life, you'll succeed if you work as a team. That's what I learned on Guadalcanal.

When VMF-121 landed there in October 1942, I'm not sure that I knew what all the medals were. But I do know that medals were as far from our minds as the far side of the moon. We were outnumbered and outgunned, short of just about everything. What we had going for us was great leadership, the kind you'll read about in these pages. We had genuine heroes, and I don't mean the blue-haired sports figures that some kids look up to today. I mean real leaders like Joe Bauer, John L. Smith, and Bob Galer, to name a few. Oh, we had some ticket punchers among regular officers who thought they were too valuable to get shot at, but those birds were weeded out pretty fast and we got on with the war, thanks to the young reservists who filled most of our squadrons.

At Guadalcanal I felt that all you had to do was show up; the rest was provided. Free gas and ammo, all the shooting you could want, and no bag limit. But I felt then and feel today that too much is made of the hero business, or what I called "the dancing bear act," involving countless speeches and appearances. At "Cactus" we were simply doing what was expected of us, whether it was flying airplanes, keeping them flying, cooking Japanese rice, or manning a Browning machine gun up on the ridge.

I learned pretty quick that combat is a dangerous occupation. There's no way to make war safe so the thing to do is make it dangerous for the other side. In the Solomons the enemy was mighty dangerous, too. Whatever we thought of the Japanese after Pearl Harbor, you didn't take them for granted.

Having been in the Congressional Medal of Honor Society for so many years, I've been privileged to know some of the finest men and greatest fliers this country ever produced. They ranged from Eddie Rickenbacker to Jimmy

Doolittle and Charlie Lindbergh, and included, of course, my fellow marines, among them Jeff DeBlanc, Kenny Walsh, and Jim Swett. For my money, the greatest fighter pilot I ever knew was Marion Carl. Why he didn't get the Medal of Honor is something I'll never figure out. But whether a man was awarded a medal or not, he was the only one who really knew the score, because he set his own standards.

Standards are important, especially for youngsters who have so many bad influences these days. That's why I'm big on history and museums. Some folks ask if I was in World War I, and I tell them "No, I missed that one," but I try to point them in the right direction. If we lose our history, we lose our national identity, and I don't ever want that to happen. That's why I'm so glad that Barrett Tillman has written this book—it's part of our history that needs to be studied for generations to come.

Joe Foss

PREFACE AND ACKNOWLEDGMENTS

This book originated with an article I wrote for *Flight Journal,* which was seen by Mark Gatlin of the Smithsonian Institution Press. He urged me to develop a book proposal, and because we had enjoyed a pleasant affiliation when he was with another publisher, we quickly sealed a deal. Then I realized how large a task I had set myself.

Apart from the number of Medal of Honor airmen (more than one hundred, depending on how they are reckoned) was the variety of related subjects, including the Navy's ill-managed Tiffany Cross between 1919 and 1942. The research was further complicated by the fact that four air arms are represented among aviation Medals of Honor: the Army, Air Force (including its iterations in both world wars), Navy, and Marine Corps. Each presented its own challenges and rewards.

Research into the Medal of Honor actions demonstrated the danger of relying on single sources—especially official sources. A surprising number of citations contained significant errors, such as location, circumstances, and even whether the recipient survived. In one instance it was necessary to consult six individuals directly or indirectly involved in an episode to determine where it occurred—disproving the official version. Many other citations contained exaggerations obviously intended to improve chances of the medal being awarded.

Other examples abound: a citation written by committee during a "lost weekend"; a medal offered to avert court martial of a favored subordinate; two or more awards to fallen comrades who probably performed none of the feats ascribed to them. Still other in-flight medals were presented in clear violation of the criteria, including at least three which were unwitnessed.

This volume may repeat some previous errors. If so, corrections are sought from knowledgeable readers.

Meanwhile, it is important to remember that Medal of Honor recipients do not write their own citations. In fact, nearly half of the awards were posthumous. Therefore, whatever the flaws of specific citations, each represents a man who willingly placed himself in harm's way. These pages contain acts of sublime courage and self-sacrifice which should—but probably will not—shame a popular culture increasingly unable to distinguish between heroism and celebrity, between warriors and mere athletes. A naval aviator who contributed to this volume wrote, "War is a full contact sport." The distinction needs to be maintained.

It took weeks to determine that the Department of Defense has no central collection of images of those who hold the nation's highest award. Therefore, it was necessary to make separate contacts in the Air Force, Army, Navy, and Marine Corps, as well as civilian sources. The situation was further complicated by nonstandard criteria for electronic images.

However, in documenting the aviation Medals of Honor I found scores of helpful, knowledgeable people. Dr. Richard Hallion, a longtime friend and colleague who also serves as Air Force Historian, backed the project literally from before the beginning. Other colleagues who consistently performed "above and beyond" include Jim Sawruk, Roy Grossnick, Hill Goodspeed, and Ron Thurlow.

Various archives provided assistance, including the Air Force History Support Office; Air Force Museum; Army Aviation Center; Army Aviation Museum; Marine Corps History and Museums Branch; Navy Historical Center; the Beuhler Library of the National Museum of Naval Aviation; Champlin Fighter Museum; National Warplanes Museum; and Pima Air Museum.

Sources and contacts were developed via the Air Force Association, the Marine Corps Aviation Association; the Marine Corps Vietnam Helicopter Association; the Tailhook Association; the Vietnam Helicopter Flight Crew Network; the B-24 Liberator Club; and Jefferson (Iowa) Area Chamber of Commerce. Unit organizations were the 43rd, 44th, 92nd, 98th, 303rd, 306th, 394th, and 452nd Bomb Group Associations; the 18th Fighter Wing Association; and the 11th Armored Cavalry Association.

Online resources proved invaluable, as did the convenience of e-mail contact with many individuals and organizations who collectively provided more than 90 percent of the basic data. I am grateful to the Aerodrome, Aerothenic.com, Australia@War, AviationArchives.com, B26.COM, Black Horse, HeavyBombers.com, Home of Heroes, Jollygreen.org, Ken's Men,

Kunsan Airbase, Misawa Airbase, Pacificwrecks.com, Twelve O'Clock High, OV-10Bronco.net, and ww1.org web sites.

More than a hundred people contributed to this project, including a cadre of Medal of Honor airmen: Jeff DeBlanc, Henry Erwin, Fred Ferguson, Ed Freeman, Joe and Didi Foss, Bob Galer, Tom Hudner, Mike Novosel, Jim Swett, Leo Thorsness, the late Jim Howard, Dave McCampbell, and Ken Walsh. Ken was especially close for three decades. I'll never forget that first visit: he had just rebuilt his lawnmower engine and he asked: "Does your car need a tuneup?" Later he liked to say, "I raised Tillman from a pup," and he made a point of phoning on my birthday.

I have also benefited from close contact with Bud Day and Jim Stockdale, cited in the "Aviation Related" segments of the Vietnam chapter.

Contact with Medal of Honor relatives included Doug Walker, Jim and Sharon Vance Kiernan, and Harl Pease's cousin Fay Benton. Michael L. Mills and Claude "Bud" Knight are great nephews of Frank Luke and Raymond Knight, respectively.

Others with connections to Medal of Honor actions include Lt. Col. Joe Forster, USAF (Ret.), and Jack Purdy, who flew with Bong and McGuire; Ed Hinrichs of Gott and Metzger's group; Norm Whalen, Kane's navigator; Col. Edward M. Jacquet, USAF (Ret.), Pease's flight leader; Russell Strong of Smith's bomb group; John Kilgore, son of Vance's navigator; Jack Leonard, an aircrewman in Van Voorhis's squadron; Brig. Gen. Bill Webster USAF (Ret.), a pilot in Wilkins's squadron; Maj. Ken Carpenter, USAF (Ret.), Levitow's pilot; Darrel Whitcomb, Bennett's fellow FAC; Brig. Gen. John C. Bahnsen, USA (Ret.), Chuck Rollins, and Mike Gorman who flew with Yano; MGYSgt. LeRoy N. Poulson, USMC (Ret.), Pless's gunner; and Comdr. John B. Nichols, USN (Ret.), Estocin's wingman.

Thanks also go to Guy Acteo; Terry Aitken; Trevor J. Allen; Nick Arabinko; Dave Armstrong; John D. Barber; Alan H. Barbour; Yvonne Barnett; Nick Beale; John Beaman; Lt. Col. Duane E. Biteman, USAF (Ret.); Capt. John H. Burton, USN (Ret.); Paul Cahill; Lt. Col. Anthony C. Cain, USAF; CMSgt. Bill Cannon, USAF (Ret.); CWO-4 Jim Casey, USMC (Ret.); Chris Charland; Michael Claringbould; Jerry Clearman; Sam Cole; John Cook; Danny Crawford; Robert C. Cressman; Ferdinando D'Amico; Vern Dander; Larry Davis; Robert F. Dorr; Maj. Hugh Dow, USAF (Ret.); Peter Dunn; Robert D. Elliot;

Dr. Steve Ewing; Robert Forsyth; Ed Gilmore; Lt. Col. Harry Gobrecht, USAF (Ret.); Skip Guidry; Herb Harper; William N. Hess; Jack Heyn; Lawrence J. Hickey; Larry Hinson; Brig. Gen. Jay Hubbard, USMC (Ret.); Toji Kakaki; Jack Kleinsorg; Jim Lansdale; Doug Lantry; Bob LaPointe; W. David Lewis; Jack Lopez; John B. Lundstrom; Harold Luntey; Lex McAulay; John McTasney; Steve Maxham; Dave Menard; Maj. Gen. John O. Moench, USAF (Ret.); Jeff Nash; Graeme Neale; Janice Olson; Terry Olson; Dr. Frank Olynyk; Brian D. O'Neill; Donald Pearson; Jerry Penry; Charlie Rains; Simon Rhodes; Comdr. Steve Riordan, USN (Ret.); Chuck Rouhier; Garry Roush; Henry Sakaida; Eldon Shook; Comdr. Doug Siegfried, USN (Ret.); Stephen Skinner; Michael A. Smith; Mike Starn; Doug Sterner; Osamu Tagaya; Justin Taylan; Henry J. Thompson; Scott Thompson; Dr. Wayne Thompson; Andrew Toppan; Capt. Dean Veremakis, USN (Ret.); Timothy Warnock; George Welsh; W. Edward White; and Dr. James W. Williams.

1

HERITAGE OF VALOR

Americans did not invent courage but they did invent aviation, and the melding of the two produced a heritage of aerial valor that spanned most of the twentieth century.

After the Cold War a new generation grew up regarding military aviation as a bloodless, risk-free enterprise; a sanitary application of sleek aircraft, precision weapons, and restrained violence eerily similar to popular electronic games. Airpower played a dominant role in the 1991 war with Iraq and frequently provided leverage elsewhere, including the Middle East and the Balkans. Indeed, airmen's long-awaited pure aviation victory in Kosovo seemed to indicate that the technological and doctrinal millennium had arrived slightly ahead of schedule. The NATO "war" in Kosovo was prosecuted with the loss of only two aircraft and no pilots. Far heavier losses occurred in stateside training than in combat.

It was not always so.

In the First World War at least 680 U.S. Air Service fliers were killed in action or in training. During World War II the Army Air Force lost some 13,000 pilots and aircrew inside the continental United States and combat attrition was more than four times that figure. Subsequently, the Korean and Vietnam Wars resulted in 2,965 U.S. Air Force combat deaths.

More than 7,100 Navy and Marine Corps airmen and crew were killed in World War II aircraft carrier operations alone, plus 253 Korean War carrier personnel and 704 from Tonkin Gulf carriers. In the Korean and Vietnam Wars, aviation was so critical to the U.S. Navy effort that nearly 80 percent of all KIAs were fliers.

In short, well over 65,000 American aviation personnel were killed in action during the twentieth century.

The Pyramid of Valor

Like their counterparts ashore and afloat, airmen were awarded the Medal of Honor "for distinguishing themselves by conspicuous gallantry and courage at risk of their own lives, above and beyond the call of duty." Originating in the War between the States, the U.S. Navy medal was established by Congress in December 1861 (hence the misnomer "Congressional Medal of Honor"); the Army version followed in July 1862. The Medal of Honor remained the only significant U.S. military decoration until 1918. As of 2001 some 3,437 individual Americans had received the Medal of Honor, though the number grows almost annually as waivers are granted or deferred awards are made.

The medal's long history is filled with contradiction and controversy, partly owing to erratic award criteria. The Army and Navy present their own versions of the medal, with differing eligibility requirements. For example, the award was not originally available to officers, and the Navy permitted awards for noncombat events until the eve of World War II. (One was subsequently awarded in violation of the combat requirement.)

The first medals presented for foreign combat went to marines and sailors involved in Korea in 1871. The Medal of Honor Legion was formed in 1890 "to protect the integrity of the medal" and foreshadowed today's Congressional Medal of Honor Society. The legion was particularly concerned with the large number of retroactive medals presented until the turn of the century, when anyone could nominate himself for the decoration.

Significant changes occurred during and after the "Great War." In 1916–17 an Army board examined all Medals of Honor awarded to date, resulting in 911 being rescinded, mostly from the Civil War. The medal had been presented for as little reason as reenlisting or for guarding President Lincoln's casket, and the board closed some egregious loopholes while authorizing "final" medals for Civil War action fifty-two years before.

The "pyramid of valor" emerged in July 1918 with the establishment of the Distinguished Service Cross and the Citation Star, which became the Silver Star in 1932, as well as the Purple Heart for combat wounds. The Bronze Star followed in World War II. The Navy Cross resulted from the Medal of Honor consolidation act of 1919, though the "cross" remained subordinate to the Distinguished Service Medal until August 1942.

With emergence of military aviation, specific medals also appeared as airmen became eligible for the Distinguished Flying Cross (1926) and the lesser Air Medal (1942). Both were presented for varying degrees of achievement "in aerial flight." Richard Byrd and Charles Lindbergh were among the first recipients of the Distinguished Flying Cross, but each later received the Medal of Honor for the same events. In subsequent cases the lesser decoration usually was rescinded so the Medal of Honor could be presented.

Another significant decoration emerged from concern over different Army and Navy criteria. In 1919, when Congress amended the warrant, the Navy established a Maltese cross version of the medal while retaining the previous five-pointed star. The intention was to present separate awards for combat and noncombat action. The new medal, known as the Tiffany Cross, was designed by the famous New York jeweler. However, even today it is uncertain which was intended as the combat decoration. The Navy web site says the Tiffany Cross was a noncombat award; the Congressional Medal of Honor Society says it was the combat decoration. Queries to both sources went unanswered.

Some sources state that twenty-one Navy men and eight marines received "the Tiffany," which is exactly the number of awards for World War I. However, five marines received both the Navy and Army awards whereas one got the Army medal, presumably leaving two recipients of the proper Navy version.

Furthermore, photographic evidence shows that Richard Byrd and Floyd Bennett received the Tiffany Cross for their polar flight, and Christian Schilt received it for Nicaraguan combat. Poorly documented, incompetently administered, and generally unpopular, the Tiffany was discontinued in 1942.

Award criteria for aviation medals broadly reflected the problems in recognizing land and sea actions. For instance, during World War I the first aviation-related Medals of Honor were Navy citations for lifesaving. At the time it was a legitimate policy since the naval warrant did not require combat action. Additionally, most Great War Medals of Honor were upgrades of Distinguished Service Crosses or Navy Crosses, presented well after the armistice.

Generally, Medals of Honor were awarded for a specific action, though several recognized consistent performance over a prolonged period, including most of the World War II Marine Corps awards. No aviation citation was more extended than Joe Foss's, covering fifty-one days at Guadalcanal during late 1942 and early 1943. Similar situations existed for other marines, including Henry Elrod, John Smith, Robert Galer, Ken Walsh, Greg Boyington, and Robert Hanson, whose actions were recognized for periods between two days and three months. Top Navy ace Dave McCampbell's citation also specified two actions four months apart.

Multiple events were recognized for a handful of Army Air Force recipients, including Harl Pease, Richard Bong, Thomas McGuire, and Raymond Knight.

Though the Air Force became an independent branch of the armed forces in 1947, the Army medal was presented for Korean War action (1950–53). A specific Air Force version was authorized in 1956 and first presented in 1967.

Criteria for the Medal of Honor are specified in Title 10, U.S. Code, under different sections for each service. Army and Air Force regulations require nomination within two years of the action and presentation within three, whereas the Navy stipulates recommendation within three years and presentation in five.

Several aviation Medals of Honor were delayed, presumably requiring withdrawal of the original decoration. The most prominent case was Eddie Rickenbacker's. His action occurred in 1918 but the medal was not presented until 1930—a lapse of twelve years.

The "escape clause" permitting awards long after the action is Section 3744(d). It allows the service secretary to present delayed medals if "no award was made because the statement was lost or through inadvertence the recommendation was not acted on." In some instances the active factor was not inadvertence but political spite, as in Theodore Roosevelt's case.

Consequently, medals are still being awarded more than a century after the fact. Some were the result of lost paperwork or bureaucratic inefficiency; others were retroactive upgrades of lesser medals presumably requiring waivers of the statutory requirements. Some were due to political patronage.

The one certainty about the Medal of Honor is that its final history will never be written.

Foreign Medals

Some foreign decorations are compared to the Medal of Honor, though the philosophy and application of each medal inevitably is different. Of all top awards, probably the British criteria for the Victoria Cross (VC) is most comparable.

The VC was established in 1856 and has been described as "the British equivalent of the Medal of Honor." In truth, the VC warrant has been more consistently adhered to, as the Medal of Honor frequently has been presented for professional excellence rather than performance above and beyond the call of duty. Because of the novel nature of air combat in World War I, the earliest aviation VCs were awarded for what later became familiar events. For example, two pilots received Victoria Crosses for destroying Zeppelins in 1915–16, but subsequent "Zep slayers" usually received the Distinguished Service Order.

Other VCs were presented for bringing back a severely damaged aircraft and saving a crewman from death or capture. One such recipient was Sergeant Tom Mottershead, who died of injuries received while dragging his gunner from their burning plane. However, perhaps the redoubtable Mottershead already should have received the VC for shooting up a German airdrome—after landing his FE-2b on the enemy field!

But even the Victoria Cross has been erratically applied. For instance, fifteen of the nineteen aviation awards in World War I represented air-to-air combat, but only two of the twenty-four in World War II went to "fighter boys," including a shipping attack. By comparison, eighteen World War II Medals of Honor were presented to fighter pilots, of whom sixteen were aces.

Two air VCs became controversial, both involving fighter pilots. In 1917 Canadian William A. Bishop received the ultimate award based on his own account of a solo attack on a German airfield, in which he claimed three planes shot down. Despite lack of the required witnesses (no German records sustain the claim), the empire's highest honor was bestowed.

Nearly a year later another controversial VC was based on the erroneous impressions of the recipient's squadronmates. Lieutenant Alan Jerrard was shot down in combat with Austro-Hungarian aircraft and was awarded the Victoria Cross while a prisoner. After the war, when enemy records were available, it was obvious that the confusion common to combat had given Jerrard's squadronmates inaccurate impressions of the fight.

In summary, an Australian historian has theorized that one-third of VCs were definitely justified; one-third possibly were not; and the remainder were awarded "for surviving a major cock-up by higher headquarters." Survival certainly was a consideration, as nearly half the "air VCs" in World War II were posthumous awards. Including men who were killed after receiving the decoration, sixteen of twenty-four were lost—a staggering 67 percent loss rate.

Although the Victoria Cross was awarded for lifesaving as well as offensive actions, the German criteria focused on life taking. Damage to the enemy was the sole requirement for the *Pour le Mérite,* with 687 issued in World War I; eighty-one went to airmen, including two senior officers. No aviation "Blue Maxes" were awarded for single acts—all represented repeated prowess, usually after long strings of aerial victories. However, the Prussian award also went to observation or bomber pilots and Zeppelin commanders, as well as to aircraft and balloon observers with consistent records of success. In a war dominated by artillery, the best "spotters" were worth more than squadrons of fighters.

Among *Jagdfliegern,* the criteria for the *Pour le Mérite* steadily climbed throughout the war. In January 1916 Max Immelmann and Oswald Boelcke were the first fliers to receive the decoration, after eight victories. By year's end the requirement had doubled, and in mid-1917 nominally twenty *abschusse* were the yardstick. At war's end about thirty shootdowns were required before Germany's highest honor was bestowed.

Whatever the flier's mission, the main distinction between the *Pour le Mérite* and the Medal of Honor or Victoria Cross was eligibility: the "Blue Max" was only presented to living officers. Of the seventy-nine combat recipients, thirty-one died in the war, a 39 percent mortality rate.

In World War II the Knight's Cross parameters were more varied. In fact, the Nazi regime was far more democratic in its decoration policies; Adolf Hitler ensured that the *Ritterkreuz* was available to enlisted men and noncoms as well as officers. Though specific performance levels were stated, they were not always observed. Fighter pilots and U-boat commanders became eligible for an escalating number of enemy planes shot down or tonnage sunk, respectively. However, actions in other combat arms were less easily quantified and a good deal of subjectivity was required. Nevertheless, there may have been less political influence in *Ritterkreuz* awards than became evident in the Medal of Honor and, to a lesser extent, the Victoria Cross.

Contrary to the U.S. and British awards, aviation Knight's Crosses seldom were awarded for a single event. Not every Knight's Cross citation would have garnered a Medal of Honor or Victoria Cross, but few if any U.S. or British citations would have won a *Ritterkreuz.*

Though relatively few Knight's Crosses were presented in error, some slip-ups did occur. In 1939 a Luftwaffe bomber pilot was decorated for "sinking" the HMS *Ark Royal.* After German intelligence confirmed that the ship was still afloat, Reichsmarshal Hermann Goering ironically told the embarrassed flier, "You owe me an aircraft carrier."

The British and German awards also differed from the medal in other ways. The Victoria Cross could be presented twice, but the survival rate among "VC and Bars" was exceedingly small, and no airman qualified. The *Ritterkreuz* was awarded in successive orders, with Oak Leaves (*Eichenlaub*), Swords *(Schwerten),* and Diamonds *(Brillanten)* added to the original medal. Only twenty-seven of the latter were presented, including twelve to pilots. On a scale of presentation (roughly one Victoria Cross per 35,000 personnel and one Medal of Honor per 25,000), the Knight's Cross and Oak Leaves came closest to matching the Allied awards, with one in 22,500 German troops. Of 159 Oak Leaves, 54 went to the Luftwaffe.

Overall, 1,716 Luftwaffe men received the *Ritterkreuz,* including paratroopers and flak personnel, who belonged to the air force. They represented about one quarter of the 7,000 Knight's Crosses presented in World War II.

Imperial Japan offered few decorations, as every Japanese soldier was expected to pursue his duty unto death. Charles Lindbergh, having seen Pacific combat, felt that almost any Japanese warrior would have been eligible for the Medal of Honor. However, in December 1944 an imperial order established the *Bukochosho* ("For Military Merit") in two grades, Class A and B, administered by the army. Contrary to the more prevalent *Kinshi-Kunsho* (Order of the Golden Kite), it was one of the few Japanese awards made to living recipients. Only eighty-nine "*Bukosho*" were known awarded, disproportionately to airmen, of whom five received the Class A. The majority were fighter pilots with reputations as B-29 slayers, though the Japanese victory claims were orders of magnitude off the mark. Seventy-four Superfortresses were known lost to Japanese fighters with another nineteen attributed to flak and fighters jointly—a total of ninety-three involving enemy aircraft. By comparison, 107 "B-san" kills were credited to just fourteen pilots, who also claimed more than thirty Boeings probably destroyed.

Shifting Criteria

The Medal of Honor has never been equitably awarded during its 150-year history. Acts of valor that received medals in one conflict or theater of war were recognized with lesser decorations just months later, and vice versa.

For instance, among nearly 1,500 American fighter aces from all wars, only five were credited with seven victories in one day. Three received Medals of Honor. Two received lesser decorations: Navy Lieutenant Stanley W. Vejtasa in the Pacific during October 1942 and AAF Major William L. Leverette in the Mediterranean a year later. Vejtasa was recommended for the Medal of Honor but received a Navy Cross, which had recently been elevated over the Distinguished Service Medal ("the senior officer's good conduct ribbon," sniped one recipient). Leverette received the Distinguished Service Cross for downing seven Junkers transports.

Of the Medal of Honor recipients, Commander David McCampbell logged two seven-kill days in 1944, including a record nine in one mission. Marine Lieutenant James E. Swett was credited with seven Japanese dive bombers off Tulagi in April 1943, and Army Captain William A. Shomo claimed six Japanese fighters and a bomber over the Philippines in January 1945. Considering that Vejtasa may have saved the only American fleet carrier remaining in the Pacific, his Navy Cross appears miserly even sixty years later. In any case, the discrepancies among the five cases remain unfathomable, especially since fighter pilots received Medals of Honor for missions with four, five, or six kills.

It may be argued what constitutes "above and beyond" for a fighter pilot, whose mission involves shooting down enemy aircraft. At what point does sublime skill transcend the obligation to perform one's duty to the best of one's ability? The extraordinary expertise displayed by aces such as Joe Foss, Dave McCampbell, Thomas McGuire, and George Davis (to mention a few) led to the medal for sustained individual performance over a period of weeks or months. Others such as John L. Smith, Joe Bauer, and Greg Boyington primarily were honored for their leadership while building notable scores along the way. Still others such as Frank Luke, Butch O'Hare, and Jim Howard received the medal for one historic mission.

Among bomber crews, several medals were presented to pilots who remained in control of damaged aircraft, enabling crewmen to bail out. Ironically, America's first significant aerial hero of World War II was widely believed to have received the Medal of Honor for just such action. Captain Colin P. Kelly perished in his B-17 over the Philippines in December 1941, permitting most of his crew to abandon ship while under fighter attack. In truth, Kelly received a posthumous Distinguished Service Cross, though later bomber pilots received Medals of Honor for similar actions.

Other examples of self-sacrifice are equally compelling, though not all circumstances can be fully known. At least four posthumous awards (Richard Fleming and Joseph Powers in World War II; Charles Loring and Louis Sebille in Korea) went to pilots who apparently dived their aircraft into the target or pressed the attack so closely that the plane was destroyed. Whether the ultimate act was deliberate or the result of battle damage or paralyzing wounds cannot be known, but the example remains.

Undoubtedly the supreme sacrifice in air action is made by a flier who gives up his parachute to a comrade. Lieutenant David Kingsley made such a decision over Romania in June 1944, choosing to die so that a wounded gunner could live.

Other lifesaving actions abound among Medal of Honor airmen, particularly for helicopter crews. All eleven in-flight helo citations were high-risk combat rescues, often in weather or darkness in addition to enemy opposition. Only one involved a gunship performing a rescue.

Perhaps the ultimate statement on awards policy (considering his own credentials) came from General Jimmy Doolittle, who said, "I have always felt that the Medal of Honor should be reserved for men who risk their lives in combat to save others, not for individual feats like shooting down a number of enemy planes or bombing enemy targets."

From 1917 to 1972, 109 Medal of Honor awards involved airmen or aircraft. Ninety-one occurred wholly or significantly in flight; eighteen involved ground or sea activity, primarily rescues or courage displayed as prisoners of war. Owing to length restraints, this book concentrates on the in-flight episodes but every aviation-related recipient is acknowledged at the end of the appropriate section for the era and branch of service.

Whatever their war, whichever their service, the surviving Medal of Honor airmen are self-effacing about the decoration. With a 48 percent combat mortality rate, most consider themselves fortunate to survive. "We were lucky" or "I was just doing my job" are frequent comments. So is the observation, "Nobody *wins* the Medal of Honor; it's not a contest." The courageous men found in these pages certainly would agree.

Notes

Though no more than two airmen have ever received the medal in one aircraft, in most instances other crew members contributed to the action. Identifying nearly three hundred additional fliers from another fifty aircraft was a major task but only eight men remain unknown, all from Vietnam. Other aircrew are identified as pilot (P), copilot (CP), bombardier (B), navigator (N), radio operator (RO), nose gunner (NG), ball turret gunner (BTG), waist gunners (WG), tail gunner (TG), and flight engineer (FE), who usually doubled as top turret gunner (TTG). Dedicated radar operators and photographers are identified as (radar) or (photo). Vietnam War weapon systems operators are (WSO), and observers for all eras are (O).

Ranks are noted as of the date of action; many citations indicate a higher rank owing to subsequent promotions, occasionally posthumous. Abbreviations are Gen. (general), Col. (colonel), Lt. Col. (lieutenant colonel), Maj. (major), Capt. (captain), 1Lt. (first lieutenant), 2Lt. (second lieutenant), F.O. (flight officer), TSgt. (technical sergeant), SSgt. (staff sergeant), Sgt. (sergeant), and Corp. (corporal). Vietnam era ranks include WO (warrant officer), A1C (Airman First Class) and Spec. (specialist). Where exact rank is unspecified, generic titles are used, such as Lt. or Sgt.

Naval ranks include Comdr. (commander), Lt. Comdr. (lieutenant commander), Lt. (senior lieutenant), Lt. (jg) (lieutenant, junior grade), Ens. (ensign), CPO (chief petty officer), and PO (petty officer). World War II rates were based on specialty such as ARM (aviation radioman) or AMM (aviation machinist mate).

Additional decorations are noted in most cases. Many recipients also were awarded foreign decorations, which generally are not listed.

Each recipient's aircraft is identified to the extent possible, by type—Boeing B-17F, for instance—followed by the serial number, squadron code letters or "buzz number" in parentheses (AB-C or 53) and name, if any, in italics such as *Bouncin' Betty.* Call signs are stated in quotes: "Yellow Two."

Among the in-flight medals, aircraft are fully known for most citations but some contradictions and gaps remain. Where previous listings have occurred, they are noted in parentheses; uncertain identifications are followed by a question mark. Readers with additional information are invited to contact the author in care of the publisher for inclusion in future printings.

2

WORLD WAR I

ARMY: 4

MARINES: 2

NAVY: 1

TOTAL: 7

The "Great War" was the first conflict in which aviation played a prominent role. The European powers—especially Britain, France, and Germany—were quick to learn the value of aerial observation in warfare, though the United States and Italy had employed aircraft in climes as diverse as Mexico and Libya.

Sparked by the Serbian assassination of Austro-Hungarian archduke Ferdinand in July 1914, the war brought into play a complex set of alliances pitting Austria and Germany against Russia, which in turn brought Britain and France into the war. Early successes by the Imperial German Air Service at Tannenburg and Mons in 1914 conclusively demonstrated that the primitive flying machines far outstripped cavalry in its traditional reconnaissance role. From there, technical and doctrinal evolution proceeded at an accelerated pace. It has been estimated that four years of war advanced aviation knowledge by as much as two decades.

America, avowedly neutral under President Woodrow Wilson, chose to sit out the first three years of the European war. In fact, Wilson campaigned for reelection in 1916 on the basis that "he kept us out of the war." However, Germany's practice of unrestricted submarine warfare rankled many Americans, as U.S. citizens who ignored the obvious peril of sailing into a war zone inevitably became casualties. The situation was aggravated by Germany's offer of restoring portions of the American Southwest to Mexico in exchange for pressure along the border. The outrage increased to the point that Wilson, nominally a pacifist, urged Congress to declare war. Anti-German hysteria swept the nation, manifesting itself in absurdly heartfelt teutonophobia: sauerkraut was renamed "liberty cabbage" and dachshunds (the Kaiser's favorite pets) were reportedly abused.

However, the infant Aviation Branch of the U.S. Army Signal Corps and its naval counterparts were committed to war without the equipment, personnel, or training suitable for the purpose. Throughout the remainder of the conflict, American aviators largely flew foreign-designed or -built airplanes. Consequently, the Medal of Honor recipients flew British, French, and Italian aircraft exclusively.

The aerial war revolved around artillery, the great killer of the western front. Artillery observers in airplanes and tethered balloons were the primary players in the complex game, as each air arm strove to deprive the enemy of his aerial vision while seeking to preserve air superiority for its own side. The fact that fighter pilots often fattened their scores at the expense of observation and reconnaissance planes has been the source of naïve criticism of some aces who seemingly "picked on" vulnerable two-seaters instead of dueling with enemy pursuit planes. Such nonsense still appears today: it would be laughable at best to Manfred, Baron von Richthofen, let alone to Sir Hugh Trenchard, father of the RAF.

Despite the fact that three-fourths of *Pour le Mérite* recipients were fighter pilots, the German air arm appreciated the efforts of its best artillery spotters. Nine aircraft observers and one balloonist received the "Blue Max," but no British or American fliers were similarly honored for their crucial work. However, four of the seven Medal of Honor airmen were DH-4 pilots and observers, so the proportion of medals among observation-bomber crews was far higher than comparable figures for Britain and Germany.

Lieutenants Harold Goettler and Edwin Bleckley of the 50th Aero Squadron received posthumous Medals of Honor for their resupply efforts on 6 October 1918. The Marine Corps team of Lieutenant Ralph Talbot and Corporal Robert Robinson was recognized for fending off German fighters that same month.

The other three medals went to fighter pilots. First was Quartermaster Charles Hammann, flying an Italian-built seaplane against the Austrians in

August 1918. Hammann's citation included combat with Austro-Hungarian aircraft, but it was his daring landing to rescue a downed squadronmate that earned him the first Medal of Honor awarded to a pilot.

September brought two Medal of Honor actions to SPAD pilots serving in France. Lieutenant Eddie Rickenbacker of the 94th Aero Squadron claimed two victories during a solo patrol behind German lines on 25 September and returned to tell the tale. Four days later Lieutenant Frank Luke of the 27th Aero closed out his sensational eighteen-day balloon-busting spree and died with pistol in hand after a forced landing, having burned three more *drachen* on his last flight. Luke's medal was the first actually awarded to a U.S. Air Service flier, as Goettler and Bleckley were recognized four years later and Rickenbacker's award was politically delayed until 1930.

The first generation of Medal of Honor airmen flew what today appear primitive machines, frightfully vulnerable with wood airframes, fabric-covered wings, and balky engines. Yet the men and the aircraft forged an image of adventure and a legacy of courage that future aviators would follow into skies around the globe, spinning slipstreams of their own to guide men toward the stars.

AVIATION BRANCH, ARMY SIGNAL CORPS (4)

FIRST LIEUTENANT EDWARD VERNON RICKENBACKER

18 OCTOBER 1890–27 JULY 1973

BORN: Columbus, Ohio

DIED: Zurich, Switzerland

ACTION: Air combat; Billy, Meuse, France; 25 September 1918 (age 27)

UNIT: 94th Aero Squadron, 1st Pursuit Group

AIRCRAFT: SPAD XIII C.1 S4523? (1)

OTHER DECORATIONS: Distinguished Service Cross (8)

A classic American success story, Eddie Rickenbacker (né Rickenbacher) arose from humble origins and overcame a rudimentary education by virtue of ability and ambition. Like Frank Luke he descended from teutonic immi-

Edward V. Rickenbacker in a SPAD XIII

grants, and he became known to auto racing fans as "the speedy Swiss." Possessing a mechanical aptitude and analytical mind, he took an engineering correspondence course and six years later he was evaluating automobiles. That pursuit naturally led to racing, and he became one of three most successful drivers in America. Speed was a core element of Rickenbacker's life.

When the United States entered the war he enlisted in the army. Because of his driving prowess Rickenbacker became a chauffeur for General John Pershing and Colonel William Mitchell. Though considered old for aviation—he was all of twenty-seven—Rickenbacker applied for pilot training and proved an apt pupil. He joined the fledgling 94th Aero Squadron in March 1918.

"Rick" quickly became a pillar of the 94th. Led by a Lafayette Escadrille veteran, Major Raoul Lufbery, the "Hat in the Ring" squadron made a name for itself by downing the first German planes credited to a U.S. unit. Lufbery was killed on 19 May, by which time Rickenbacker was credited with three victories. He claimed his fifth victory on 28 May, adding a sixth by month's end to become one of a handful of Nieuport 28 aces.

Then misfortune struck. Rickenbacker succumbed to mastoid problems in July, and the ear infection nearly ended his career. However, he recovered in Paris and returned to the front with a new SPAD XIII. The geared Hispano-Suiza engines caused serious problems for the First Pursuit Group, but Rickenbacker's intimate knowledge helped overcome the difficulties. By mid-September he was back in harness, marking his seventh notch on the fourteenth.

As a squadron commander Rickenbacker made a point of logging more hours over the lines than any of his pilots. It was in keeping with his lead-from-the-front philosophy, but it prompted him to fly solo patrols which did nothing to enhance the squadron's effectiveness. On 25 September, his first day as CO, unaccountably he decided on a lone flight behind German lines. At 0840 near Billy-sous-Mangiennes, fifteen miles northeast of Verdun, he spotted two Halberstadt observation planes escorted by five Fokkers. He stalked the enemy formation and pounced, claiming one fighter downed in his first pass. Using the momentum built from his dive, he reversed, selected one of the two-seaters, and fired, leaving it tumbling earthward. He then disengaged, returning to claim two "Boche" out of control. Because an air combat that date was observed by a French soldier west of Verdun—many miles from the scene—Rickenbacker's claims were credited as his ninth and tenth victims.

German records are inconclusive for 25 September. *Flieger Abteilung* 36 lost a crew at Jametz, ten miles west-northwest of Billy, but the time is unknown. Apparently no German fighter casualties occurred in that area during the day.

At month's end, with Luke's death, Rickenbacker inherited the ace of aces title with an even dozen victories. He never relinquished it. He led the 94th to the top rank of American pursuit squadrons, finishing with twenty-six personal victories by Armistice Day.

Of Rickenbacker's twenty-six credited victories, at least ten were listed as out of control and two were grounded balloons. In World War I, moral as well as physical victories counted in the U.S. and British air arms, and the byword was, "every kill is a victory but not every victory is a kill." Rickenbacker's tally included several "e/a dived east" and, on one occasion, "Fokker

Rickenbacker's wartime record catapulted him to even greater postwar acclaim than he had known as a racer. He published his first book, *Fighting the Flying Circus,* and committed himself to the transportation industry. With close ties to automotive and aviation circles he became one of the nation's leading technology advocates. He founded Rickenbacker Motor Company with an innovative design featuring disk brakes. The car was a technical success and commercial failure, so Rickenbacker joined Cadillac. He was also co-owner of the Indianapolis Speedway.

With former squadronmate Reed Chambers, Rickenbacker started Florida Airways, which foundered. However, in the early 1930s he became a prime force behind American Airways and North American Aviation before joining Eastern Airlines in 1935, where he became president and general manager. He gave commercial aviation a tremendous boost by endorsing the Douglas series of transports.

During World War II Rickenbacker traveled tirelessly on morale-building missions and functioned as a high-level courier. In 1942 the B-17 he was aboard became lost in the South Pacific and ditched 600 miles from Samoa. Rickenbacker's acerbic style kept most of the crew alive for three dreadful weeks, and upon rescue the emaciated warrior admitted, "I wanted them to hate me so much that they'd live to see me dead!" His *Seven Came Through* was a candid account of the ordeal.

"Captain Eddie" enjoyed meeting a new generation of aces. The first American to match Rickenbacker's World War I tally was Marine Corps Captain Joe Foss in January 1943. Subsequently the former SPAD pilot was genuinely pleased when, in April 1944, Major Richard Bong downed number twenty-seven.

Rickenbacker published his definitive memoir in 1970. He died in his ancestral Switzerland at age eighty-two, and subsequently Columbus Air Force Base was named in his honor.

last seen in a vertical bank." These claims would not even have been credited as probables in World War II, but they were considered valid in 1918.

Aside from his undisputed record as the top American ace (Frederick Gillet claimed twenty destroyed in the Royal Air Force), Rickenbacker was easily the most-decorated flier of the American Expeditionary Force. He had eight Distinguished Service Crosses as well as the French *Croix de Guerre* with three palms, and he was made a Chevalier of the Legion of Honor.

Rickenbacker had support for the Medal of Honor, but his cause immediately became political. Chief among his supporters was Congressman Robert Clancy of Detroit, who urged the top award for a decade or more. However, the influential Senator Hiram Bingham of Connecticut bitterly resented Rickenbacker's support of Billy Mitchell and resisted the Medal of Honor nomination. Additionally, many people disliked Rickenbacker's commercial use of the hat-in-the-ring emblem.

An unknown factor is Rickenbacker's own impetus toward the award. Until Lindbergh's flight in 1927, "Captain Eddie" had been America's top aviator. He may have felt that if a peacetime event (awarded in contravention of Army requirements) merited the medal, so did his combat record. Biographer W. Edward White feels there was a rivalry between the two, largely from Rickenbacker's side, but Lindbergh lent his immense prestige to the motion for Rickenbacker's medal. The Distinguished Service Cross for 25 September 1918 was rescinded and the award was presented by President Herbert Hoover at Bolling Field on 6 November 1930.

SECOND LIEUTENANT FRANK LUKE JR.

19 May 1897–29 September 1918

Born: Phoenix, Arizona

Died: Murvaux, Meuse, France

Action: Air combat; Meuse Valley, France; 29 September 1918 (age 21)

Unit: 27th Aero Squadron, 1st Pursuit Group

Aircraft: SPAD XIII C.1 S7984

Other decorations: Distinguished Service Cross (2), Purple Heart

Evening was casting long shadows across the valley of the Meuse and some of the most sanguinary fields of the world war. East of the fortress of Verdun, at an outlying field used by American pursuit pilots, a twenty-one-year-old Arizonan was strapped into a SPAD XIII so new that it did not yet bear the 27th Aero Squadron's eagle emblem.

It was 29 September 1918. In the previous seventeen days Lieutenant Frank Luke had destroyed eleven German observation balloons and four airplanes. Now he had spotted three more *drachen* ("dragons") clustered about twelve miles to the north, around Dun sur Meuse. Luke intended to take off, burn them, and return to his field—perhaps twenty minutes flying time.

Eager to take advantage of the waning daylight, Luke fidgeted in his wicker seat. But the flight commander told him to sit tight: Major Harold Hartney, commanding the First Pursuit Group, was inbound. Luke was not to take off before talking to Hartney, who likely knew that Luke's squadron commander had ordered the headstrong youngster detained for insubordination.

British-trained, with experience dating from 1916, Hartney arrived in his Sopwith Camel. He blipped his way down to a landing and taxied up to the SPAD. He climbed out and ambled over to Luke's plane.

Frank Luke Jr.

Harold Hartney knew a lot about Frank Luke.

The fifth of nine children, Frank Luke Jr. was the grandson of a Prussian immigrant who settled in Arizona Territory, the surname Leucke having been anglicized. The irony could not have been lost on those involved in the stellar career of Frank Jr., who made his reputation against his ancestral homeland.

He shared his father's blond, blue-eyed appearance, but in personality young Frank was active, outgoing, and aggressive. He enjoyed competition, excelling in baseball and football, and proved an above-average student in high school. He did not live long enough to attend college.

When war hysteria (there is no other term for it) swept America in April 1917, Luke was immediately drawn to the Army Signal Corps, responsible for America's pitiful air service. It was not a pleasant time for a German descendant wishing to serve America. However, Luke graduated from Phoenix Union High School in May and, just turned twenty, he enlisted that September. He had twelve months to live.

Following training, in July 1918 Luke joined the 27th Aero Squadron in France, one of four outfits in the fledgling First Pursuit Group. Luke was regarded with suspicion by some colleagues, and he was drawn to another pilot of German background. Joseph F. Wehner of Boston was a year and a half older than Luke and far more worldly. In 1916 he volunteered for YMCA service in Germany and saw the results of twentieth-century warfare. Eventually he concluded that the only way to end the suffering was to win the war, so he volunteered for flying. Twice detained by the FBI, he was finally deemed reliable enough to die for his country.

Originally the 27th flew Nieuport 28s, elegant rotary-engined biplanes led by Major Hartney, who knew talent when he saw it. Though Luke's occasionally abrasive personality riled some, Hartney saw the white flame of ambition burning behind those blue eyes. The CO gave the Arizonan his head as much as he dared, and after a bumpy start Hartney's confidence was rewarded.

However, when Hartney was promoted to lead the group, squadron command fell to Captain Alfred Grant, a disciplinarian. Luke's unconventional attitude rankled some: he enjoyed helling around on a motorcycle, trick shooting with his Colt .45 pistol, and playing with captured Maxim machine guns. But he got results.

When the 27th converted to SPAD XIIIs, Luke hit his stride. Standing orders called for attacks on any German observation balloons found in the patrol sector, creating an atmosphere rich in potential for aggressive young males. Luke and Wehner formed a potent team, attacking the *drachen* in both impromptu and planned missions. Their assault on the enemy balloon line was a major contribution to the American war effort, as balloons were the primary platform for German artillery observers.

Beginning 12 September, Luke and Wehner waged serious war. In seven days they claimed sixteen victories between them, including four airplanes. On the seventh day, 18 September, they hit their peak: they burned three balloons and Luke dropped two Fokkers and a Halberstadt. However, in the swirling, confused combat Joe Wehner disappeared. He had fallen protecting his wingmate. Heartsick, Luke took nine days off. When his next wingman was killed, Luke became more of a loner.

On 28 September, Luke announced his return with another balloon and a Hannover observation plane destroyed. With fifteen victories he was America's ace of aces. But he had a bad habit of disappearing overnight, staying with his French friends at the Stork Group or lodging with artillery observers. Frank Luke may have been headstrong, but he was cunning. He cultivated friends among Allied troops who could confirm his claims.

At the advanced field the evening of the twenty-ninth, Hartney chewed his mustache, pondering Luke's request for another solo patrol. Finally he said, "Permission granted." At the appointed time Luke gunned his SPAD off the ground, headed north. He diverted only long enough to drop a note to the U.S. 7th Balloon Company, asking observers to watch for burning German balloons along the Meuse.

Luke's flight path took him to Liny, Doulcon, and Milly. At each spot a garish gout of hydrogen-fed fire erupted in the evening sky as he methodically burned three balloons in seven minutes. Reports that he strafed enemy troops and downed one or two Fokker D.VIIs undoubtedly refer to nearby incidents earlier that day.

In flaming the *drachen* Luke was wounded by AA fire and landed near tiny Murvaux, where he exited his SPAD and drew his M1911 pistol. German soldiers approached and may have called on him to surrender. He replied with pistol shots and—accounts vary—immediately succumbed to his wound or was killed by a volley of rifle fire. In any case, the Arizona gunfighter died with Colt in hand.

Luke's grave was identified in January 1919, and affidavits were obtained from villagers who recounted his last flight. The officer who found the grave and proposed the Medal of Honor was Merian C. Cooper, later famous as the director of *King Kong*. Luke already held the Distinguished Service Cross and was due to receive a second for his 18 September mission, but Hartney felt he deserved more. The Medal of Honor nomination proceeded rapidly, and the award was presented to Frank Sr. in 1919. The family donated the medal to the Air Force Museum in 1984.

Luke's body was moved to the Meuse-Argonne Cemetery on 1 November 1921, where it rests today with 14,245 other Americans.

In 1919 the new military airfield at Pearl Harbor, Hawaii, was named in Luke's honor, as was the Army Air Force base west of Phoenix in 1941. Another heartfelt tribute was paid to the Arizona Balloon Buster eighty-two years after his death. Led by sportscaster Stephen Skinner, a group of World War I enthusiasts from "The Aerodrome" website contributed more than $2,000 to restore the monument at Murvaux erected by the 388th Fighter Wing in 1958. The original plaque had long since disappeared but the identical replacement was dedicated with suitable honors in November 2000.

LIEUTENANTS EDWIN RUSSELL BLECKLEY AND HAROLD ERNEST GOETTLER

30 DECEMBER 1894–6 OCTOBER 1918 (BLECKLEY)

21 JULY 1890–6 OCTOBER 1918 (GOETTLER)

BORN: Wichita, Kansas (Bleckley); Chicago, Illinois (Goettler)

DIED: Near Binarville, France

ACTION: Aerial resupply; Argonne, France; 6 October 1918 (age 23—Bleckley; 28—Goettler)

UNIT: 50th Aero Squadron, 1st Observation Group

AIRCRAFT: DH-4s 32169 (2) and 32517 (6)

OTHER DECORATIONS: Purple Heart (1 each)

One of the enduring tales of the American Expeditionary Force was rescue of "the lost battalion" of the 77th Infantry Division. Actually, in extraordinarily rough terrain of the Argonne Forest, most of two battalions of the 308th Infantry Regiment were outflanked and cut off on 2 October. Occupying an area hardly bigger than four football fields, Major Charles Whittlesey's doughboys held on by their fingernails over the next five days. The Germans literally had the Yanks under their guns, as "Whittlesey's Bench" was beneath the surrounding high ground from which machine guns, grenades, and flame throwers kept up frightful pressure. Casualties mounted by the hour.

Desperate to locate the stranded battalions, the 77th Division asked the 50th Aero Squadron to search the tree-choked area. Captain Daniel Morse's Liberty DH-4 crews accepted the challenge. Flying at extremely low level through fog and rain, their search was hampered by Whittlesey's reluctance to lay out recognition panels for fear of drawing more fire. Yet the airmen found Whittlesey and reported his position. Then, knowing that days would pass before a relief column could break through, the DeHavillands began perhaps the first sustained aerial resupply operation in military history. The fliers were right: the lost battalions' casualties were approaching 50 percent.

Low-flying DH-4s made repeated sorties, attempting to drop ammunition and supplies in the face of determined German rifle and machine gun fire. But the ravine—only seventy-five yards wide in places—was a difficult target, even from 1,000 feet. Three planes were shot down, with one flier dead and two wounded, but the others remained grimly determined to succor the infantry.

Edwin R. Bleckley

Harold E. Goettler

On 6 October the crew of Lieutenants Harold E. Goettler (pilot) and Edwin R. Bleckley (observer) had been frustrated in their morning mission. Enemy gunfire forced them to drop supplies from too high an altitude, and even then their plane, squadron number two, took hits.

Nevertheless, Goettler, one of the 50th's flight commanders, resolved to fly lower on the next mission of the day, hoping to make more accurate drops. Knowing that they would be subjected to more intense German ground fire, the crew switched to an undamaged aircraft, number six, and took off once more.

Bleckley and Goettler were a solid crew from disparate backgrounds. At six feet two inches, "Dad" Goettler (he was all of twenty-eight) had been a standout athlete at the University of Chicago who played on the 1913 conference champion football team. He built a promising business as a real estate broker and was engaged to a Red Cross ambulance driver. Five years younger, Bleckley was from Kansas, a former bank teller whose family objected to aviation.

Both men had entered the service in July 1917 and both had been in the squadron two months. Bleckley, originally of the 130th Field Artillery, had volunteered for aerial observer training and was teamed with Goettler. They had flown their first mission together on 12 September at the start of the St. Mihiel offensive. It had been a long three weeks.

Approaching the embattled gorge, Goettler throttled back the 400-horsepower V-12 and made his lowest run yet—barely off the tree tops, below the adjoining cliffs where Maxim gunners actually fired down on the khaki and gray airplane. During its low, slow approach the big DeHavilland presented an easy target, and 8mm bullets shredded the airframe. Though both fliers were shot, they made their drop and banked toward the allied lines. Goettler managed a crash landing but was killed on impact. Bleckley was pulled from the wreckage of his DH-4 and died before reaching a French aid station.

Both fliers received posthumous Distinguished Service Crosses, but the magnitude of their sacrifice was such that the decorations were rescinded and the Medal of Honor was awarded in December 1922.

Thanks in no small part to the 50th Aero Squadron the lost battalions were saved. General John Pershing awarded Medals of Honor to Whittlesey and three of his subordinates, making five medals in all—probably the most decorated American event of the First World War.

MARINE CORPS (2)

SECOND LIEUTENANT RALPH TALBOT AND CORPORAL ROBERT GUY ROBINSON

6 JANUARY 1897–25 OCTOBER 1918 (TALBOT)

30 APRIL 1896–5 OCTOBER 1974 (ROBINSON)

BORN: South Weymouth, Massachusetts (Talbot); Wayne, Michigan (Robinson);

DIED: France (Talbot); St. Ignace, Michigan (Robinson)

ACTION: Bombing missions; France and Belgium; 8 and 14 October 1918 (age 21—Talbot; age 22—Robinson)

UNIT: Squadron C, 1st Marine Aviation Force

AIRCRAFT: DeHavilland 4 A3295 (D-1); also listed as A3279

Ralph Talbot had enlisted in the Navy at age twenty and was promoted to seaman second class in October 1917. He was commissioned an ensign in

Ralph Talbot

Robert G. Robinson

April 1918 and passed pilot training at Miami. Mustered out of the Navy in May, he was commissioned a Marine Corps second lieutenant and arrived in France on 1 August with the First Marine Aviation Force.

Despite the New York City birthplace noted on his Medal of Honor citation, Robert Robinson was a Michigander who enlisted in the Marine Corps in May 1917. Upon joining Squadron C of the First Marine Aviation Force the twenty-two-year-old gunner was crewed with the twenty-one-year-old pilot. Their aircraft were American-built DH-4s with 400-horsepower Liberty engines.

As part of the Northern Bombing Group, U.S. Marines flew joint missions with the Royal Air Force, though equipment was slow to arrive. The Marines did not receive their own aircraft until late September and even then were seldom up to strength. Nevertheless, Talbot and Robinson had logged three previous bombing raids with the British, and on the morning of 8 October they were part of a formation of No. 218 Squadron, RAF, bombing Ardoye, Belgium. They were attacked by nine German fighters and, in the running battle near Kortemark, fourteen miles south-southeast of Ostend, Robinson was credited with downing a Fokker D-VII. The victory was shared with Lieutenants H. W. Mathews and H. W. Murray of No. 218.

Six days later Talbot and Robinson were in action again.

An attack against Thielt, Belgium, on 14 October was the first all-Marine mission, flown from Le Fresne aerodrome. Seven DHs dropped a metric ton of bombs on rail targets and were homeward bound when attacked by eight Fokkers and four Pfalz. The squadron commander, Captain Robert Lytle, signaled the formation to close up for mutual support. In the early going one German was claimed down out of control, but the rest were aggressive, concentrating on the left side of the formation. Lytle noted Talbot lagging and tried to cover him, but then he went down with a dead engine. Talbot and Robinson were largely alone.

Robinson swiveled his Lewis Gun as the black-crossed, white-tailed Fokkers closed in, and he fired short, accurate bursts. One enemy plane was observed diving away, but the others pressed their advantage.

Robinson was hit in the left arm, the 8mm bullet tearing away most of his elbow. Almost immediately Robinson's gun malfunctioned and Talbot pulled away, giving the crippled gunner time to clear the jam. With the Lewis again operational, the marines continued the fight with Robinson firing one-handed. He continued shooting until the interceptors departed, then collapsed on the floor of the rear cockpit. He had sustained a dozen more wounds in the chest, stomach, hip, and legs.

Meanwhile, Talbot used his forward-firing Vickers, claiming a Fokker and a Pfalz shot down. With an opportunity to disengage, he dived headlong through German gunfire, making for Allied territory barely fifty feet off the ground.

Talbot located a field hospital inside the Belgian lines, landed at Hondschoote airdrome, and quickly summoned help for his critically injured gunner. Robinson's life was saved by the surgeon general of the Belgian Army, who also reattached the severed tendon in the young marine's left elbow.

German records indicate two fighter casualties on the Fourth Army front during the day: an army flier wounded and a Marine Flieger Korps pilot killed near Snelleghem. Neither can be attributed to the U.S. Marines, but Germany's nonfatal aircraft losses were seldom recorded.

Talbot survived less than two weeks. Flying D-1 on a 25 October test flight, he crashed because of engine failure. His passenger (future Virginia governor Colgate Darden) was thrown clear of the wreckage, but Ralph Talbot burned to death.

Robinson was discharged in 1919 with the rank of gunnery sergeant and was appointed a reserve second lieutenant. He retired from the reserves in May 1923, though subsequently he was advanced to first lieutenant. He died in a rural cabin near St. Ignace, Michigan, at age seventy-eight and is buried in Arlington National Cemetery.

Both marines were further recognized after the war. The USS *Ralph Talbot* (DD-390), a Gridley-class destroyer, was commissioned in October 1937. She was one of the fightingest ships of the Pacific War, with twelve battle stars from Pearl Harbor to Okinawa. A test vessel for the Bikini Atoll atomic explosion, she was scuttled in 1948.

The Robinson Award is presented annually to the Marine Flight Officer of the Year.

Navy (1)

LANDSMAN FOR QUARTERMASTER CHARLES HAZELTINE HAMMANN

16 March 1892–14 June 1919

Born: Baltimore, Maryland

Died: Langley Field, Virginia

Action: Combat rescue; Pola, Austria; 21 August 1918 (age 26)

Unit: Naval Air Station Porto Corsini, Italy

Aircraft: Macchi M-5 M13015

Landsman for Quartermaster Charles Hammann banked his single-seat Macchi flying boat over Pola Harbor, Austria. The twenty-six-year-old Hammann, known to his friends as a dedicated gambler, was concerned about the increasing odds against him. That morning he had taken off with six other aviators on the first U.S. Navy mission launched from Porto Corsini, Italy. Another M-5 fighter and an M-8 bomber had turned back with engine

Charles A. Hammann in front of a Macchi M-5

trouble, leaving four M-5s and an M-8 to continue the mission across the Adriatic Sea.

Approaching the drop point at 8,000 feet, the bomber released its "ordnance," propaganda leaflets. Enemy gunners opened fire from the harbor entrance, posing little danger to the Americans, but a more serious threat appeared: five Albatros fighters followed by two seaplanes. The latter pair climbed slowly but the Daimler-powered Albatrii were another matter.

As the M-8 withdrew, Ensign George Ludlow took his wingmen down to intercept the Austrians. In the ensuing dogfight Ensign Pete Parker followed one Austrian down and out of the combat. Then Ensign Dudley Vorhees had to disengage when both guns malfunctioned, leaving Ludlow and Hammann to continue the fight against five Albatrii.

Ludlow sent one Austrian away smoking, then took multiple hits to his engine and propeller. He glided to a water landing only five miles from the harbor mouth.

Hammann, after eluding his opponents, saw his friend's Macchi riding roughly in the fifteen-knot swell. Knowing that the Austrians considered propaganda equivalent to espionage, he feared for Ludlow's life. Therefore,

Hammann made a skillful landing and taxied close aboard the crippled M-5 while Ludlow opened the cock in the hull to let in water. He then jumped aboard Hammann's plane, straddling the fuselage behind the cockpit. Hammann managed a takeoff with the unaccustomed load but smashed his bow against the breaking waves. He banked around to fire his remaining ammunition into Ludlow's plane and circled until it sank.

The sixty-mile flight back to Porto Corsini was uneventful, but upon landing, water poured in through the broken bow, cartwheeling the M-5. Both men surfaced in the canal and were rescued with minor injuries.

Hammann was commissioned an ensign in October and remained at Porto Corsini until after the armistice. He returned to America in January 1919 but soon was flying again, evaluating foreign aircraft at Hampton Roads, Virginia. Ironically, on 14 June he died in a Macchi M-5 while participating in an Army "flying circus" at Langley Field, Virginia, less than ten months after the Pola action. Crippled by a control failure, Hammann's Macchi spun in from 1,200 feet and he died before he could be lifted from the wreckage. He was buried at Oak Lawn Cemetery in Baltimore.

Charles Hammann retroactively became the first pilot awarded the Medal of Honor, with presentation of the award in November 1920. He was remembered in the USS *Hammann* (DD-412), a Sims-class destroyer sunk with the USS *Yorktown* (CV-5) at the Battle of Midway in June 1942. The name was perpetuated in DE-131, an Edsall-class destroyer escort launched that December and stricken in 1972.

Navy Aviation Related (2)

Ship Fitter Patrick McGunigal; aboard the cruiser USS *Huntington* (ACR-5) in the Atlantic; 17 September 1917. The ship's kite balloon observer became trapped underwater when his balloon unexpectedly dropped from 200 feet and trailed overboard. McGunigal, a fifty-year-old veteran, scaled down the side of the ship, disentangled the lines, and pulled the observer to safety. McGunigal's citation was the first ever involving aviation, occurring eleven months before Hammann's action.

Chief Francis E. Ormsbee Jr.; Pensacola Naval Air Station, Florida; 25 September 1918. The twenty-six-year-old machinist was airborne with Ensign J. A. Jova when they saw a plane spin into the bay. Jova landed nearby and

Ormsbee dived to the sinking wreckage and pulled the observer to the surface. When a speed launch arrived, Ormsbee dived for the pilot. Despite repeated efforts, Ormsbee was unable to rescue the flier but he had saved the observer's life. Ormsbee subsequently became the twenty-fifth noncommissioned naval aviation pilot.

3

THE INTERIM YEARS

NAVY: 4

MARINES: 1

ARMY: 1

TOTAL: 6

Six aviators were among the twenty-one Medal of Honor recipients during the interwar period from 1919 to 1939. Only one of the six aviation awards involved combat valor; five were presented for exploration or lifesaving efforts.

Naval aviators Richard Byrd and Floyd Bennett as well as Marine Lieutenant Christian Schilt received the "wartime" Tiffany Cross. It is unknown which version of the medal went to William Corry and Carlton Hutchins. However, the submarine rescuers in 1939 were awarded the original star design presumably reserved for noncombat actions. The reasons for the contradictory policies remain unexplained and are probably unknowable.

Whatever the legal or administrative anomalies of the Tiffany Cross, the fliers who received the Medal of Honor for exploration received wide recognition. Byrd and Bennett were Navy pilots on extended leave for their 1926 polar flight, and in 1927 Charles Lindbergh held a reserve commission in the air service, though he had not been on active duty for two years.

Corry and Hutchins, active-duty naval aviators, both perished attempting to save fellow airmen, in 1920 and 1938, respectively.

More successful was Schilt, who made repeated short-field landings and takeoffs through Nicaraguan gunfire to deliver supplies and evacuate wounded. Though technically not a war, the prolonged conflicts in Caribbean "banana republics" yielded benefits to the Marine Corps. Even salty leathernecks such as Brigadier General Smedley Butler (a two-time Medal of Honor recipient) objected to the politics—he felt the Marine Corps had become the action arm of United Fruit Company—but there were long-term advantages. In Nicaragua, Haiti, and the Dominican Republic, marines gained institutional experience in bush fighting and close air support, both of which proved useful in the Pacific between 1942 and 1945.

Most of the other interwar medals were presented for naval rescue efforts such as the sunken submarine *Squalus* (SS-192) in 1939. However, in 1935 Congress awarded a Medal of Honor to retired Major General Adolphus W. Greely who had left the Army twenty-nine years before. The brief citation alluded to his "life of splendid public service," which included arctic exploration in the 1880s. Greely died that year, aged ninety-one. Though awarded in clear violation of the charter, his medal was not unique, as political patronage has featured in many awards before and since.

A source of considerable confusion is the case of Colonel (previously Major General) William "Billy" Mitchell, America's foremost airpower advocate before his death in 1936. Mitchell's public feud with the Army and the U.S. Government led to court martial for insubordination in 1925. Though some of Mitchell's theories were extreme, in large part he was vindicated by events in World War II, and in 1946 Congress voted him a posthumous congressional gold medal which was not *the* Medal of Honor. Photos clearly reveal the award as a medallion rather than the highest award for valor.

ARMY AIR SERVICE (1)

CHARLES AUGUSTUS LINDBERGH

4 FEBRUARY 1902–26 AUGUST 1974

BORN: Detroit, Michigan

DIED: Maui, Hawaii

ACTION: Transatlantic flight; 20–21 May 1927 (age 25)

AIRCRAFT: Ryan NYP NX-211 *The Spirit of St. Louis*

OTHER DECORATIONS: Distinguished Flying Cross

Charles Lindbergh was an essential American type: remote by choice, reserved by nature, with a self-reliance that grew into supreme self-confidence.

Charles A. Lindbergh

How else to explain a twenty-five-year-old, unemployed flier who invested his savings, his future, and his very existence in an all-or-nothing grab for history's golden ring? In achieving his goal—the first transatlantic flight between New York and Paris—he extended the boundaries of glory and practically invented celebrity. In the Golden Age after World War I, Lindbergh's star shone brighter than all.

He cared nothing for any of it. The flight of *The Spirit of St. Louis* was a quest of a young man in search of himself, having already exhausted the frontiers of challenge. Ironically, in so doing he launched himself into the adulation of the human race and quickly came to regret the remorseless attention of his species.

Charles Lindbergh was captivated with flying, yet more so with flight. Writing eloquently, as usual, he said, "I live only in the moment in this strange, unmortal space, crowded with beauty, pierced with danger." Certainly he was on speaking terms with danger: he saved his life by parachute four times. He earned his Army wings in 1925 and, following his release in 1926, he became an airmail pilot between Chicago and St. Louis. Lindbergh was lucky and then some: of the first forty airmail pilots hired, thirty-one died on the job.

Following barnstorming and flying the mail, Lindbergh was attracted by the $25,000 Ortieg Prize, announced in 1919 for the first direct flight between New York and Paris, in either direction. By 1927 the prize remained unclaimed, though other transatlantic flights had been made between Europe and North America. Americans and Frenchmen were prepared to risk their lives in the endeavor, and during May some valiantly unsuccessful efforts were made. Six men already had died in the attempt.

Every other contender chose multiengine aircraft or additional pilots or navigators. All but Lindbergh. Shrewdly analytical, he turned down Bellanca's offer to sell his St. Louis consortium a plane when the factory required a pilot of its choosing. Lindbergh took his own funds and those of his backers and visited a small company in San Diego. Ryan Aircraft, which had built mailplanes, produced the NY-P (New York to Paris) in record time. A tiny single-seater powered by a Wright radial engine, *The Spirit of St. Louis* was delivered on 10 May 1927. "Slim" Lindbergh flew it cross-country with almost no time to spare. He sweated out the poor weather on Long Island and, on 20 May, decided to go. Shunning a parachute's weight, he pulled on his flight suit, helmet, and goggles, cached his sack lunch, and gunned the Wright's 200 horses down the muddy track of Roosevelt Field. The silver Ryan became unstuck at the far end, lifting a full load of fuel and aspirations over the phone lines.

At that point Lindbergh had been without sleep for two days. He faced thirty-three and a half more hours in the air.

The magnitude of Lindbergh's feat defies widespread comprehension today. When transcontinental air travel is commonplace, with near-infallible aircraft and pinpoint navigation, the pioneering flights of Lindbergh and his contemporaries remain monuments to optimism and courage.

Lindbergh received tumultuous welcomes in Paris and in America. He received 100,000 telegrams and cables, 14,000 packages and nearly four million letters: three and a half million New Yorkers heralded his return. Congress authorized the Medal of Honor on 14 December 1927, and President Calvin Coolidge presented it on 21 March 1929. It took a special act of Congress, as Lindbergh was neither on active duty (officially he was a reserve captain) nor engaged in combat. It did not matter. He also was awarded the Distinguished Flying Cross and a promotion to colonel. His memoir, *We*, became a huge best seller.

The Medal of Honor citation, one of the shortest ever written, lauded Lindbergh's "heroic courage and skill as a navigator, at the risk of his life," adding that he "achieved the greatest individual triumph of any American citizen."

The rest of Lindbergh's life was spent in the shadow of his thirty-three hours over the spume-flecked Atlantic Ocean.

Following his incredible feat in 1927, Lindbergh embarked on one of the most remarkable lives of the twentieth century. With his wife, Anne Morrow, whom he married in 1929, he pioneered commercial air routes to South America and the Orient, most prominently for Pan American Airways. Arguably, he did more to promote aviation than anyone since the Wright Brothers.

Tragedy followed triumph. The Lindberghs' infant son was kidnapped and killed in 1932, and the ensuing media circus drove the parents from America. They settled in Britain, raising four other children, until returning to the United States in 1940. During the interim, Charles pursued varied interests, including pioneering medical work with French doctor Alexis Carrel. They developed equipment and procedures enabling heart surgery and coauthored a text, *The Culture of Organs.* It seemed there was nothing Lindbergh could not achieve—except success in politics.

Increasingly concerned about America's growing support of Britain under President Franklin Roosevelt, "Lucky Lindy" became a spokesman for neutrality. He was widely criticized for his seeming friendship with Luftwaffe chief Hermann Goering, and many Americans were stunned when, in 1938, he accepted a Nazi decoration, the Order of the German Eagle. Outspoken in the America First movement, Lindbergh expounded a hard line in favor of the caucasian race, distrust of orientals, and hostility toward the Soviet Union. He frankly regarded German domination of Europe as favorable to Russian domination. Roosevelt was livid.

Unknown for decades, Lindbergh's apparent friendliness with high-ranking Nazis concealed an intelligence mission on behalf of the U.S. Army Air Corps. His unique ability to move in elevated circles gave him exposure to Luftwaffe capabilities, enabling him to sort the facts from the propaganda.

Lindbergh's rancor toward the Roosevelt administration led to his resigning from the Army Air Corps in April 1941. However, following the Japanese attack on Pearl Harbor eight months later, Lindbergh immediately applied for active duty. Roosevelt promptly denied the request on the grounds that Lindbergh's "fascist sympathies" precluded his commissioning. Charles Lindbergh, the consummate aviator (he probably had more time over 30,000 feet than anyone in America) was forced to find other ways to contribute.

He found them.

Over the next four years Lindbergh consulted with Ford's aviation program and served as a United Aircraft "tech rep" in the United States and abroad. He perfected cruise control for Vought F4U Corsairs and Lockheed P-38 Lightnings in the Pacific Theater, where he flew unauthorized combat missions and shot down a Japanese aircraft in 1944. His *Wartime Journals* (1938–45) were published in 1970.

After the war Lindbergh remained engaged across the globe. He won a Pulitzer Prize for his beautifully written memoir, *The Spirit of St. Louis,* which was made into a successful movie. He also received an Air Force reserve commission as brigadier general, but by then the Lone Eagle had become highly introspective about technology. In some ways the ultimate technologist, he became more interested in earth's environment and deep sea exploration. Increasingly reclusive, he died in Hawaii in 1974.

When the U.S. Postal Service honored the former airmail pilot in 1977, the stamp depicting the lone Ryan merely said, "50th Anniversary, First Solo Transatlantic Flight."

MARINE CORPS (1)

FIRST LIEUTENANT CHRISTIAN FRANK SCHILT

1 MARCH 1895–9 JANUARY 1987

BORN: Richland Country, Illinois

DIED: Norfolk, Virginia

ACTION: Lifesaving; Quilali, Nicaragua; 6–8 January 1928 (age 32)

UNIT: VO-7M

AIRCRAFT: Vought O2U-1 BuNo 7529 (7-O-3)

OTHER DECORATIONS: Legion of Merit, Distinguished Flying Cross, Bronze Star Medal, Air Medal (5)

From 1925 to 1932 the U.S. Marine Corps maintained nearly a continuous presence in the Central American republic of Nicaragua. Internal disputes and violence were frequent during the civil war, which prompted American and other nationals to request protection that Washington was pleased to provide. A Marine brigade was dispatched to help maintain order and to train a nominally nonpolitical gendarmerie that would become capable of performing the mission itself.

Meanwhile, lawlessness continued, sometimes under the growing aegis of robber barons who controlled large tracts of land. One such episode occurred near Quilali in early January 1928. An insurrection erupted, resulting in a marine detachment with Nicaraguan government forces being trapped in the town about 100 miles north of Managua. Lieutenant Christian F. Schilt of Marine Observation Squadron Seven (VO-7M) offered to land in the beleaguered village—a challenge to his airmanship, as the available landing areas were narrow, rough streets. The situation was further complicated by hostile gunfire and reduced visibility from burning buildings. Weather over the mountains added to the peril but the thirty-two-year-old "mustang" was willing to try.

Schilt was already a veteran aviator with a proven record of achievement. He had joined the corps in 1917 and served as an enlisted marine in the Azores. Applying for flight training after the war, he received his wings and commission in June 1919. His first flying assignment was with Squadron D in Santo Domingo.

From 1920 to 1922 Schilt flew with the First and Second Marine Brigades in Haiti and the Dominican Republic. He was based primarily at Quantico, Virginia, for the next five years and gained notice by placing second in the Schneider Cup seaplane race of 1926. His Nicaraguan tour had begun in November 1927. VO-7M at Ocotal had been the first to receive O2Us the year before and nominally operated six Voughts with five other aircraft.

Christian F. Schilt

Schilt faced a varied challenge. Apart from the rebel troops, he would have to cross the mountainous terrain of Neuva Segovia Province, often in poor weather. He was also concerned about conditions in Quilali so he had an O2U's standard wheels replaced with the oversize wheels and tires of a DH-4. Without brakes, he wanted as much traction as possible. For three days Schilt sustained the garrison by delivering a new commanding officer and 1,400 pounds of badly needed supplies. Beside gunfire from the insurgents, the rough, narrow street posed a major obstacle, so the besieged marines burned down some buildings to clear a manageable runway. The available street was so short that Schilt's plane was dragged to a stop by riflemen grasping the lower wings, but he made ten risky landings and ten overloaded takeoffs. The latter were particularly notable, as he evacuated eighteen wounded men, repeatedly making the thirty-mile flight to Ocotal. His success demonstrated not only courage and perseverance, but exceptional airmanship, and the Tiffany Cross Medal of Honor was approved.

Following return to the United States in August 1929, Schilt commanded a fighter squadron and became chief test pilot at the Naval Aircraft Factory in Philadelphia. By 1941 he was assistant naval attaché in London, absorbing developments of modern air warfare. During the 1942 Guadalcanal Campaign he was on the staff of the First Marine Aircraft Wing and commanded two wings during 1944–45.

Schilt commanded the First Marine Aircraft Wing in South Korea during 1951–52 and received a fifth Air Medal as a general officer. The old warrior observed the 176th birthday of his corps by flying his pet F7F Tigercat over the front lines on 10 November 1951. Subsequently, as a lieutenant general, he was director of marine aviation from 1955 until retirement in 1957.

Both popular and respected, soft-spoken Chris Schilt was rightly regarded as one of the genuine pioneers of Marine Corps aviation.

NAVY (4)

LIEUTENANT COMMANDER WILLIAM MERRILL CORRY JR.

5 OCTOBER 1889–7 OCTOBER 1920

BORN: Quincy, Florida

DIED: Hartford, Connecticut

ACTION: Attempted rescue; Hartford, Connecticut; 3 October 1920 (age 40)

UNIT: Staff, Atlantic Fleet

AIRCRAFT: Curtiss JN-4H AS 38062

Lieutenant Commander William M. Corry Jr. and Lieutenant Arthur C. Wagner were stranded at the Hartford, Connecticut, golf club on the afternoon of 3 October 1920. Their borrowed Army trainer was due back at Mitchel Field, New York, but reportedly there were problems with the seventy-octane gasoline available at Hartford. After some tinkering, the prop was swung and the OX-5 clattered into life.

Corry and Wagner were experienced pilots. Only the twenty-third naval aviator (the first from Florida), Corry had graduated from Annapolis in 1910. Following battleship duty he became disappointed with Navy life and attempted to resign his commission, but the attempt was rejected. Applying for flight training, he reported to Pensacola in July 1915 and received his wings of gold eight months later.

William M. Corry Jr. in a Curtiss A-1 floatplane

During World War I, then-Lieutenant Corry commanded the first U.S. naval air station in France, at Le Croisic in the mouth of the Loire. He also commanded NAS Brest. Holder of the Navy Cross, he was currently on the staff of the Commander, Atlantic Fleet.

Wagner, age thirty-eight, was attached to the Naval Reserve Force at Mineola, Long Island. He had learned to fly at his own expense in 1911, joined the Navy in 1917, and became a naval aviator in October 1918. Following service in the battleship *Nevada* (BB-36) he joined the Ship-Plane Division at Hampton Roads, Virginia, in June 1920.

It was Wagner's turn to fly on the return trip, and he had just lifted the Curtiss Jenny to about seventy-five feet when the engine quit. Trying to avoid a tree, he banked and stalled. The Curtiss dropped off on one wing and smashed to earth—a classic takeoff accident.

Corry was thrown thirty feet from the crash but hit the ground relatively uninjured. Shaking himself, he saw the JN-4 burning from spilled gasoline. He did not see Wagner and assumed his friend was trapped in the burning wreck, which had flames reaching nearly thirty feet high. As Wagner struggled in agony, Corry tried to penetrate the fire but was repulsed by the searing heat. Somehow, Wagner broke free and staggered from the blazing Jenny, his clothes consumed in flames. Witnesses, including four doctors, rolled him on the ground, suppressing the fire. Help was quickly summoned.

Corry had broken ribs as well as burns on his face and hands, but at the Hartford hospital his condition was assessed as "not critical." Wagner, however, suffered severe burns and was not expected to last more than a few hours. He expired at 10:00 P.M.

Corry's condition worsened, and on the fifth a navy dispatch said that he was not expected to live. He lingered until the morning of the seventh, two days after his forty-first birthday. His funeral was held at St. Thomas Church in New York City the following Saturday.

The cause of the fatal crash was not conclusively proven. By some accounts, there was trouble with the gasoline, which both pilots strained through a chamois. The official report attributed probable cause to failure of the fuel line from the tank in the top wing, allowing raw gas to ignite on the hot engine manifold.

Corry's memory was perpetuated in three destroyers: DD-334, a Clemson-class vessel of 1921, scrapped under the London Naval Treaty of 1930; DD-463 of the 1941 Bristol Class, sunk by German mines off Normandy in June 1944; and the Gearing-class DD-817 commissioned in 1945.

Corry Field near Pensacola was named on 1 November 1922, but the name was transferred to the new air station in 1934. At least five of Corry's Annapolis classmates died in early aviation, including Clarence Bronson, Henry Cecil, and Godfrey Chevalier, who were memorialized with air station names. Other notables from the class of 1910 included Marc Mitscher, Charles Pownall, and Earl Spencer, first husband of Wallis Warfield, later Duchess of Windsor.

RICHARD EVELYN BYRD JR. AND FLOYD BENNETT

25 October 1888–11 March 1957 (Byrd)

25 October 1890–25 April 1928 (Bennett)

Born: Winchester, Virginia (Byrd); Warrensburg, New York (Bennett)

Died: Boston, Massachusetts (Byrd); Quebec, Canada (Bennett)

Action: North Pole flight; 9 May 1926 (age 37—Byrd; age 39—Bennett)

Aircraft: Fokker F.VIIA-3M Trimotor *Josephine Ford* (designated BA-1 for Byrd Arctic One)

Other decorations: (Byrd) Navy Cross, Distinguished Flying Cross

Despite the social and military gap between them, Commander Richard E. Byrd and Chief Machinist Floyd Bennett were close friends; they even shared the same birthday.

Byrd graduated from Annapolis in 1916 and was designated naval aviator number 608 in April 1918. While at Pensacola he met Chief Floyd Bennett, only the ninth noncommissioned pilot in the U.S. Navy. Byrd's World War I service included duty on Nova Scotia, where he became intrigued with long-range, overwater flight. After the war he developed aerial navigation aids, helped plan the NC boats' transatlantic flight in 1919, and worked on lighter-than-air designs for oceanic crossings. In 1924 he led the aviation detachment supporting a Navy arctic expedition in Greenland. There he again crossed paths with Floyd Bennett.

Floyd Bennett

Bennett had grown up in New York, where he worked as a mechanic. He joined the Navy in 1917 and became an enlisted pilot highly regarded for his mechanical knowledge and technical ability. After the war his duties included flight testing new and experimental aircraft.

Two years later Byrd teamed with Bennett to fly a Fokker Trimotor over

Richard E. Byrd Jr. with President Franklin D. Roosevelt and Eleanor Roosevelt

Richard E. Byrd Jr. in flight gear

the North Pole, unexplored since Robert Peary's 1909 sled expedition. Because it was a private venture, Byrd and Bennett took a leave of absence from the Navy with funding provided by the Ford and Rockefeller families as well as the *New York Times.* The Fokker, named *Josephine Ford,* took off from Spitzbergen, Norway, on 9 May 1926 with Bennett flying and Byrd navigating. Fifteen and a half hours later the Fokker returned to base, with Byrd claiming a 1,320-mile round trip between Spitzbergen and the North Pole. The average groundspeed was eighty-five miles per hour—faster than some observers felt possible with a heavy fuel load and skis on the aircraft.

Two days later, 11 May, aeronauts Roald Amundsen of Norway and Umberto Nobile of Italy, with American Lincoln Ellsworth and a crew of twelve, lifted off from Spitsbergen in the airship *Norge.* In seventy-two hours they flew 3,382 miles, crossing the North Pole and landing in Alaska. Their undisputed achievement was widely acclaimed.

Bennett subsequently flew an 8,000-mile tour within the United States, demonstrating the greater potential for airline passenger business at a time when airmail service garnered most attention.

Byrd continued his interest in long-range navigation, the next year competing for the $25,000 Ortieg Prize for first flight between New York and Paris. The Fokker *America* sustained damage in an accident in late April, and in the interim Charles Lindbergh flew into history. Far from resenting Lindbergh's success, Byrd had assisted "The Lone Eagle" with navigational preparation and helped arrange permission for Lindbergh's use of the lengthened runway on Long Island.

A month later, 29 June, Byrd took off with his crew, including Norwegian Arctic colleague Bernt Balchen, Lieutenant George Noville, and Bert Acosta. *America* reached Paris but was unable to land owing to fog. Balchen skillfully ditched off the Brittany coast, saving all on board.

Lindbergh's success inaugurated a succession of transatlantic crossings, not all of which were successful. In April 1928 an Irish-German crew disappeared and Bennett immediately set off from Detroit to join the search. Though he was running a high fever and did not know the missing airmen, he felt compelled to lend a hand. It was his undoing. He contracted influenza and died in Quebec on 25 April.

New York City's first airport began construction in 1928 and in 1931 was dedicated as Floyd Bennett Field. It became a naval air station in 1941, being decommissioned thirty years later.

Byrd was deeply saddened by his friend's premature death but remained determined to continue exploration. The following year, relying on grants and public subscription, Byrd and his companions established the base known as Little America on the Ross Ice Shelf. In November 1929—spring in the Antarctic—Byrd navigated to the South Pole with Bernt Balchen in a Ford Trimotor named *Floyd Bennett.* Byrd received the Navy Cross for planning and directing the nineteen-hour flight.

During World War II, Byrd joined the staff of the chief of naval operations. Shortly after the war he returned to Antarctica in programs such as Operation High Jump and Operation Deep Freeze; he made his fifth and last trip to the bottom of the world in 1956. A rear admiral, he died in Boston on 11 March 1957 at age 68. Among his popular writing was *Skyward,* an account of the 1926 flight; *Little America,* describing the Antarctic flight; and *Alone,* which described his five-month solitary ordeal and narrow rescue in 1934.

Close examination of Byrd's 1926 log and related materials has led to doubt whether *Josephine Ford* actually reached the North Pole. (See Richard Montague, *Oceans, Poles, and Airmen,* [1971].) Bennett, whose reticence may have been based on embarrassment, never seized the limelight that could have been his. Reportedly, he told Bernt Balchen that an oil leak forced the Fokker to turn back some 150 miles south of the goal.

Regardless of the actual circumstances of the 1926 expedition, Richard Byrd and Floyd Bennett unquestionably advanced the cause of aerial navigation and exploration.

Meanwhile, Byrd and Bennett returned to a triumphal reception in the United States, capped by presentation of the Tiffany Cross. Medal of Honor eligibility was questionable since Byrd and Bennett were not on active duty at the time of their polar flight, but in the euphoria of the moment it did not matter. Byrd was soon promoted to commander and began planning additional exploration.

LIEUTENANT CARLTON BARMORE HUTCHINS

12 SEPTEMBER 1904–2 FEBRUARY 1938

BORN: Albany, New York

DIED: California coast

ACTION: Lifesaving; California coast; 2 February 1938 (age 33)

UNIT: Patrol Squadron 11

AIRCRAFT: Consolidated PBY-3 BuNo 0463 (11-P-4)

It was one of the largest exercises ever conducted by the Pacific Fleet: ninety-eight ships, hundreds of aircraft, and 40,000 men testing the Navy's ability to defend the West Coast. Seventy miles off San Diego, PBY flying boats of Patrol Squadron 11 cruised overhead four battleships escorted by destroyers and cruisers on the night of 2 February 1938.

The weather was not conducive to surface-air coordination. Rain squalls swept by heavy winds compounded the problem, and Lieutenant Carlton B. Hutchins struggled with his controls. Hutchins had been flying naval aircraft for nine years, but seldom in such adverse conditions. The high-winged PBY bucked and protested at the gusts that tossed it in the dark sky. Hutchins had reason for additional concern, as he knew that other Consolidated P-boats shared the same airspace.

Despite a scholarship to Cornell, Hutchins entered the U.S. Naval Academy. He graduated in the class of 1926, a vintage year that produced aviation leaders such as Admiral James S. Russell; Vice Admirals P. D. Stroop, Robert B. Pirie, and Fitzhugh Lee; and Rear Admirals C. Wade McClusky and Clifford H. Duerfeldt. At Annapolis "Hutch" starred in football and crew, making friends easily and creating a minor legend when, on his "youngster" cruise to Europe, he offered to buy a drink for a classmate's prohibitionist Scottish uncle.

Carlton B. Hutchins

Following service in the battleship *Pennsylvania* (BB-38), Hutchins was accepted for flight training and received his wings of gold in February 1929. Over the next three years he flew dive bombers and fighters from the *Saratoga* (CV-3), then returned to Pensacola as an instructor. Subsequently he studied engineering, receiving a master's degree from California Institute of Technology in 1934.

Returning to the fleet, Hutchins was an observation pilot aboard the light cruisers *Memphis* (CL-13) and *Concord* (CL-10) until 1936. After ten years of active duty he was promoted to full lieutenant that June and served fourteen months at NAS Anacostia, the navy's aviation research facility.

Having flown carrier planes and scout-observation types, Hutchins's next professional step was patrol planes. He reported to VP-17 in the Panama Canal Zone in 1937 and later that year joined PatRon 11 in San Diego. Shortly he became commander of a Consolidated PBY-2, then the Navy's most capable flying boat.

It had been a new year of mixed fortunes in the PBY community. On 7 January the full seven-man crew of a San Diego boat had perished but twelve days later eighteen PBYs executed a flawless 2,570-mile flight from San Diego to Hawaii.

On the night of 2 February, something went terribly wrong. It was later theorized that uncommonly violent downdrafts threw Hutchins's 11-P-4 into Lieutenant Elmer G. Cooper's 11-P-3. Whatever the cause, the two PBYs collided in a rending crash. Cooper's plane caught fire and fell in flames; all seven men perished. Both planes were brand new, being completed in October 1937 and delivered to the squadron on 31 December.

Hutchins's PBY, only one serial number later than Cooper's, dropped toward the unseen ocean. Damaged beyond hope, 11-P-4 became even more unmanageable; Hutchins gave the order to bail out. He was unable to leave the pilot's seat, as it was necessary to maintain control of the PBY's unchecked descent. It is uncertain whether his noncommissioned copilot, Chief Marion Woodruff, was able to function, but four of his crew jumped into the rainy, storm-tossed blackness.

Of the fourteen men aboard the two P-boats, eleven perished including all seven of Cooper's crew. Jumping from Hutchins's boat were Chief Petty Officers Vernon Hatfield and Donald McKay, Machinist Louis Carpenter, and Radioman Jesse Hester, who died early the following morning. The survivors owed their lives to the courage of Carlton Hutchins.

Hutchins's crew: ACMM (NAP) Marion W. Woodruff (CP); ACMMs Vernon O. Hatfield and Donald B. McKay; AMM1/c John G. Niedzwiecki; AMM2/c Louis S. Carpenter; RM 1/c Jesse H. Hester.

Consolidated PBY-3 BuNo 0462 (11-P-3): Lt. Elmer G. Cooper; ACMM Maurice J. Fitzmaurice; AMM1/c George G. Griffin; AMM2/c (NAP) Joe E. Walton and William P. Landgrebe; RM2/c Julian Rawls; Cadet Edwin J. Koch.

4

WORLD WAR II

ARMY AIR FORCE: 36
MARINE CORPS: 11
NAVY: 6

TOTAL: 53

Official American involvement in World War II was more than twice as long as World War I, and the direct combat phase lasted nearly four times longer. During the forty-five months between December 1941 and September 1945, fifty-three in-flight Medals of Honor were awarded, including twenty-six posthumous citations. The 49 percent mortality rate did not include the four living recipients who died before VJ-Day: Bong, Kearby, O'Hare, and Vance.

Army Air Force casualties were particularly high, running at 58 percent posthumous awards; the combined naval services rate was about 33 percent.

Twenty-five in-flight medals were awarded for actions against Germany (including seven over Romania) and twenty-eight against Japan, of which eleven went to marines and six to Navy aviators.

Reflecting airpower's enormous growth since 1918, 12 percent of World War II Medals of Honor were in-flight awards, a relative increase of 100 percent. However, the philosophical concepts were unchanged. As before, it was asked what truly represents "above and beyond"? If a bomber pilot is killed, is his copilot not doing his duty by continuing to fly the aircraft? However, if that bomber has wounded aboard who would perish if the copilot bailed out, the decision to remain at the controls assumes greater importance. The problem arises not so much in what is determined to be above and beyond, but in erratic application from one war theater to another and among the various services. In one command, a pilot remaining at the controls of his doomed airplane received the Medal of Honor; in another, the Distinguished Service Cross.

In short, no awards system is perfect. But some are less imperfect than others.

Aerial combat claims have always been the subject of controversy. Among the seventeen World War II fighter pilots awarded the Medal of Honor largely for aircraft destroyed, one incident cannot be found in enemy files at all, and most other recipients downed fewer than were credited. However, the violence and turmoil of air combat have always resulted in erroneous claims, the large majority being made in good faith. Readers should recognize that errors of 100 to 500 percent represent confusion and optimism more than any intent to deceive, as even gun camera film can be misinterpreted.

A striking contrast exists between USAAF medals in Europe and the Pacific. Of twenty-five in-flight awards against Germany, only two went to fighter pilots; of thirteen against Japan, four flew fighters. Additionally, no troop carrier, liaison, or glider pilot in any theater was so recognized. The lesson could not be plainer: against "the main enemy" in Europe, the AAF was about bombardment aviation.

In the naval services the ratio was reversed: a dozen fighter pilots (ten marines) versus three dive bomber pilots and two patrol plane commanders. In an oversight that defies explanation, no torpedo pilots received the Medal of Honor, and only one carrier aviator was decorated after 1942.

Perhaps a partial answer lies in service politics.

In the aftermath of the Pearl Harbor debacle, fifteen Navy Medals of Honor were awarded for 7 December and none went to Army personnel. The situation continued over the next twelve months: twenty-five naval awards (including twelve marines and one coast guardsman) to eleven Army men, excluding a few postwar medals awarded for the 1941–42 period. Many of the presentations actually were made in 1943, but at the end of 1942 the naval services had garnered forty Medal of Honor citations—nearly four times the Army figure.

The plain fact was that in the first year of the war, the U.S. Army was not as heavily engaged as the naval services and claimed few successes. Therefore, it should not have surprised anyone that the medal count reflected that situation.

Although it is doubtful that anyone specifically tracked the aviation awards, again the Navy and Marines exceeded the Army Air Force. Nine naval aviators earned Medals of Honor for 1942 actions compared to four Army officers, two of whom were decorated for a diplomatic mission in North Africa.

One yardstick of public acclaim was the relative standing of American fighter pilots. At the end of 1942 marines occupied the top three slots in the pantheon of U.S. aces: Joe Foss with twenty-three victories (soon twenty-six); John L. Smith with nineteen; and Marion E. Carl with sixteen and one-half. Next in line came members of the flying Tigers, whose two top aces also were Navy trained. Foss and Smith received the Medal of Honor; Carl was nominated for it but was passed over. His case may be illustrative of the political nature of the medal.

Carl, who later held the world altitude and speed records, was a superb fighter pilot. Skilled and aggressive, he was widely regarded as the finest naval aviator of his generation. He felt that he did not receive the Medal of Honor because his commanding officer, John L. Smith, had received it. (Carl later advocated withholding all Medals of Honor until a war was ended.) However, Navy Department insiders insisted that Secretary of War Henry Stimson resented the large number of medals going to marines, especially in the relatively short period between August and December 1942.

One measure of Stimson's concern about the medal count was his action in May 1943. When Sergeant Maynard Smith was approved as the AAF's first living recipient in the European Theater, Stimson boarded an aircraft with a Medal of Honor in his pocket. The secretary of war personally carried the decoration to Britain to ensure that an Army Air Force man received the nation's highest decoration.

Without tracking other individual cases, the Army's enmity toward the Marine Corps is indisputable. The chief of staff, General George C. Marshall, was typical of his generation of Army officers, who bitterly resented the corps's fame in the "first War," gained under Army control at places such as Belleau Wood. Later, President Harry Truman—an Army artillery officer in 1918—drew fire by comparing the leathernecks' propaganda machine with Soviet premier Joseph Stalin's.

Interservice rivalry continued at the upper levels, particularly when the Marines siphoned off 600,000 high-quality young men whom the Army badly needed. Things were not improved when Marshall's attitude was returned in spades by the abrasive chief of naval operations, Admiral Ernest J. King. Yet as frosty as relations sometimes may have been among the U.S. Joint Chiefs, they seldom descended to the outright enmity between the Imperial Japanese Navy and its Army counterparts. Just one example will suffice: the Japanese Army Submarine School at Hiroshima.

Whatever the political wrangling in Washington, at the sharp end of the war the operating forces usually cooperated splendidly. No better examples exist than the Doolittle Raid launched from the carrier the USS *Hornet* (CV-8) or the truly joint nature of air operations at Guadalcanal. In the Solomon Islands—the meat-grinder of attrition warfare that chewed up Japan's most capable forces—Army, Navy, and Marine Corps squadrons proudly shared title to the "Cactus Air Force."

In the following year the medal count clearly favored the AAF, with ever larger air operations in Europe, Africa, and the Pacific. Fourteen Army fliers logged Medal of Honor actions during 1943 compared to four marines. One Navy pilot was decorated posthumously after the war.

During 1944 the industrial and organizational capacity of the United States achieved staggering heights. Numbered air forces emerged fully fledged; fleets that did not exist three years before ruled the Atlantic and Pacific. Sixteen AAF fliers achieved Medal of Honor status, as did two Navy pilots and a marine. Thereafter, General Henry H. Arnold's silver-winged airmen dominated the field, earning the war's final aviation Medals of Honor in 1945. If any proof of American air dominance was required, the last two aerial medals were awarded for actions two weeks apart—over Italy and Japan.

On VJ-Day only twenty-three of the fifty-three men who received in-flight Medals of Honor were still living. The oldest was then forty-eight; the youngest twenty-two. Whatever their age, they still had full lives ahead of them; nearly 300,000 of their comrades did not.

ARMY AIR FORCE (36)

LIEUTENANT COLONEL JAMES HAROLD DOOLITTLE

14 DECEMBER 1896–27 SEPTEMBER 1993

BORN: Alameda, California

DIED: Pebble Beach, California

ACTION: Tokyo raid; 18 April 1942 (age 45)

UNIT: First Special Aviation Project

AIRCRAFT: North American B-25B 40-2344

OTHER DECORATIONS: Distinguished Service Medal (2), Silver Star, Distinguished Flying Cross (3), Bronze Star Medal, Air Medal (4)

The lead B-25 was flown by America's greatest aviator. Behind him, fifteen more Mitchells waited their turn, Wright engines barking a staccato cacophony.

In the left seat of number 40-2344, Lieutenant Colonel Jimmy Doolittle tapped his brake pedals and the bomber lurched slightly on its nose wheel. Seawater splashed its salty spray across the Army bombers and Navy crewmen on the wooden flight deck of the USS *Hornet* (CV-8). Following the plane director's pantomime motions, Doolittle nudged sixteen tons of aircraft, fuel, and ordnance into position for takeoff.

James H. Doolittle

With the 19,000-ton carrier cresting the Pacific swells, the launch officer raised an arm and twirled a small flag in a circle—the signal for maximum power. Doolittle stood on the brakes, advanced the throttles and prop controls, and checked that his flaps were lowered for maximum lift. Then, as the ship's bow began to rise, the Navy lieutenant slashed forward with his hand.

Had he never won a race, bombed Tokyo, or commanded one (let alone three) air forces, James Harold Doolittle still would remain one of the most significant figures of aviation history. An exceptional pilot from the beginning, he was retained as an instructor during World War I. In 1920 he was sent to Massachusetts Institute of Technology, where he received a doctorate in engineering. He then began a series of pioneering flights, including the first transcontinental crossing in less than twenty-four hours. Ten years later, 1932, he was first to cross the country in under twelve hours.

Later Doolittle worked on what he regarded as his most significant contribution—development of blind flying equipment and techniques. Working with the Sperry Company, he helped perfect instruments such as the artificial horizon and, in 1929, he made the first blind takeoff and landing in history. Had he done nothing else, his place in aviation history would have been assured. At that point he had already won the Schneider Cup and the Mackay Trophy in 1925.

Lieutenant Doolittle left the army in 1930 to manage Shell Oil's aviation department. No deskbound aviator, he continued his winning ways: the Harmon Trophy in 1930, the Bendix race in 1931 and the Thompson in 1932. His racing triumphs gained him a reputation as a "daredevil," but nothing was farther from the truth. He was aptly described as "the master of the calculated risk" and proved it repeatedly.

Deeply committed to the art and science of flight, Doolittle was a near unique combination of aviator and scientist. His aerobatic performances stunned fellow fliers, and among his lesser achievements was making the first outside loop. Renowned as a superb pilot and champion drinker, he made infrequent lapses of judgment that soon passed into legend. While selling Curtiss aircraft in South America he did a handstand on the window sill of a hotel room, lost his balance, and fell two stories. The former tumbler regained his orientation, landed feet first and saved his life but broke both ankles. Two days later, with his feet tied to his P-1's rudder pedals, he won a mock dogfight.

Doolittle also provided intellectual contributions

Sailors pulled the chocks and Doolittle released the brakes. The twin-tailed Mitchell slowly accelerated but with thirty knots of wind over the deck, the airfoil took the weight.

The bomber cleared the blow in a dangerously nose-high angle at minimum airspeed. Doolittle and his copilot, Lieutenant Richard Cole, shoved forward on the yoke and raised the landing gear while their plane sank visibly. Sailors held their breath.

Number 344 reappeared into view, nose level with the flaps coming up. Doolittle banked around, made a low pass over the deck to check his compass heading, and disappeared into leaden skies. One by one the other fifteen planes lumbered down *Hornet*'s deck, each with more room than its predecessor. Their target was the Japanese homeland.

to aviation. In 1924 and 1925 he wrote the first aviation master's thesis and doctoral dissertation. One of his photos showed him standing before a GeeBee racer, earflaps raised on his leather helmet, Phi Beta Kappa key on his belt. That picture spoke volumes.

Doolittle also was politically astute. Realizing that neither the armed forces nor the petroleum industry would independently develop high-octane aviation fuel, he midwifed the project by assuring the Army and Shell Oil that the other was interested—before either was prepared. The result led to greater performance from aircraft engines.

Following the Tokyo raid, Doolittle was promoted to brigadier general. Subsequently he ran General Dwight Eisenhower's Twelfth Air Force in North Africa in late 1942, and subsequently the Fifteenth, often logging combat missions. When Doolittle took over the Eighth Air Force in early 1944 he kept his hand in, usually by flying hot aircraft on inspection tours. He was airborne in a P-38 on D-Day, surveying the Normandy landings. His decision to cut the fighters loose from close bomber escort sounded the death knell of the Luftwaffe over northern Europe. Doolittle's Mustangs and Thunderbolts hunted the Germans to destruction in the air and on the ground.

After VE-Day, Doolittle prepared to lead the Mighty Eighth against Japan. He landed a B-29 on Okinawa in August 1945 and was among the Allied leaders present when Imperial Japan surrendered in September.

Retirement for "General Jimmy" was if anything as active as his military career. He became an insurance executive in Los Angeles, and at age eighty he shunned the elevator to his third-floor office, preferring the stairs, "so I'll be in shape for World War III."

Congress granted Doolittle a fourth star in 1985, and while it may have been satisfying, it meant less to him than his professional reputation. His precise, clipped speech bespoke the mathematical precision of his scientific bent (he still said, "aeroplane"), and his unmatched accomplishments insist that when the most significant names of the first century of flight are compiled, Jimmy Doolittle will stand near the top of the list.

The concept for the first Special Aviation Product belonged to a naval officer, Captain Francis Low. Of necessity, the Army-Navy plan involved joint service cooperation, and General Hap Arnold of the Army Air Force immediately signed on. He chose Doolittle to organize the event in the ten weeks available, never thinking that his old friend would fly the mission. Doolittle had other ideas, and on 18 April 1942 he led seventy-nine Army fliers off *Hornet*'s heaving deck.

At 200 feet Doolittle settled onto a westerly course. The plan, carefully crafted in the four months since Pearl Harbor, already had come adrift. Early detection by Japanese picket boats forced a daytime launch more than 600 miles from the target cities of Tokyo, Yokohama, and Nagoya. It meant little fuel reserve upon reaching the China coast, based on the proposed 400-mile flight. Instead, they departed 220 miles and thirty hours early.

Nevertheless, Doolittle pressed ahead, his bomb bay packed with incendiaries to light the way for his hand-picked crews. For James H. Doolittle, it was the chance of a lifetime. He understood what was at stake. "I don't intend to be taken prisoner," he announced. In the precise, clipped tones of an engineer, he said that if his plane became disabled over Japan he would bail out his crew and dive into the most lucrative target he could find. Nobody doubted his words.

Making landfall that afternoon, Doolittle followed the direction of Lieutenant Henry Potter, the navigator who placed them eighty miles north of Tokyo. They dropped their fire bombs five hours after launch, drawing little attention from the astonished defenders, and headed westerly across the Sea of Japan. That night, in worsening weather after thirteen hours aloft, they had no choice but to bail out over the China coast. Doolittle followed Cole, Potter, and Staff Sergeants Fred Braemer and Paul Leonard. Doolittle's parachute descent—his third—ended in a reeking rice paddy.

Next morning a disconsolate Doolittle surveyed the wreckage of his B-25. His crew regrouped, and Sergeant Braemer snapped a photo of his forlorn CO. "I guess they'll send me to Leavenworth," Doolittle gloomed.

"No sir," Braemer smiled. The bombardier predicted that Doolittle would be promoted to general, adding, "They're going to give you the Congressional Medal of Honor."

Thirty-two days later Braemer's prediction came true. Headlines proclaimed, "Doolittle Do'ed It!" and on 20 May, Doolittle stood in the Oval Office while President Roosevelt awarded him the first Medal of Honor bestowed upon an airman in World War II. Astonished at the turn of events following an apparent failure, Doolittle solemnly intoned, "I will spend the rest of my life trying to earn this honor." He insisted that he accepted the medal on behalf of all his airmen, three of whom had been killed and eight of whom were captured by the Japanese. Three of the latter were executed in captivity.

Jimmy Doolittle's war had just begun.

Crew: 1Lts. Richard E. Cole (CP) and Henry A. Potter (N); SSgts. Paul J. Leonard (B) and Fred A. Braemer (FE).

CAPTAIN HARL PEASE JR.

10 April 1917–8 October 1942

Born: Plymouth, New Hampshire

Died: Rabaul, New Britain

Action: Bombing mission; Rabaul, New Britain; 6–7 August 1942 (age 25)

Unit: 93rd Bomb Squadron, 19th Bomb Group, 7th Air Force

Aircraft: Boeing B-17E 41-2429 (often listed as 2439)

Other decorations: Distinguished Flying Cross (2), Air Medal, Purple Heart

The 19th Bombardment Group was one of the major players of the U.S. Army Air Force in the Pacific Theater, even before the war began. In May 1941 twenty-one B-17s flew from Hamilton field, California, to Hickam field, logging the first mass flight of land-based aircraft to Hawaii. On 7 December a dozen 19th Group bombers were caught in the Pearl Harbor attack, and others fought throughout the Philippines and Java campaigns. It was no coincidence, then, when the 19th became heavily involved at Guadalcanal, the first American offensive of World War II.

Despite its losses, the 19th Group received four Distinguished Unit Citations in that low ebb, with two more before the war's end. One of the factors in the group's exceptional record was a young officer named Harl Pease.

Hailing from Plymouth, New Hampshire, Pease attended Tilton Prep School and graduated from the University of New Hampshire in 1939. He completed pilot training in June 1940 and qualified in B-17s at March field, California. In May 1941 Pease participated in the first mass flight of B-17s from California to Hawaii, and in October from Albuquerque, New Mexico, to the Philippines and on to Australia.

In the Philippines, Pease flew with the 93rd Bomb Squadron until Clark field became untenable. In January 1942 he was among the personnel evacuated by submarine to Java, where he continued flying combat missions until the group withdrew to Australia.

By the summer of 1942 Pease was a captain and operations officer of the 93rd Squadron. In conjunction with the Marine Corps landing at Guadalcanal on 7 August, the 19th Group was ordered to send a maximum effort to the Japanese naval-air complex at Rabaul, New Britain. It was an ambitious

Harl Pease Jr.

undertaking, staging from Mareeba, Northern Australia, through Horn Island to Port Moresby, New Guinea.

En route to Moresby on the sixth, Pease's bomber developed engine trouble, requiring a return to Mareeba. There Pease and his crew "confiscated" a war-weary B-17E used for familiarization and training. Though only nine months old, it had four high-time engines, no electric fuel transfer, and needed long-range tanks installed. With Pease's men at the point of exhaustion, two or three other crews helped arm and fuel his plane, directed by his best friend and flight leader, Captain Ed Jacquet.

Following intense field repairs to the multihued Fortress, Pease's crew was airborne that night. They landed at Moresby at 1:00 A.M. on the seventh, having flown almost continuously since 6:00 the previous morning. They had less than three hours sleep before manning up for Rabaul.

Fifteen Fortresses were assigned to the mission but one crashed on takeoff at Horn Island and another aborted, so Lieutenant Colonel Richard Carmichael led thirteen unescorted bombers. The target was Vunakanau Airfield, one of Rabaul's outlying fighter fields. Approaching the target at 22,000 feet, the Fortresses were intercepted by as many as twenty-six Mitsubishi A6M3 Zeros of the Tainan Wing and Second Naval Air Group. The Japanese fighters were tenacious and aggressive but did not prevent the 19th from bombing. The Americans claimed six Zeroes shot down, and though no A6Ms were lost, a dozen were hit by B-17 gunners.

Pease's Fortress was the last over the target, and the Zeroes pursued the Boeings for twenty minutes or more, concentrating on Pease's aircraft. Cannon and machine gun fire holed the auxiliary tank, which caught fire and was seen to drop from the bomb bay. It did no good. Pease's war-weary bomber was unable to maintain formation and dropped behind. Pursued by eleven Zeros, the B-17 lost altitude until crashing into the jungle near the juncture of the Maulo and Powell Rivers. No parachutes were seen and the crew was declared lost.

For his extreme devotion to duty, Harl Pease was awarded the Medal of Honor, the Distinguished flying Cross, and the Air Medal, which President Roosevelt presented to his parents on 2 December. Pease was also recognized in 1957, when Portsmouth Air Force Base was renamed in his honor. When the base closed, Pease's name was perpetuated in the Air National Guard facility.

After the war survivors of the Rabaul prison camps returned with a grim tale. Pease and at least one other man survived the shootdown and were taken to Rabaul. Pease had been wounded in one leg when Japanese fighters shot at his parachute. However, in captivity he impressed his guards, some of whom called him "Captain Boeing," as the Japanese respected the B-17.

On 8 October, two months after his shootdown, Harl Pease and at least three other prisoners were killed by their captors.

The crash site was found in June 1946, and the full story gradually emerged. Veterans of the 19th Group, who bore little regard for Douglas MacArthur, felt that his public relations office bent the facts of Pease's case in a number of ways. The citation included the assertion that on 6 August, Pease's flying Fortress lost an engine over a New Guinea target and returned to base that evening. In truth, of course, Pease was staging to Moresby on the sixth. According to the citation, he queried his crew if they would volunteer for the "extra" Rabaul mission when in fact they went as a matter of routine. The citation's statement that Pease made a second pass over Rabaul to divert enemy flak gunners also is erroneous.

Whatever the details of his last mission, Harl Pease and the 19th Bomb

Group typified the American airmen who fought tenaciously with diminishing assets against the best efforts of a determined enemy.

Crew: F/Sgt. Frederick W. Earp, RAAF (CP); 1Lt. Robert B. Burleson (B); 2Lt. Richard M. Wood (N); SSgt. Rex E. Matson (FE); Sgts. Alavar Liimatainen (RO), Chester Czechowski (G), David Brown (G), and Fred Oettel (G).

BRIGADIER GENERAL KENNETH NEWTON WALKER

17 July 1898–5 January 1943

Born: Cerrillos, New Mexico

Died: New Britain

Action: Bombing mission; Rabaul, New Britain; 5 January 1943 (age 42)

Unit: 5th Bomber Command (43rd Bomb Group), 5th Air Force

Aircraft: Boeing B-17F 41-24458 *San Antonio Rose II*

Other decorations: Silver Star, Legion of Merit, Purple Heart

Ken Walker was a true believer. Among the early U.S. airpower advocates, none worked harder to develop the theory and practice of bombardment aviation.

Twenty-year-old Lieutenant Walker won his wings in November 1918, the month the Great War ended in Europe. However disappointed he may have been at missing combat, he devoted himself to bringing the potential of airpower to hard reality. Both a practitioner and theorist, he rose to command bombing squadrons in the United States and the Philippines, and attended the Air Corps Tactical School in 1928–29. It was a seminal organization in the history of the U.S. Air Force, and Walker was in his element. He was retained as an instructor teaching the theory of aerial bombardment.

In the company of like-minded airmen, Walker not only taught theory but evolved a modern doctrine for employing airpower against an industrialized enemy. With Harold George, Haywood Hansell, Laurence Kuter, and Donald Wilson, Walker foresaw that the headlong rush of technology would cross the line on the chart representing the bombardment mission. At that point—only several years downstream—long-range bombers would execute the principles advocated by the Tactical School brain trust.

Kenneth N. Walker

Their optimism was not widely shared, even within the air service. Walker clashed with a senior officer named George C. Kenney, who advocated low-level attack aviation over strategic bombardment. Additionally, in 1934 Walker was among the true believers asked to appear before the Howell Commission on military aviation. The five fliers laid their professional lives on the line, advocating strategic bombing at a time when the Depression-strapped Army hierarchy was unable to purchase enough small-arms ammunition or gasoline for training. Walker and his friends offered to travel at their own expense, incurring the ire of hidebound superiors, and told their tale. Their commitment was ultimately rewarded as all five became generals.

Meanwhile, in 1941 Walker was a lieutenant colonel with the War Plans Division of the Army Air Forces staff. Again the five horsemen of the Tactical School pooled their talents, producing AWPD-1, essentially the blueprint for waging aerial warfare against Germany and Japan. In the years before computers, the awesome task was completed in merely nine days during August. When Japanese naval aircraft attacked Hawaii that December, the U.S. Army Air Forces had the foundation it needed for training, equipping, and fighting a global war.

By mid-1942 Walker's experience and ability were too extensive to ignore. He pinned on his brigadier's star and became commander of V Bomber Command in Lieutenant General George Kenney's Fifth Air Force. As of that fall, Walker still had precious few resources: about thirty operational "heavies" and perhaps one hundred twin-engine bombers. Despite the paucity of aircraft, Walker firmly believed what he had written before the war: "a well-planned and well-conducted bombardment attack . . . cannot be stopped."

However, the reality of the Pacific War collided with the doctrine that the Tactical School had evolved. As an apostle of strategic airpower, Walker intuitively supported high altitude precision bombing. Fifth Bomber Command's primary targets often were ships, which were virtually immune to such techniques. Consequently, lower altitudes for multiengine and masthead attacks for twin-engine bombers became necessary. It was not an easy transition, but Walker often led from the front, in the air.

Though Kenney cautioned his former rival against undue risk, Walker wanted to observe operations to assess his groups' tactics. He received a Silver Star for repeated combat missions but also drew Kenney's ire. After a rough Rabaul mission Walker's bomber landed with three feet missing from one wing and Kenney laid down the law: Walker was too valuable as a commander and possessed too much intelligence data to risk over Japanese bases. In October and December 1942 Kenney prohibited Walker from further combat missions.

Perhaps considering Fifth Bomber Command his fiefdom, Walker ignored the directive. On 5 January 1943 he led a dozen B-17s and B-24s to strike Japanese shipping at Rabaul, New Britain. He would fly in a B-17 named *San Antonio Rose II.* It was his seventeenth mission—perhaps a record for a general officer.

Walker rode with the 43rd Group's air exec, Lieutenant Colonel Jack Bleasdale, and Major Allen Lindberg, skipper of the 64th Squadron. Another officer objected to so much seniority in the same aircraft but Walker overruled the staffer. Additionally, it is possible that the shift from a dawn to a daylight raid was based on concern over poor night bombing accuracy and turbulent weather that would make a predawn rendezvous virtually impossible. In any case, the weather over the target was good.

The B-17s led the Liberators with each plane bombing individually. Pressing through heavy flak, Walker's formation was intercepted by Japanese fighters (mainly 11th *Sentai* Ki-43s with a few Zeroes), which shot down one Fortress. The remainder bombed visually, claiming hits on nine ships in the harbor. *San Antonio Rose* limped away with one engine idle and trailing smoke, pursued by other Oscars, and the crippled Boeing was lost to sight. Searches produced no trace of Walker, his plane, or crew.

The Americans had lost two B-17s while at least one 5,800-ton freighter was sunk. Two Oscars and one pilot also were lost in the engagement.

Despite the fact that Walker had violated direct orders, Kenney recommended him for the Medal of Honor. Theater commander Douglas MacArthur endorsed the nomination, which quickly made its way through the review process. Ken Walker had many admirers in the States, and approval was a foregone conclusion. President Roosevelt presented the medal to Walker's sixteen-year-old son Kenneth less than three months later, on 25 March 1943. Subsequently ten-year-old Douglas received his father's Legion of Merit, presented for Walker's WPD work.

More than half a century later, the search continues for Ken Walker and the crew of *San Antonio Rose.*

Crew: Lt. Col. Jack W. Bleasdale (P); Maj. Allan Lindbergh (CP); Capt. Benton H. Daniel; 2Lts. John W. Hanson and Robert L. Hand; TSgt. Dennis Craig; Sgt. Leslie A. Stewart; PFC William G. Fraser; Pvts. Liland W. Stone and Quentin W. Blakely.

FIRST LIEUTENANT JACK WARREN MATHIS

25 September 1921–18 March 1943

Born: San Angelo, Texas

Died: Over Germany

Action: Bombing mission; Vegesack, Germany; 18 March 1943 (age 21)

Unit: 359th Bomb Squadron, 303rd Bomb Group, 8th Air Force

Aircraft: Boeing B-17F 41-24561 (BN-T) *Sure Stuff/The Duchess*

Other decorations: Air Medal (2), Purple Heart

On 18 March 1943 twenty-two flying Fortresses of the 303rd Bomb Group attacked submarine pens at Vegesack, Germany. During the run to the target the B-17s met heavy flak which pummeled the low squadron, the 359th, at 24,000 feet. Leading the squadron was Captain Harold L. Stouse in *Sure Stuff/The Duchess.* His bombardier was first Lieutenant Jack W. Mathis, a twenty-one-year-old Texan designated the squadron's lead bombardier for

Jack W. Mathis

the mission; the other Forts would "drop on lead" when they saw *The Duchess* release.

It was Mathis's fourteenth mission, putting him over the halfway mark to completing his tour—no easy task in European skies in 1943. The "Hell's Angels" had flown their first missions in November 1942, ranking them high in seniority in "The Mighty Eighth."

Growing up in the West Texas town of San Angelo, Jack Mathis enlisted in the field artillery at Fort Sill, Oklahoma, in June 1940. His older brother Mark's interest in aviation drew him to aircrew training at San Angelo's Goodfellow field in January 1942. Commissioned as a bombardier on 4 July, he served with groups in the Southwest before joining the original complement of the 303rd in Utah. Upon arrival in Britain the group was based at Molesworth, Huntingdonshire. There he wrote informative letters to his former CO at Goodfellow field—Major Leon R. Vance, another future Medal of Honor airman.

Mathis was on the Norden sight, his crosshairs tracking toward the release point when, less than sixty seconds from drop, a shell detonated near the right side of *The Duchess*'s nose. Metal shards blasted the plexiglass with such force that Mathis was hurled to the rear of the compartment, mortally wounded. Incredibly, the young Texan found the strength to ignore his nearly severed right arm and severe wounds in his body, crawl back to his sight, and drop his bombs. The navigator, Lieutenant John Stupe, also had been bowled over by the explosion but escaped injury and did not realize Mathis's critical wounds until the bombardier collapsed while reaching to close the bomb bay doors.

Though the group lost a plane on the Vegesack mission, Stouse brought *The Duchess* home to Molesworth. She flew a total of fifty-nine missions before being retired, and her sole loss was Jack Mathis, the dedicated bombardier who became the Eighth Air Force's first Medal of Honor recipient and the first against Germany. He was buried at Fairmont Cemetery in his native San Angelo, where on 21 September 1943 his medal was presented to his family at Goodfellow field.

In one of the tragic ironies of the Eighth Air Force, Jack's brother Mark replaced him as a bombardier in the 359th Squadron. Mark's plane was lost in the North Sea after a mission to Kiel on 14 May 1943.

In 1988 San Angelo's airport was named Mathis Municipal for Jack W. and R. Mark Mathis. Nine years later Jack's Medal of Honor was presented to the Mighty Eighth Air Force Museum in Savannah, Georgia.

Crew: 1Lt. Harold L. Stouse (P); 2Lts. Squire T. O'Connor (CP) and John R. Stupe (N); SSgts. Eldon Audiss (E) and Calvin Owen (TG); Sgts. Donald Richardson (R), Theron Tupper (WG), and John Garriott (BT).

STAFF SERGEANT MAYNARD HARISON SMITH

19 MAY 1911–11 MAY 1984

BORN: Caro, Michigan

DIED: Unknown

ACTION: Bombing mission; France; 1 May 1943 (age 31)

UNIT: 423rd Bomb Squadron, 306th Bomb Group, 8th Air Force

AIRCRAFT: Boeing B-17F 42-29649

OTHER DECORATIONS: Air Medal (2)

Son of a circuit judge, "Snuffy" Smith enlisted in the Army Air Force in 1942 and was trained as an aerial gunner. He was assigned to the Eighth Air Force, joining the 306th Group at Thruleigh, Bedfordshire, in early 1943 but was not immediately assigned to a crew.

Smith's first combat was a May Day mission to St. Nazaire, which encountered serious opposition compounded by navigational error. A seven-tenths cloud cover hindered ground observation, placing the group's return leg too close to the French coast. As the formation descended through the clouds, flak batteries opened fire from the Brest Peninsula. Attrition was appalling: the 306th lost ten of its sixteen Fortresses committed to the mission.

Maynard H. Smith with Browning .50 caliber in B-17 "waist" position

The bomber piloted by Lieutenant Lewis P. Johnson sustained multiple hits, setting fires in the radio compartment and tail. In the ball turret, rookie gunner Smith may not have appreciated the seriousness of the situation. (According to one group veteran, Smith forgot to bring his parachute aboard the plane.) With his turret inoperative, he crawled out of the confined space in time to see both waist gunners and the radio operator bail out. With previous combat experience, all three men concluded that their plane was doomed.

Snuffy Smith felt otherwise. Without even knowing whether the pilots remained aboard, he used a sweater to cover his face from the smoke and flames, grabbed an extinguisher, and fought the fire in the radio compartment. At that point he noticed the plane remained in formation and realized that somebody was still flying.

Smith headed aft, intending to douse the smaller fire around the tail wheel when he found a wounded man. "The tail gunner had blood all over him," Smith related. "He had been hit in the back . . . probably through the left lung." Smith applied first aid, then scrambled back forward to resume his battle with the radio compartment fire.

At that point Focke-Wulf 190s attacked the formation and the gunner alternated firing both waist .50 calibers. When fighter attacks abated, he returned to fire fighting and tending to the wounded tail gunner. The radio compartment fire was fed by punctured oxygen lines, heating the blaze even more and "cooking off" machine gun ammunition. Smith grabbed the ammo boxes available to him and tossed them through a large hole burned in the fuselage. He pulled others away from the persistent fire.

In all, Smith fought the fires, blazed away at FW-190s, and treated his crewmate for an hour and a half, without help. Toward the end, out of fire extinguishers, he emptied a water bottle, smothered the flames with clothing and even urinated on the persistent, smoldering portions.

Lieutenant Johnson landed the crippled Fort at Predannack, Cornwall, the first available field after Land's End. At that point, number 649 was a flying wreck: steel and aluminum parts had melted inside the fuselage; one prop was hit; the top turret, flaps, and a fuel tank had been damaged and the tail wheel burned off.

The St. Nazaire mission depleted the crew: the radio operator and both waist gunners drowned; the tail gunner was severely wounded. The copilot and nose gunner–togglier were killed later that year and the navigator, later wounded, prematurely ended his tour.

Nominated for the Medal of Honor on his first mission, Smith flew at least four more sorties before he was reassigned to ground duties (later he claimed thirteen additional missions). When approved for the Medal of Honor, it was discovered that none existed in the European Theater so Secretary of War Henry Stimson carried the medal with him on his way across the Atlantic. Smith was awarded the second ETO Medal of Honor on 12 July, and reportedly took to signing his name in British fashion: "SSgt. Maynard H. Smith, CMH."

The citation concluded, "This soldier's gallantry in action, undaunted bravery, and loyalty to his aircraft and fellow crew members, without regard for his personal safety, is an inspiration to the U.S. armed forces."

Smith's subsequent career was less than inspirational. His rebellious conduct was indulged far longer than many contemporaries felt warranted. In December 1944 the group operations officer recommended Smith's reduction to private owing to his "insufferable" attitude and lack of "any desire to perform his duties in a manner becoming his rank." He was discharged in May 1945, far too late to suit many of his comrades at Thurleigh.

After the war Smith became a self-described "promoter," falling afoul of the law on at least two occasions involving fraud. Nevertheless, he remained philosophical about life and living and offered modern Air Force noncoms some advice: "Get out of the house and run around. If you're not married, get a girlfriend. It keeps you young."

Crew: 1st Lt. Lewis P. Johnson (P); 2Lt. Robert McCallum (CP); 1Lt. Stanley M. Kissebrth (N); TSgts. William W. Fahrenhold (FE) and Henry R. Bean (RO); SSgts. J. C. Melaun (NG), Joseph S. Bukackek Jr. (WG), Robert V. Folliard (WG), and Roy H. Gibson (TG).

CAPTAIN JAY ZEAMER AND SECOND LIEUTENANT JOSEPH RAY SARNOSKI

25 July 1918– (Zeamer)

30 January 1915–16 June 1943 (Sarnoski)

Born: Carlisle, Pennsylvania (Zeamer); Simpson, Pennsylvania (Sarnoski)

Died: Solomon Islands (Sarnoski)

Action: Reconnaissance mission; Solomon Islands; 16 June 1943 (age 24—Zeamer; age 28—Sarnoski)

Unit: 43rd Bomb Group, 5th Air Force

Aircraft: B-17E 41-2666 (Nicknamed *Lucy*)

Other decorations: (Zeamer) Silver Star (2), Distinguished Flying Cross (2), Air Medal (2), Purple Heart; (Sarnoski) Silver Star, Air Medal, Purple Heart

Aerial reconnaissance was a dangerous occupation in the Southwest Pacific during 1943. Perennially short of assets, the Fifth Air Force could not afford many dedicated "recce" units so the role often fell to bombers for long range missions and fighters for shorter hops.

Previously a B-26 copilot, Captain Jay Zeamer was a member of the 43rd Bomb Group, a B-17 pilot with forty-seven missions during the previous eight months. On 16 June 1943 his crew volunteered for a single-plane photo-

Jay Zeamer *(far left)*, 16 January 1944, with mother and General H. H. Arnold *(far right)*

Joseph R. Sarnoski

mapping mission to the Solomon Islands, 600 miles northeast of its base at Port Moresby, New Guinea. Zeamer's crew was famous for its jack-of-all-trades attitude; no job was too daunting.

Zeamer was briefed to scout the Japanese airfield on Buka, a small island north of Bougainville. With Allied forces planning a major amphibious landing at Empress Augusta Bay later that year, detailed intelligence was important. The sixteenth looked promising for weather, so the mission was a "go." The 43rd Group had flown to Bougainville previously and most of the missions were "milk runs." All that was about to change.

Zeamer's bombardier was Second Lieutenant Joseph Sarnoski, a fellow Pennsylvanian. A few years before the war Sarnoski had been a "rookie" soldier at Langley Field, Virginia. There he participated in an experimental program to determine whether the Norden bomb sight could be used by large numbers of enlisted men in case of sudden, massive requirements. Since then Sarnoski had been provided with far more thorough training.

Overflying Buka, the Fortress crew counted twenty-two Japanese fighters taking off. However, the B-17 was well above them and cleared the area without difficulty. Moments later Zeamer turned onto his mapping run along the

Bougainville coast. Less than one minute from completing his mission, the Boeing was met head-on by five enemy fighters. The Japanese had learned the same lessons as their Luftwaffe counterparts: the B-17 was most vulnerable from the nose. The fighters came in shooting. In the nose, Sarnoski returned fire. Both sides scored hits.

The interceptors were eight A6Ms from the 251st *Kokutai* under Chief flight Petty Officer Yoshio Oki. He led the head-on attack but his Zero was struck by return fire, holing a fuel tank. Oki returned to Buin, escorted by a wingman, but the remaining Japanese pressed their attacks.

Manning his machine gun, Sarnoski was wounded in both arms and legs but continued shooting. Other crewmen thought that his fire was accurate; they reported two fighters shot down. Zeamer thought that Sarnoski broke up the first attack and possibly saved the B-17 from immediate destruction.

On the flight deck, Zeamer also contributed to the bomber's defense. Some 43rd aircraft had field modifications with forward-firing guns activated by a trigger on the control yoke. He lined up his improvised sight on a Zero, pressed the button, and was rewarded with hits on the attacker.

But the other Japanese pressed their advantage. Unknown to Allied briefers, as many as 400 enemy fighters had been transferred into the area. According to one Air Force source, Bougainville and Rabaul had become hornets' nests.

On another pass the Japanese scored repeatedly. A 20mm shell exploded in the bombardier's position, knocking Sarnoski backward. The same shell wounded Zeamer, breaking one leg and cutting his arms. Critically wounded, Sarnoski pulled himself back to his position, grasped his gun and continued firing. When his Browning fell silent, he was found dead over his weapon.

The same attack punctured the bomber's oxygen system, holed the hydraulics, and destroyed the flight instruments on Zeamer's panel. He realized that to continue a straight flight path would ensure destruction so he used the only option available: gravity.

Zeamer shoved forward on the yoke, nosing over from 25,000 feet. The descent was so steep and fast that he could only estimate his altitude by the increasing inches of mercury reading on his manifold pressure gauges. He hauled the damaged bomber into level flight at 10,000 feet.

The six remaining Zeros made so many passes that the Americans estimated seventeen fighters. Beset from all angles, Zeamer jinked the damaged bomber as best he could. Incredibly, the Fortress held together after some thirty minutes of desperate maneuvering by a half crippled pilot. The fighters finally disengaged, low on fuel and nearly out of ammunition. (They fired 1,257 rounds of 7.7 and 20mm.) Zeamer's gunners had claimed two shot down and two probably destroyed, though three Zeros were damaged and one ditched with engine trouble. By then only the copilot and two gunners were uninjured.

Jay Zeamer's battle was not over. Weak from blood loss, he remained in his seat, directing the crew. Said the flight engineer, Sergeant Johnnie Able, "Capt. Zeamer, although severely wounded and losing blood continuously, remained conscious throughout the trip. Although in great pain he kept his head and kept command of the ship until we landed. I have never seen a man with so much 'guts.'"

Approaching New Guinea, Zeamer doubted that the B-17 could clear the Owen Stanley Mountains so he had his copilot, Lieutenant John Britton, head for Dobodura on the east coast. Britton did a marvelous job: without brakes or flaps, the bomber ran off the runway and ground-looped to a halt. The ambulance crew found one dead and six wounded aboard. Originally Zeamer was thought dead as well: he lost half his blood from 120 puncture wounds. For three days he lay between life and death.

Colonel Merian C. Cooper of Fifth Air Force headquarters (who had recommended Frank Luke for the Medal of Honor in 1919) compared Zeamer's feat to those of Luke and Rickenbacker, adding, "Both of these officers were awarded the Congressional Medal of Honor [*sic*]." The next day, 17 July, Major General Ennis Whitehead, the Fifth's deputy commander, endorsed the medal recommendation. Sarnoski's posthumous award was authorized in December 1943.

Zeamer was evacuated "stateside." He received the Medal of Honor from General Hap Arnold in January 1944 and was medically discharged as a lieutenant colonel in Janary 1945. The rest of his crew received Distinguished Service Crosses, making 41-2666 easily the most-decorated military aircraft in U.S. history.

Summarizing his exceptional survival, Zeamer said, "In a tight spot you'll come out better if you grab the long chance and plow through rather than run away."

Crew: 2Lts. John T. Britton (CP) and Ruby Johnston (N); SSgts. Jonnie J. Able (FE) and William Vaughn (RO); TSgt. Forrest E. Dillman (WG); Sgts. Herbert Pugh (TG) and George Kendrick (photo).

FLIGHT OFFICER JOHN CARY MORGAN

24 AUGUST 1914–17 JANUARY 1991

BORN: Vernon, Texas

DIED: Nebraska

ACTION: Bombing mission; Germany; 28 July 1943 (age 28)

UNIT: 326th Bomb Squadron, 92nd Bomb Group, 8th Air Force

AIRCRAFT: Boeing B-17F 42-29802 (JW-C) *Ruthie II*

OTHER DECORATIONS: Distinguished Flying Cross, Air Medal (2), Purple Heart

John Morgan took the long way 'round the world to become a Medal of Honor airman. Born in Texas and educated in New Mexico, he worked on a fiji Island pineapple plantation between 1934 and 1937, then returned to his roots as a salesman in Texas. He was rejected by the U.S. Army Air Force six times owing to a neck injury that led to a 4F classification.

Undeterred, Morgan joined the Royal Canadian Air Force in August 1941, and upon completion of pilot training, he arrived in Britain the following summer. His RCAF flight sergeant's stripes brought him a warrant (flight officer) commission when he transferred to the USAAF in August 1943.

Upon assignment to the 92nd Bomb Group at Bovington, Hertfordshire, Morgan was rated as a B-17 copilot. On the 28 July mission to Hanover, flying in the right seat of *Ruthie II,* he was teamed with first Lieutenant Robert L. Campbell, whose first B-17 was a writeoff on the July Fourth mission.

Approaching the enemy coast, the 92nd's formation was attacked by company-front swarms of FW-190s. Campbell was struck in the head by machine gun or cannon fire and reflexively lurched forward, locking his arms around the control column. Morgan, though a 200-pound six-footer, needed all his strength to overcome the dying pilot's inert weight and keep the plane on course. Morgan called for help on the intercom but received no reply. He was on his own.

At first unknown to Morgan, the top turret gunner also was hit by German gunfire. Staff Sergeant Tyre C. Weaver's left arm was amputated just below the shoulder, and he slid to the deck of the navigator's compartment. There Lieutenant Keith J. Koske found a morphine needle bent and too little remaining of Weaver's arm for a tourniquet. Out of touch with the rest of the crew, the navigator made a fast decision. He dragged Weaver to the nose hatch, placed the gunner's right hand on the ripcord, and pushed him into space. The ball turret gunner saw the parachute open.

John C. Morgan

The formation was still west of Hanover at 24,000 feet while "Red" Morgan continued the struggle with his dying pilot. He heard no gunfire and assumed the rest of the crew had abandoned ship, when in fact four men were unconscious from severed oxygen lines. Meanwhile, the bombardier and navigator knew only that *Ruthie II* was proceeding on course. Somehow, Morgan maintained formation during the bomb run, flying with one hand on the controls and the other trying to restrain Campbell's spasms.

Only when approaching the coast outbound did anyone else realize the ghastly drama on the flight deck. Koske pulled Campbell out of the left seat so that Morgan could move over and look forward, as the right windscreen was shattered. Morgan had flown largely blind, restraining his unconscious pilot's death struggle, for nearly two agonizing hours.

Morgan searched for the first available airfield and landed at RAF Foulsham. There it was learned that the four unconscious crewmen had sustained frostbite, and Captain Campbell had died.

Weeks later the Red Cross reported that Sergeant Weaver had been picked up by the Germans and was safe in a hospital.

Morgan received the Medal of Honor in Britain in December 1943. The month after his notable mission he transferred to the 482nd Bomb Group. Commissioned a second lieutenant in November, he became assistant operations officer of the 813th Squadron.

Morgan was shot down on his twenty-sixth mission, flying with the 385th Group over Berlin on 16 March 1944. He was abandoning a dying Fort, carrying his parachute, when a tremendous explosion blew him into space. He managed to attach his chute, landed near a flak battery, and spent the next fourteen months in Stalag Luft 1. He was liberated shortly after VE-Day in May 1945.

After the war Morgan returned to Texaco's aviation products department, but he was recalled to active duty for Korea. Subsequently he rejoined Texaco again and completed forty-five years with the company, retiring as general manager of aviation sales in Los Angeles.

Crew: 1Lt. Robert L. Campbell (P); 2Lts. Keith J. Koske (N) and Asa J. Irwin (B); TSgt. John A. McClute (RO); SSgt. Tyre C. Weaver (TTG); Sgts. James L. Ford (BTG), Reece A. Walton (WG), John F. Foley (WG), and Eugene F. Ponte (TG).

LIEUTENANT COLONEL ADDISON EARL BAKER AND MAJOR JOHN LOUIS JERSTAD

1 January 1907–1 August 1943 (Baker)

12 February 1918–1 August 1943 (Jerstad)

Born: Chicago, Illinois (Baker); Racine, Wisconsin (Jerstad)

Died: Romania

Action: Bombing mission; Ploeşti, Romania; 1 August 1943 (age 36—Baker; age 25—Jerstad)

Unit: 93rd Bomb Group, 9th Air Force (8th Air Force detached)

Aircraft: Consolidated B-24D 42-40994 (D) *Hell's Wench*

Other decorations: (Baker) Silver Star, Distinguished Flying Cross, Air Medal (3), Purple Heart; (Jerstad) Silver Star, Air Medal (4), Purple Heart

In 1991 some American journalists described Operation Desert Storm as the world's first war fought over oil. The depth of their ignorance was matched only by the depth of the oil wells in Kuwait. Much of the Second World War

Addison E. Baker

John L. Jerstad

revolved around petroleum; it was the primary reason that Japan attacked Hawaii, as the U.S. Navy had to be neutralized before the Dutch East Indies could be seized. And it was the reason for one of the legendary air missions in military history.

The Allied Combined Bomber Offensive identified two primary targets: German transportation and petroleum. The former depended largely upon the latter; other targets were secondary.

Consequently, in the summer of 1943 an extraordinarily ambitious plan was conceived. Five B-24 groups were assigned to destroy the major center of Nazi oil production—seven refineries around Ploeşti, Romania, which collectively accounted for one-third of Hitler's petroleum, including aviation fuel. Such was the importance that three Liberator groups were temporarily transferred from the Eighth Air Force in Britain to the Ninth Air Force in North Africa.

Operation Tidal Wave called for 178 Liberators to conduct an extremely long-range attack. Following a 1,350-mile flight from Benghazi, Libya, to

Ploeşti, they would bomb from minimum altitude. Planning was meticulous, involving specially produced films, scale models of the target complexes, and two dress rehearsals. The plan turned on accurate navigation, surprise, and daring. Nothing like it had ever been attempted. During briefings the aircrews were told to expect 50 percent losses, but the target was considered worth the cost.

From their desert airfields the B-24s launched behind Brigadier General Uzal Ent, flying with Colonel Keith Compton, leading the 376th Bomb Group. Taking off before dawn on 1 August (a Sunday, to minimize casualties among forced labor), the Liberators flew north to the Greek coast, climbed the rugged terrain of Albania and Yugoslavia, then descended to minimum level to avoid German radar. The initial point was Piteşti, from which the 389th Group would head for the Campina refinery. The other four groups proceeded at 500 feet, seeking Floreşti, which marked the thirteen-mile run to Brazi and Ploeşti itself.

But things had already come undone. Near the Greek isle of Corfu the bomber with the mission's lead navigator mysteriously crashed. General Ent was positioned to assume the tactical lead during the bomb run but lost his backup navigator whose pilot decided to search for survivors.

Operating under radio silence, the task force's cohesion came unraveled. High clouds over the Balkan mountains delayed the trailing groups, which emerged over the Danubian Plain half an hour behind the leaders. Tidal Wave's timing—crucial to success—was irretrievably lost.

The situation only worsened. The 93rd and 376th Groups identified Piteşti and turned for floreşti but misidentified an interim town. Turning to the briefed southeasterly heading, the Liberators actually passed west of Ploeşti and did not catch the error until nearly over Bucharest. With little option, Ent opened up and radioed the groups to head north, striking opportune targets in the refinery complexes.

Leading the 93rd Group was Lieutenant Colonel Addison Baker, an erstwhile auto mechanic who had become an Army pilot in 1930. Depression budget cuts forced him out of the service, but he returned to active duty in 1940 and became a charter member of the "Traveling Circus" bomb group as well as the Eighth Air Force. He had commanded the group since May, logging fifteen missions. For Tidal Wave he flew as copilot in Major John L. Jerstad's Liberator, named *Hell's Wench*.

Jerstad had taught high school in St. Louis, Missouri, before enlisting as an aviation cadet in July 1941. Like Baker, he had originally joined the 98th Group at Barksdale field before being moved to the 93rd. As a headquarters officer he subsequently joined the staff of the 201st Provisional Combat Bombardment Wing in May. He had finished his tour—a rarity in 1943—but insisted on making the Ploeşti mission.

Baker spotted a target—the 44th Group's Columbia Aquila refinery—but bored in regardless. Aquila's defenses were imposing: 230 antiaircraft guns plus barrage balloons and smoke generators. An estimated 400 German and Rumanian fighters were reported in the region.

Nevertheless, Jerstad pressed through the awesome flak. Three miles from the refinery, *Hell's Wench* took successive hits and caught fire. Jerstad jettisoned his bombs. The wingmen expected their leader to make a belly landing in nearby fields, as did some other stricken Liberators, but Jerstad and Baker never wavered. Holding the bomber in the air as long as humanly possible, they remained at the head of "The Traveling Circus." Reaching the bombing point, the *Wench* abruptly nosed up, indicating both pilots were on the controls. A few crewmen bailed out before the big Consolidated nosed over and crashed. Later it was learned that the entire crew had perished.

For exceptional leadership and devotion to duty, John Jerstad and Addison Baker received posthumous Medals of Honor, authorized in October 1943 and March 1944, respectively. Three other medals were awarded for Operation Tidal Wave, an aviation record that remains unapproached to this day.

Baker is buried in the American Battle Monument Cemetery in Florence, Italy; Jerstad in ABMC Ardennes, Belgium.

Crew: 1Lts. Alfred W. Pezzela (B) and George J. Reuter (N); TSgts. Charles E. Bennet (TT) and John H. Carrol (RO); SSgts. Morton O. Stafford (G), Edgar C. Faith (G), William O. Wood (G), and George P. Allen (G).

COLONEL LEON WILLIAM JOHNSON

13 SEPTEMBER 1904–10 NOVEMBER 1997

BORN: Columbia, Missouri

DIED: Fairfax, Virginia

ACTION: Bombing mission; Ploeşti, Romania; 1 August 1943 (age 38)

UNIT: 44th Bomb Group, 9th Air Force (8th Air Force detached)

AIRCRAFT: Consolidated B-24D-5 41-23817 (L) *Suzy Q*

OTHER DECORATIONS: Distinguished Service Medal, Silver Star, Legion of Merit, Distinguished Flying Cross (2), Air Medal (4)

Leon Johnson became one of the notable combat commanders of the Army Air Forces. A West Pointer from the class of 1926, he served initially as an infantry officer, then caught the flying bug. He completed pilot training in 1930, serving in the United States and Philippines until 1941.

As one of the first four flying officers of the nascent Eighth Air Force, Johnson accompanied the tiny staff to Britain in June 1942. Six months later he was appointed commander of the 44th Bomb Group, which had initiated the Liberator to operational service. Calculating that four plus four equals eight, the men called themselves "The flying Eightballs."

On the Ploeşti mission Johnson flew as copilot to Major William Brandon in order to concentrate on the tactical aspects of the operation. Johnson's Eightballs and Colonel John Kane's 98th Group passed the initial point at floreşti more or less together. At that juncture there was no doubt about the target's location—a huge cloud of black smoke from burning oil tanks showed the way, roaring red-orange at the base. The seething cauldron had been ignited by the preceding 93rd and 376th Groups.

The peril in continuing the attack was immediately evident. Apart from near-zero visibility in the smoke, Johnson knew that steel cables suspended from barrage balloons waited to snag his bombers, and the low-level approach risked damage from exploding bombs intended to detonate after the Liberators departed. The careful timing of the mission schedule had turned to hash.

Nevertheless, Johnson decided to accept the risk. The flight into smoke, flames, flak, and explosions turned into an aerial inferno undreamt of by

Dante. Flying that low, the big Liberators were tossed and buffeted by the searing heat. Sometimes the updrafts were so violent that both pilots had to wrestle the controls to keep the wings level. Upon plunging into the dense smoke cloud, some 44th crews gasped at near misses with 376th Group B-24s that had just bombed their own target.

Leon W. Johnson

Of the sixteen planes that Johnson took into the blazing Columbia Aquila refinery, only nine emerged on the far side. His *Suzy Q* sustained multiple flak hits but pulled off target, still airworthy. He landed at Benghazi after 2,400 miles and nearly fourteen hours in the air, learning that the balance of his group—twenty-one planes under Lieutenant Colonel James Posey— had razed the Brazi refinery at a cost of two planes downed by fighters.

The month after Tidal Wave, Johnson received his brigadier general's star and assumed command of the 14th Combat Bombardment Wing, a position he retained until the end of the European war. He led the Third Air Division in Britain during 1948–50.

Aside from the Medal of Honor, presented in November 1943, General Johnson also received eight other U.S. decorations, the British DFC, French Legion of Honor, plus the French and Belgian *Croix de Guerre.* Enormously popular with his troops, Johnson seldom missed a 44th Group reunion. He often wore the nation's highest award at such gatherings to share it with "my guys." Typically he asked a veteran of the Ploeşti mission, "Would you like to hold your Medal of Honor? I'm just wearing it for you."

Crew: Maj. William H. Brandon (P); 2Lts. Charles J. Selasky (B) and Berthal Swenson (N); TSgt. John F. Irwin (FE); SSgts. Kelly L. Morrison (WG), Frank Paliga (WG), and William R. Brady Jr. (TG); Sgt. Thomas C. Ray (TTG).

COLONEL JOHN RILEY KANE

5 JANUARY 1907–29 MAY 1966

BORN: McGregor, Texas

DIED: Unknown

ACTION: Bombing mission; Ploeşti, Romania; 1 August 1943 (age 36)

UNIT: 98th Bomb Group, 9th Air Force

AIRCRAFT: Consolidated B-24D 41-11825 (V) *Hail Columbia*

OTHER DECORATIONS: Silver Star, Legion of Merit, Distinguished Flying Cross (2), Air Medal (5)

"Killer" Kane's 98th Group called itself the Pyramiders, heralding its Desert Air Force origins in Egypt. For Operation Tidal Wave the 98th had flown near the head of the bomber stream until reaching the cloud-covered Balkan mountains. In the ensuing confusion, other groups arrived prematurely and attacked his briefed target, the Columbia Aquila refinery.

Flying with the 344th Squadron, Kane chose Lieutenant John Young's crew. Contrary to usual practice, the radio compartment was occupied by an officer, Lieutenant Ray Hubbard, the squadron communications officer on his first ("and I presume his last!") mission, according to another crew member.

Kane, a 1928 graduate of Baylor University, had won his wings in 1932 and reverted to reserve status in 1934. However, he returned to active duty the next year at Barksdale field in Louisiana. He rose to squadron command at Lackland field, florida, before assuming responsibility as a group commander.

Kane began flying combat in North Africa during the summer of 1942. The Pyramiders liked to say that their CO was dubbed "Killer Kane" by Luftwaffe intelligence officers, but whatever the case, he had logged forty-three missions by early August. None of them had prepared him for the forty-fourth.

Like Leon Johnson, Kane made an on-the-spot command decision to press ahead with his Liberators despite horrific conditions over the Columbia Aquila refinery: poor visibility, heavy turbulence, murderous flak, barrage balloons, and tall smokestacks. Collision was as big a risk as enemy action. The losses were dreadful as fifteen of his forty-one bombers fell to the flak and Luftwaffe or Romanian fighters in the target area; three more B-24s were shot down over Bulgaria. Kane's *Hail Columbia* was badly hit, losing one engine at Ploeşti with serious airframe damage. Upon landing at an RAF field on Cyprus, the battered Liberator was written off as irrepairable.

John R. Kane

Kane's Medal of Honor was approved immediately after the mission. It was awarded by Major General Louis H. Brereton, commander of the Ninth Air Force, at the Gezira Sporting Club in Cairo.

Recalled navigator Norman Whalen, "Everyone who participated in the raid was promoted one grade regardless of how recent their previous promotion. Also, every participant was awarded the Distinguished flying Cross or higher (Silver Star or, more rarely, the Distinguished Service Cross). In the 98th Bomb Group, only four of the latter were awarded. Strangely, all four were from New Jersey. Of the four Distinguished Service Crosses, three were posthumous; only one lived to receive it."

Kane returned to the United States in February 1944 and commanded bases in Idaho and Nebraska. After the war he rose to command a military air transport wing and retired as commander of Smoky Hill Air Force Base, Kansas, in 1954.

Crew: 1Lt. John S. Young (CP); 2Lts. Norman M. Whalen (N) and Harold F. Korger (B); 1Lt. Raymond B. Hubbard (RO); TSgt. Fredrick A. Leard (FE-WG); SSgts. Harvey L. Treace (TT) and Neville C. Benson (WG); Sgts. Joseph J. Labranche (BTG) and William Leo (TG).

SECOND LIEUTENANT LLOYD HERBERT HUGHES

12 July 1921–1 August 1943

Born: Alexandria, Louisiana

Died: Romania

Action: Bombing mission; Ploeşti, Romania; 1 August 1943 (age 22)

Unit: 564th Bomb Squadron, 389th Bomb Group, 9th Air Force (8th Air Force detached)

Aircraft: Consolidated B-24D-95 42-40753 (J) *Eager Eagle*

Other decorations: Purple Heart

The last group over the Ploeşti target area was Colonel Jack Wood's 389th, which turned northeast and bombed the Campina refinery. The intense flak knocked down four Liberators, including *Eager Eagle,* flown by Lieutenant Lloyd Hughes, a twenty-two-year-old who had logged only four previous missions.

The son of Welsh immigrants, Hughes grew up in Texas, attending A&M for three years. His studies were interrupted in December 1941, when he enlisted for pilot training. After completing multiengine school in early 1943 he joined the 389th Bomb Group at Biggs field near El Paso and accompanied the group to Britain in June.

Approaching the target, Hughes's plane streamed fuel from wing and bomb bay tanks which had been holed by flak splinters. Rather than put the '24 down in the wheatfields beneath him, he continued the attack, climbed to bombing height, and waited for the "bombs away" call. The attack was delivered from so low an altitude that the venting gasoline was ignited by flames from the burning refinery.

Upon emerging from the seething oil fires, *Eager Eagle's* right wing was engulfed in flames. With nowhere to go but down, Hughes turned to approach a riverbed that offered prospects of a belly landing. Somehow he lifted the blazing bomber over a bridge and settled toward the ground. Too low, the B-24 snagged a wing on the riverbank or an obstacle, veered, and crashed. Three men miraculously survived the impact but one of them, Lieutenant Sidney Pear, died of his injuries. Two gunners—Sergeants Edmond Smith and Thomas Hoff—owed their lives to Lloyd Hughes. His Medal of Honor was approved 26 February 1944.

Lloyd H. Hughes

Exact losses in Tidal Wave have been difficult to verify owing to the confused nature of the attack and the scattered nature of the survivors. After the war, senior airmen arrived at a consensus. Of 177 Liberators dispatched, one crashed on takeoff; 161 bombed a target; forty-four were shot down or crashed in the target area; and seven landed in Turkey, where they were interned. Overall, nearly 30 percent of the bombers were lost to the Allied cause and with them more than 530 airmen.

Operation Tidal Wave had succeeded in reducing Romania's oil production. But repairs were made and the oil continued to flow to Germany. American airmen would return to Ploeşti again and again.

Crew: 2Lts. Ronald H. Helder (CP), John A. McLoughlin (B), and Sidney A. Pear (N); TSgts. Louis M. Kase (RO) and Joseph E. Mix (TTG); SSgts. Malcolm C. Dalton (WG), Edmond H. Smith (WG), Avis K. Wilson (BTG), and Thomas A. Hoff (TG).

MAJOR RALPH CHELI

29 October 1919–c. 5 March 1944

Born: San Francisco, California

Died: Rabaul, New Britain

Action: Bombing mission; Wewak, New Guinea; 18 August 1943 (age 23)

Unit: 405th Bomb Squadron, 38th Bomb Group, 5th Air Force

Aircraft: North American B-25D 41-30117

Other decorations: Distinguished Flying Cross, Air Medal, Purple Heart

Land-based airpower determined the length of stride for each step of General Douglas MacArthur's trek through the Southwest Pacific Theater. Lieutenant General George C. Kenney's Fifth Air Force had secured bases at Port Moresby and Dobodura, New Guinea, which put bombers within reach of Japanese airfields around Wewak, about 300 miles west of Lae. Three main airdromes in that area harbored an estimated one hundred Japanese aircraft that had to be destroyed before the next amphibious operation.

Following preliminary strikes on 16–17 October 1943, involving eighty bombers and a similar number of fighters, the Fifth Air Force prepared for its longest medium bomber mission to date. B-25s based at Port Moresby faced a 520-mile one-way trek to Wewak. Leading the Mitchells was Major Ralph Cheli of the 38th Bomb Group, regarded as one of the finest combat leaders in the theater. He had been commissioned in November 1940 and flew anti-submarine patrols from MacDill Field, Florida, in 1942. That August he had led the first in-flight transit of B-25s from the United States to Australia. Shortly after arrival at Moresby he was promoted to major and command of the 405th Squadron. Since then Cheli had flown thirty-nine missions against some of the toughest targets in the New Guinea region. During the Battle of the Bismarck Sea in March 1943 he gained notice for leading the 405th's masthead attacks against a Japanese reinforcement convoy—reportedly the first such daylight mission in the Southwest Pacific.

The briefed target on the eighteenth was Dagua airdrome, just west of Wewak. The route covered jungled, mountainous terrain with rugged peaks jutting as high at 15,000 feet. The situation was compounded by two-mile visibility due to rain and haze. Barely half the "heavies" bombed their targets through cloud cover.

Ralph Cheli

Meanwhile, the mediums attacked through heavy flak and determined air opposition. Ten or more Japanese Army fighters descended from the laden clouds, hoping to head off the B-25s before they hit the field. One of the Oscars concentrated on the lead Mitchell, and two miles out Cheli's aircraft took heavy damage; the right engine caught fire and the flames took hold on the wing.

Cheli still had sufficient airspeed from his descent to pull up and permit his crew to bail out. But he knew that doing so would loosen his squadron's formation and therefore diminish the effect of the attack. He elected to remain in his dive, pressing onto Dagua's runways and revetments with bombs and strafing. Japanese on the ground must have marveled at the determination of the American leader in his dragon-head bomber, continuing his attack with flames streaming behind him. The Mitchells bombed with parafrags and strafed fifteen or more planes on the field.

Pulling off target, Cheli radioed his number two, turning over the lead, and crossed beneath his left wingman. Others thought they heard him say he was attempting a water landing. As is common to combat, observers returned to base with different impressions. Some said the Mitchell crashed into the jungle; some that it dived into the sea. Still others thought the squadron CO had made a safe ditching. In any case, Ralph Cheli and his four crewmen were missing in action.

Cheli's devotion to duty was beyond question, and the Medal of Honor was authorized in barely two months, on 28 October. It was hoped that he might yet emerge to receive the award in person, and that hope was raised some months later when a Japanese broadcast reported that Cheli and some of his crew were prisoners.

Postwar investigation showed that Cheli had successfully ditched about 300 yards offshore. His copilot and Australian observer died in the aircraft but Cheli and both gunners had been captured and taken to Dagua Airdrome. There the victory was credited to Captain Shigeki Namba of the 59th *Sentai.* Namba landed and, apparently with aid of a doctor, interrogated the Americans before they were removed to Rabaul, New Britain. One gunner apparently died of wounds and the other was routinely killed.

Reportedly Cheli had been burned and sustained other injuries but he determined to resist the Japanese as much as possible. In succeeding months, as the senior American present, he was interrogated and beaten but yielded only name, rank, and serial number. Returning prisoners reported that Cheli remained cheerful and optimistic, despite typically abusive treatment from his captors.

Cheli's ultimate fate remains uncertain. After the war the Japanese reported that he and as many as thirty-one other prisoners were killed in an American bombing attack on 5 March 1944, either while boarding a ship for Japan or while sheltering at Talili. Other evidence indicates that Cheli and the others may have been executed.

Crew: F. O. Don Yancey (CP); 1Lt. Vincent Raney (N); TSgt. Raymond C. Warren (RO-G); SSgt. Clinton H. Murphree (FE-TTG); Capt. John H. Massie, RAAF (O).

COLONEL NEEL EARNEST KEARBY

5 JUNE 1911–5 MARCH 1944

BORN: Wichita Falls, Texas

DIED: Wewak, New Guinea

ACTION: Air combat; Wewak, New Guinea; 11 October 1943 (age 32)

UNIT: 343rd fighter Group, 5th Air Force

AIRCRAFT: Republic P-47D

OTHER DECORATIONS: Silver Star (2), Distinguished Flying Cross (4), Air Medal (5), Purple Heart

On 11 October 1943 Colonel Neel Kearby, commanding the 348th fighter Group, led a flight of four "razorback" P-47Ds on a sweep in the Wewak area, more than 500 miles northwest of Port Moresby, New Guinea. His wingman was Captain Bill Dunham, operations officer of the 341st Squadron, with Major Raymond Gallagher and Captain John Moore of the 342nd in the second element. Staging through Tsili Tsili, the Thunderbolts arrived near Boram Airdrome at 28,000 feet that morning. Kearby, with three kills already, hoped to pick a fight.

He got his wish. Alerted by radar, the Japanese Army responded with elements of the 13th and 68th *Sentai.*

Winning his wings in February 1938, Neel Kearby moved up fast. In December 1940, less than three years after being commissioned, he commanded the 14th Pursuit Squadron, flying Bell P-39s in Panama. Rotated back to the States, he formed the new 348th Group in October 1942, determined to make the Thunderbolt a success. When he took the 348th to Australia in June 1943, Kearby had two things in mind: proving the P-47 in the Pacific Theater and proving himself the top shooter in Fifth Fighter Command. Lieutenant General George Kenney, commanding the Fifth Air Force, recalled that Kearby's first question was, "Who has shot down the most planes?" Before long it was common knowledge that the slightly built group commander intended to bag fifty Japanese aircraft before going home.

Meanwhile, it was necessary to solve the "Jug's" limited range, the dominant factor in the Pacific air war. Kenney arranged for drop tanks to be produced in Australia, and by August the 348th was ready for action. So was

Neel E. Kearby

Neel Kearby, who entered combat as a mature 2,000-hour fighter pilot.

Now, near Boram Airdrome, Kearby sighted a fighter below them at about 20,000 feet. Diving on the Kawasaki Tony (Kearby called it a Zeke) from the left rear, he fired at 300 yards, and the Ki-61 exploded.

After his kill, Kearby climbed back to 26,000 feet in near clear conditions. Major Gallagher was missing, having chased another Japanese in and out of clouds. Soon, four miles below, Kearby sighted a dozen bombers inbound from a mission as perhaps twenty-five fighters climbed to intercept. Odds meant nothing to Kearby — he saw targets rather than danger — and gave the attack signal. In less than a minute he claimed a Zeke and two Hamps (they were Ki-43 Oscars), and Dunham and Moore reported a Tony apiece.

Momentarily satisfied, Kearby climbed to 20,000 feet, intending to regroup and head for home. But from his perch he saw a Thunderbolt chased by two Tonys. The friendly was Moore. Rolling into a 400-m.p.h. dive, Kearby descended onto the Kawasakis and shot them off Moore's tail. Dunham and Moore then saw Kearby engaged with six more Ki-61s. The colonel fired at one, apparently missed, then ducked in and out of clouds at 7,000 feet. Moore claimed another and the fight ended.

Now short on fuel, Kearby regrouped and nursed his flight homeward. The Jugs diverted to Lae's emergency strip but had enough fuel to indulge in victory rolls. Kearby rolled seven times before landing. Exultant after the mission, he claimed seven kills; he was credited with six. (Japanese records show two losses and four damaged against the nine claimed by the P-47s, but the losses were significant: a wing commander and squadron leader.)

Kearby's record was unparalleled in the Fifth Air Force, and Kenney immediately recommended him for the Medal of Honor. Two Thirteenth Air

Force pilots had become aces in a day that summer, and worldwide just two U.S. Fighter pilots had exceeded a sextuple kill: Navy Lieutenant Swede Vejtasa a year previously and Twelfth Air Force's Major Bill Leverette merely two days before, in the Mediterranean. Neither had the patronage of a theater commander so neither received the highest award.

Kearby transferred to Headquarters Fifth Fighter Command in November but continued flying combat. By year's end he had run his string to seventeen, four behind Dick Bong; one up on Tommy Lynch and Tommy McGuire. MacArthur decorated Kearby in Brisbane, Australia, on 23 January 1944, when Kearby's nineteen kills matched Bong's tally. However, the pug-nosed Lightning ace was due back from stateside leave in February. Kearby felt the need to seize the opportunity but Kenney advised him against getting greedy, urging him to settle for one kill at a time. Kearby recognized the wisdom but it didn't fit his goal of fifty planes before he went home.

On the morning of 5 March, Kearby had claimed twenty-one kills, maintaining a dead heat with Bong. Flying to Wewak with Captains Sam Blair and Bill Dunham, Kirby spotted fifteen Japanese aircraft: Nell bombers escorted by Oscar fighters. Kearby attacked, burning a Nell on his first pass and then zoom-climbing back for position. Meanwhile, Blair and Dunham each claimed a kill before the Oscars intervened. Two jumped the lead P-47 and one put a killing burst into the Thunderbolt. Dunham shredded the Oscar with his eight .50s but Kearby's Jug, *Fiery Ginger IV,* went into the jungle. Heartsick, his wingmen returned to base.

Neel Kearby's body was recovered by Australian searchers in early 1946. Unseen by his wingmen, he had bailed out and either sustained injuries in the jump or was shot in his parachute.

Ironically, it took the end of the war to validate Kearby's faith in the Thunderbolt. By then—eighteen months after his death—P-47s had shot down very nearly as many Japanese aircraft and produced more aces than the Curtiss P-40.

MAJOR RAYMOND HARRELL WILKINS

28 SEPTEMBER 1917–2 NOVEMBER 1943

BORN: Portsmouth, Virginia

DIED: Rabaul, New Britain

ACTION: Shipping attack; Rabaul, New Britain; 2 November 1943 (age 26)

UNIT: 8th Bomb Squadron, 3rd Bomb Group, 5th Air Force

AIRCRAFT: North American B-25D 41-30311 (A) *Fifi*

OTHER DECORATIONS: Silver Star, Distinguished Flying Cross (4), Air Medal (2), Purple Heart

The seventy-five B-25s came in low and fast, dropping down Rabaul's volcanic slopes to the large harbor. The Mitchells' intended targets were twenty-seven Japanese transports photographed the day before, though overnight enemy cruisers and destroyers had arrived. They were lucrative targets but they put up an incredible volume of flak: small arms, tracers, and bursting stuff.

Fifth Air Force intended to shut down Rabaul both as a naval and air complex. Sitting at the end of New Britain, it posed a threat to Allied forces in the Solomons and New Guinea, and General George Kenney's bomb groups had been working on Rabaul since mid-October. Between Japanese fighters and flak, as well as weather, losses often were heavy but the medium and heavy bombers kept up the pressure.

At the end of the bomber stream, leading the Third Bomb Group's Eighth Squadron, was Major Raymond Wilkins, barely twenty-six but veteran of eighty-six previous missions. Wilkins was a survivor: he was the last member of the Third Group's original contingent that had arrived in Australia nearly two years previously. It had been a long journey.

Barely six weeks before Pearl Harbor, Raymond Wilkins pinned on his wings and gold bars. It was what he expected of himself: his father was a Regular Army sergeant. Lieutenant Wilkins soon embarked for the Philippines but the Japanese attacked and the ship was diverted to Australia, where Wilkins joined the Third Group just before New Year's.

In February the group entered combat in the New Guinea theater. Assigned to dive bombers, Wilkins flew Douglas A-24s, formerly Navy SBDs. Losses were unsupportable: Wilkins was the only one of seven pilots to return from an antishipping strike in July, but he kept flying. By January 1943 he had logged more than fifty missions, mainly in B-25s, and wore captain's bars and the Silver Star. Having twice declined rotation home, Wilkins decided to stay awhile longer. He had moved up from squadron executive officer to CO, and he was all business. When he assumed command he moved away from his pilots, saying, "You can't be both a good friend and a good combat commander at the same time, and I'm choosing the latter."

Raymond H. Wilkins

Since then Wilkins had led nearly every hard mission. The night before Rabaul (twice postponed for weather) he told a colleague that he had set a December wedding date with his fiancée. After eighty-six missions during twenty-two months in combat, he was going home—following the Rabaul strike.

Flying a B-25 named *Fifi,* Wilkins realized that the plan had turned to hash. The first-wave Mitchells were defense suppressors, bombing and strafing flak batteries ringing the harbor. The suppressors also laid smoke screens on either side of the approach route, denying enemy gunners a clear view of the strikers. But the heavy volume of fire from the warships and reduced visibility caused the preceding 13th Squadron to alter its briefed approach, swinging too far north. Wilkins tried to make sense of the situation, but his radio call elicited no clear response. Rather than follow the 13th, he took his eight planes in a 180-degree turn, formed in right echelon, and turned hard left back to the planned ingress between Rabaul's two volcanoes.

In making two unplanned turns the Eighth became strung out line astern instead of the "company front" attack that maximized the bombers' firepower. Furthermore, valuable time was lost—time that benefited the enemy gunners. Meanwhile, there were bandits all around the clock as Lightnings fought Japanese interceptors from 20,000 feet to the deck.

Cresting the slope and diving into the harbor basin, Wilkins found only a narrow corridor between the smoke, perhaps one hundred yards wide. It was too late to abort the attack so he pressed on, hemmed in by bombers on either side.

With so many warships crowded into a relatively small space, the automatic weapon fire was heavy and accurate. Doing about 240 m.p.h., *Fifi* was hit early in the approach but Wilkins returned fire with his forward guns, scything .50 caliber rounds into a cluster of small craft. With bomb bay doors already open, he selected a destroyer and dropped a thousand-pounder that possibly struck the target. But the ship's crew kept firing, reportedly shooting off part of Wilkins's left vertical stabilizer.

Fighting the damaged controls with his copilot, Lieutenant Bob Murphy, Wilkins continued the attack. He put his remaining bomb into a transport that other crews observed afire as they pulled off.

The rest of the squadron claimed hits on three ships and probably two more. Whatever the results, *Fifi* took additional damage, possibly losing the rest of the damaged stabilizer. Unable to maneuver, Wilkins was committed to fly directly toward a cruiser whose automatic weapons opened fire at close range. The Mitchell staggered visibly and rolled belly side to the cruiser, which shot off the left wing. *Fifi* plunged into the water near the harbor mouth; another B-25 was shot down nearby. Total losses were nine bombers and ten fighters. Strike photos showed poor results but Fifth Air Force said as many as three Japanese destroyers and eight merchantmen may have been sunk.

One version of the mission held that Wilkins had intentionally continued the uncommanded roll caused by vertical stabilizer damage, rather than risk a midair collision in the confined airspace. Pilots who were there observed no such action, citing combat focus and reduced visibility. Fifty-eight years later, squadron members felt that mentions of the damaged stabilizer and intentional sacrifice were "slightly glamorized" by MacArthur's headquarters.

Wilkins's posthumous award was approved in March 1944 and was presented to his family in Vandalia, Ohio, in December.

Crew: 2Lts. Robert E. Murphy (CP) and Howard R. Bunce (B-N); SSgt. George H. Chamberlain (TTG?); TSgt. Miles L. Rowe (TG?).

TECHNICAL SERGEANT FORREST LEE VOSLER

29 July 1923–17 February 1992

Born: Louisville, New York

Died: Titusville, Florida

Action: Bombing mission, Germany; 20 December 1943 (age 20)

Unit: 358th Bomb Squadron, 303rd Bomb Group, 8th Air Force

Aircraft: Boeing B-17F 42-29664 (VK-C) *Jersey Bounce Jr.*

Other decorations: Air Medal, Purple Heart

The Luftwaffe was up in strength on 20 December 1943. More than 470 heavy bombers bound for Bremen were intercepted by German single- and twin-engine fighters, which barged through escorting P-38s and P-51s to fire cannon shells and aerial rockets into the Fortresses and Liberators. The defenders knocked down twenty-seven bombers, but nearly all were victims of Messerschmitts and Focke-Wulfs since the Eighth Air Force had chosen this mission to introduce "window," aluminum strips cut to match enemy fire-control radars. It was good timing, as the *Jagdflieger* were trouble enough.

Among the Fortresses of the 303rd Bomb Group was *Jersey Bounce Jr.*, flown by Lieutenants John Lemmon and Elmo Clark. The radio operator was a twenty-year-old New Yorker, Forrest Vosler, who left school as a teenager and worked in a machine shop until 1942. Accepted into the AAF that October, "Woody" Vosler was trained as a radioman and qualified as a gunner before assignment to a combat aircrew pool. Subsequently he joined the 303rd Bomb Group at Molesworth, Huntingdonshire, in the summer of 1943.

Jersey Bounce Jr. was damaged by flak over the target, lost airspeed, and dropped behind the formation. German fighters noticed the vulnerable bomber and pounced on it, scoring numerous 20mm hits. One shell exploded in the radio compartment, where Vosler was standing to fire his single .50 caliber. Though wounded in both legs, he remained at his gun and kept up his defensive firing. Then another cannon round detonated, damaging the radio and spewing steel fragments into Vosler's face and chest. Small splinters penetrated his eyes, and his vision was further reduced by blood running down his face. Nevertheless, he refused first aid in preference to shooting at the vague shapes making repeated runs on his plane.

Forrest L. Vosler

Continued fighter attacks inflicted additional damage to the Boeing, including the tail guns with serious wounds to the gunner, Sergeant Virgil Brown.

Losing blood and suffering from mild shock, Vosler lapsed in and out of consciousness. But during the moments he revived, he tended to the radio, expertly tracing tubes and wires by touch since he could not focus on the parts. With the set working again, Vosler transmitted the plane's position and situation.

Despite the crew's efforts, *Jersey Bounce Jr.* was unable to reach England and Lieutenant Lemmon ordered everyone to prepare for a water landing. Vosler sent out a final SOS and assumed his position.

Once the crippled Boeing splashed to a stop, the crew scrambled from ditching stations to deploy life rafts. Vosler, unable to see any better than before, nonetheless helped the badly wounded Sergeant Brown from the bomber and kept him on the wing until the rest of the crew could ease him into a dinghy. The crew was rescued by a coastal vessel off Cromer, Norfolk.

Vosler was in serious condition: blinded by face wounds and with injuries to his legs. He was returned to the United States in early 1944 and entered Valley Forge Hospital in Pennsylvania. He regained his vision seven months after his last mission and received the Medal of Honor from President Roosevelt that summer, the second 303rd Group flier so recognized. He left the service with an honorable discharge the next month. His citation lauded his selfless actions as "an inspiration to all serving with him."

Forrest Vosler passed away at age sixty-eight and was buried at Arlington National Cemetery. His medal was donated to the Eighth Air Force Museum in 1997.

Crew: Lts. John Lemmon (P), Elmo Clark (CP), Darrell Gust (N), and Elbert Stone (B); Sgts. Caryl Zeller (R), Andrew Berzansky (FE), Clayton Bagwell (BTG), Wayne Briggs (WG), Albert Beavers (WG), and Virgil Brown (TG).

MAJOR JAMES HOWELL HOWARD

8 April 1913–18 March 1995

Born: Canton, China

Died: Bay Pines, Florida

Action: Air combat; Halberstadt, Germany; 11 January 1944 (age 30)

Unit: 356th fighter Squadron, 354th Fighter Group, 9th Air Force

Aircraft: North American P-5B (AJ-X)

Other decorations: Distinguished Flying Cross (2), Bronze Star Medal, Air Medal (9)

Major Jim Howard learned the hard way: it *was* possible to be lonely in a crowd. His was the only Mustang in a crowd of Messerschmitts and Focke-Wulfs. Minutes previously he had been leading the 356th fighter Squadron; now he was the lone defender of a box of heavy bombers deep in German airspace.

The Eighth Air Force sent 650 heavies to the Brunswick area; the first Division was to bomb the Oschersleben FW-190 factory, 140 miles west-southwest of Berlin. Many groups aborted because of weather, but the Oschersleben region was clear under an overcast. Forty-nine Mustangs of the 354th fighter Group provided target support for the 174 Forts attacking Oschersleben.

It had happened so fast. Somebody—the pilot did not give his call sign—had spotted bandits climbing to intercept the B-17s. In the 354th Group pragmatism ruled: whomever made the first sighting took the lead. It was unusual doctrine—especially for a West Pointer—but Colonel Ken Martin, leader of the Pioneer Mustangs, insisted on tactics over protocol.

Howard's squadron was cruising just below the overcast at 17,000 feet. The anonymous young pilot who had seen *staffeln* of 109s and 110s clawing for position to attack the bombers called, "Go down and get the bastards!"

James H. Howard

Recalled Richard E. Turner, a flight leader, "The voice sounded enough like Major Howard's to satisfy us." As the CO nosed down, he was overtaken by a squadron of youngsters eager to exploit their altitude advantage.

Air discipline vaporized. Without awaiting identification or proper procedure, the entire 354th Group shoved over. Howard pulled up to avoid a collision. He was largely on his own.

Because all three squadrons had jumped on the vulnerable Messerschmitts, Howard realized that the bombers were unprotected. Therefore, he led his flight back to the bombers' level, providing miniature escort to dozens of B-17s. In the next few minutes he was going to have more shooting than he wanted.

Jim Howard had already lived a fighter pilot's fantasy: prewar carrier aviator, flying Tiger mercenary, and ultimately one of the original Mustang squadron commanders. He fought both major Axis powers, scoring against each in a combat career spanning two and a half years.

Born in China, the son of a surgeon working for the Rockefeller Foundation, Howard graduated from Pomona College in 1937. He became a naval aviator in 1939 and flew the delightful Grumman F3F biplane series. However, he resigned in June 1941 to join the American Volunteer Group as a flight leader. From January to July 1942 he claimed 2.33 aerial victories and four planes on the ground. When the Tigers were absorbed into the Army Air Force, he elected to go along and received a captain's commission in January 1943. He joined the 354th in May.

As the first Merlin engine P-51 group committed to combat in November 1943, the 354th was assigned to the Ninth Air Force. But the Mustang's seven-league boots were just what the Eighth needed: fighters with the range and performance to take the "big friends" all the way to the Reich—and back. The 354th was temporarily loaned to the Mighty Eighth.

Howard had bagged a Bf-109 on 20 December, his fourth kill of the war. Now, northwest of Halberstadt in only his second ETO combat, he had a skyful of black-crossed fighters to himself.

Howard cut off a Bf-110 tracking the bombers and shot it down but lost his wingmen in the process. Then a squadron of Bf-109s drove in for an attack. Howard, the consummate professional, headed them off. He feinted and dodged, taking shots when he could, but mainly spoiling the Germans' firing runs even when down to one gun functioning. Incredulous bomber crews watched Howard ride a wild Mustang across the sky in a high noon shootout. For twenty-five minutes he jousted with as many as thirty opponents from three fighter wings: Bf-109s of II *Gruppe* JG-11; Bf-110s of I *Gruppe* ZG-26; and FW-190s of II *Gruppe* JG-1. Undeterred at the odds, he spoiled repeated attacks on the bombers, whose crews counted six planes shot down or damaged.

Back at base the Pioneer Mustangs claimed fifteen kills with no losses. When Howard landed and debriefed, his share of the total was two Bf-110s and a FW-190 destroyed, plus a 109 probably destroyed and one damaged. Without the P-51s the toll in bombers would have been appalling. As it was, it was bad enough: 34 of the174 attacking Oschersleben, or nearly 20 percent.

Howard won praise from Colonel Harold Bowman's 401st Bomb Group, which was subjected to gun and rocket attacks. The B-17 men insisted that the pilot in the P-51 coded AJ-X be decorated.

Interviewed shortly after the action, Howard provided one of the most memorable quotes from the ETO: "I seen my duty and I done it." It was a facetious comment but nonetheless accurate.

Uncommonly reticent for a fighter pilot, Howard felt he had done no more than "my duty" and was undeserving of the Medal of Honor. If not for the glowing reports of the bomber crews, his action probably would have been passed over. It was service politics: the AAF lived and died by the self-defending bomber, and Medals of Honor to "little friends" might draw attention away from the "big friends." In any case, no other ETO fighter pilot received the Medal of Honor. Howard's medal was presented in Britain on

27 June, by which time he was a lieutenant colonel. His final European score was six kills.

Howard entered the reserves in November 1945 and was promoted to brigadier general in March 1948. He led the 419th Troop Carrier Wing in 1949–50 and retired from the Air Force Reserve in 1966. His memoir, *Roar of the Tiger,* was published in 1991.

FIRST LIEUTENANT WILLIAM ROBERT LAWLEY JR.

23 August 1920–30 May 1999

Born: Leeds, Alabama

Died: Montgomery, Alabama

Action: Bombing mission; Germany; 20 February 1944 (age 23)

Unit: 364th Bomb Squadron, 305th Bomb Group, 8th Air Force

Aircraft: B-17G 42-38109 (WF-P)

Other decorations: Legion of Merit, Air Medal (2), Purple Heart

They called it "Big Week," the Eighth Air Force's concentrated offensive against the German aircraft industry from 19 to 25 February 1944. On Sunday, 20 February, the Mighty Eighth launched 1,000 bombers into weather that hinted at decent visibility over the continent—and heavy Luftwaffe resistance.

Takeoff from Chelveston, Northamptonshire, was a dreary process for Colonel Ernest Lawson's 305th Bomb Group, one of three in the 40th Wing. Amid cold, low-hanging clouds that sprinkled snow showers, the Flying Fortresses lifted into the dank air, assembled, and headed east for the Greater German Reich.

Coming off the target, the 305th Group was subjected to head-on attacks by German fighters. A twenty-three-year-old Alabaman, William R. Lawley, was in the left seat of a 364th Squadron Fortress, frustrated at his plane's inability to release its bombs owing to frozen racks. Then things turned to hash.

Luftwaffe fighter pilots aggressively attacked the "Can Do" group, firing head-on from close range. In the cannonade, copilot Lieutenant Paul Murphy was killed by a 20mm shell. The explosion inflicted facial wounds on Lawley;

Lawley's B-17 crash-landed after his Medal of Honor mission, 20 February 1944.

William R. Lawley Jr. *(left)* with Lt. Gen. Carl Spaatz

five other crewmen also were injured. One engine was set afire as the Boeing staggered under the blows and dropped out of formation.

Bill Lawley had entered the Army Air Force in 1942 and completed pilot training in April 1943. Seven months later he became a B-17 replacement pilot for the Eighth Air Force, assigned to the 305th. Little in his training had prepared him for the challenge he now faced on his tenth mission.

Much like John Morgan six months before, Lawley had to contend with a broken, bloody windscreen and Murphy's weight on the controls. With difficulty he recovered from the descent as the B-17's inertia was augmented by the bombs still aboard. With blood on his face, he cast nervous glances at the blazing engine, concerned that the fire would spread to the bomb bay with catastrophic results. He rang the bailout bell while there was still time.

Only then did Lawley learn that two gunners were too badly injured to jump. After a hurried conference, the entire crew elected to remain aboard.

With the engine fire quenched, the battered Boeing seemed capable of making England, though it was difficult maintaining altitude. When more German fighters attacked, they shot out a second engine before losing their potential victim. By then the bombardier, Lieutenant Harry Mason, had managed to jettison his ordnance and rid the bomber of useless weight.

Crossing the sea for England, Lawley's injuries and steady bleeding overcame him. On the verge of shock, he fainted at the controls. Mason climbed into the right seat, steering the damaged bomber until Lawley revived. It was just in time; as the Fort crossed the coast one engine died from fuel exhaustion.

Lawley cleared his mind, focusing on the developing problem. He decided to set down on the first available field, which was Redhill, Surrey. During the straight-in approach, a previously damaged engine reignited but Lawley smoothly settled the flying wreck onto the sod in a wheels-up landing that prevented additional injuries to the crew.

He remained on operations until June, by which time he had flown fourteen combat missions for a total 121 hours. His Medal of Honor was presented by General Carl Spaatz in August and he returned to the United States in September, assigned as a public relations officer. Subsequently he served at Headquarters Army Air Forces.

Lawley stayed in the service after the war, and as a major he undertook projects for the Air Research and Development Command in 1950. Later he became assistant air attaché to Brazil and commanded the 55th Air Refueling Squadron. Promoted to colonel in 1959, he retired as director of curriculum at the Air War College.

Lawley maintained contact with his crew and retained the men's undying respect. Waist gunner Ralph Braswell said it best after a visit with his former pilot in the 1990s. "He had arthritis," Braswell said, "but after I shook his hands I said, 'They're beautiful. They saved my life.'"

Crew: 2Lts. P. F. W. Murphy (CP), R. B. Seraphine, (N), H. G. Mason (B); SSgts. T. A. Dempsey (RO) and C. W. Rowley (TTG); Sgts. H. S. Speers (WG), R. E. Braswell (WG), J. T. Kobierecki (BTG), and H. A. Malone (TG).

SECOND LIEUTENANT WALTER EDWARD TRUEMPER AND STAFF SERGEANT ARCHIBALD MATHIES

31 October 1918–20 February 1944 (Truemper)

3 June 1918–20 February 1944 (Mathies)

Born: Aurora, Illinois (Truemper); Scotland (Mathies)

Died: Polebrook, Northamptonshire, England

Action: Bombing mission; Germany; 20 February 1944 (age 25—Truemper; age 25—Mathies)

Unit: 510th Bomb Squadron, 351st Bomb Group, 8th Air Force

Aircraft: Boeing B-17G 42-31763 (TU-A)

Other decorations: Purple Heart (1 each)

On the same day of Lieutenant Lawley's mission, two other Eighth Air Force fliers became Medal of Honor recipients for valiantly trying to save a fellow airman.

In the 510th Squadron of the 351st Bomb Group, Second Lieutenant Clarence Nelson commanded a very junior crew. He had two other "brown bars," a flight officer, and five buck sergeants. Staff Sergeant Archibald Mathies, dual qualified as gunner and engineer, was the senior NCO but like everyone else he was new to combat. Three of the other six 510th planes were commanded by "second louies," but they all had more experienced aircrew.

Nelson's navigator, Walter Truemper, intended a career in business and accounting rather than dropping bombs over occupied Europe. However, he enlisted in June 1942 and transferred to the AAF in November. He was commissioned a second lieutenant bombardier in August 1943 and arrived in Britain just before year's end. There he joined the 351st Bomb Group; 20 February was his second combat mission.

Approaching Leipzig, an estimated forty Messerschmitts attacked. It was a churning, confused battle with bomber gunners shooting at P-51s as well as Bf-109s. "A-Able" of the 510th Bomb Squadron took a cannon shell in the cockpit, much as Lawley's plane had. In this instance the 20mm round entered from the right, killing the copilot and knocking Lieutenant Nelson unconscious. Shot out of formation, without a hand on its controls, the Fort

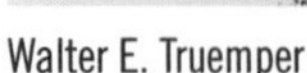

Walter E. Truemper

Archibald Mathies

swerved wildly. The bombardier assumed the plane was going down and called for a bailout, then jumped from the nose.

Sergeant Mathies climbed from his ball turret and made his way to the cockpit to check the situation. Like Truemper he was only flying his second mission, and he was appalled at what he found.

By wartime standards Mathies was an old-timer, having enlisted in 1940. His parents had emigrated from Scotland to Pennsylvania, and the irony of finding himself flying from Britain must have struck him on occasion. Upon joining the Army Air Force, he was trained as a mechanic and later qualified as an aerial gunner. He joined the 351st Bomb Group in January 1944 and flew as flight engineer and gunner.

With little option, Mathies leaned forward between the bloodstained, inert pilots and pulled "Able" into level flight. Soon Truemper and other crewmen assembled there, pondering what to do. They decided to try for a return to base, but it would not be easy. Apart from subzero temperatures in the blasted cockpit, the copilot's body resisted removal. While that task was underway, Mathies and Truemper alternated steering by yoke only, as they could not reach the rudder pedals from behind the throttle console.

As a flight engineer, Mathies had limited experience controlling an aircraft, but he slid into the bloody right seat, subjected to an unrelenting icy blast through the windscreen. He could only remain there for short periods, so Truemper and other crewmen relieved him periodically.

Descending into somewhat warmer air on a westerly heading, the stricken Boeing seemed assured of reaching Britain. Though there was little immediate hope of anyone landing the aircraft, the crew radioed for suggestions once over home base. The unconscious pilot was unable to jump but Truemper and Mathies directed the other crewmen to bail out at Polebrook.

The group commander, Colonel Eugene Romig, joined the crippled Fort in another B-17, hoping to talk his desperate airmen down. However, he was unable to establish radio contact with Truemper and Mathies and directed the control tower to transmit his orders: turn back toward the coast and take to their parachutes. The risk in landing a damaged aircraft was too great, but the bombardier and gunner refused to abandon their pilot. Faced with such determination, the tower operator agreed to radio detailed instructions for a landing attempt. Fuel, mixture, propeller controls, indicated airspeed—all had to be explained quickly and lucidly.

On the first approach the B-17 was too high to land safely and the tower radioed the two men to take it around. They accelerated, gained airspeed, and made a circuit of the pattern. Turning on final approach a second time, they were again too high and the tower waved them off.

Obviously determined to land on the third attempt, the impromptu flight crew allowed the airspeed to degrade. The bomber stalled, fell off on a wing, and smashed into a field four miles east of base. Donald Truemper and Archie Mathies were killed on impact. Clarence Nelson, whom they had died trying to save, also perished of his injuries.

Truemper and Mathies's medals were approved four months later, in June 1944. Truemper is buried in Aurora, Illinois; Mathies at Finleyville, Pennsylvania.

Crew: 2Lts. Clarence R. Nelson (P) and Joseph R. Martin (B); F.O. Roland E. Bartley (CP); Sgts. Carl W. Moore (TTG), Joseph F. Rex (RO), Thomas R. Sowell (WG), Russell R. Robinson (WG), and Magness A. Hagbo (TG).

FIRST LIEUTENANT EDWARD STANLEY MICHAEL

2 MAY 1918–10 MAY 1994

BORN: Chicago, Illinois

DIED: Fairfield, California

ACTION: Bombing mission, Europe; 11 April 1944 (age 25)

UNIT: 364th Bomb Squadron, 305th Bomb Group, 8th Air Force

AIRCRAFT: Boeing B-17G 42-38131, (WF-D), *Bertie Lee* (also listed as 37931)

OTHER DECORATIONS: Distinguished Flying Cross, Air Medal (3), Purple Heart

The bombers pierced German airspace in ordered ranks of squadrons, groups, wings, and divisions: more than 900 Eighth Air Force "heavies" escorted to six targets by ten fighter groups.

In the high squadron of the 305th Bomb Group formation was a B-17 named *Bertie Lee,* flown by first Lieutenant Edward Michael, who had been in bombers for a year. Though three airmen were relative newcomers, his was a veteran crew that belonged to a veteran squadron; Lieutenant William Lawley had flown a Medal of Honor mission in the 364th less than two months before.

The 305th's target that April morning was a ball-bearing factory at Stettin, eighty miles northeast of Berlin.

Edward Michael graduated from Chicago High School in 1936, enlisted in November 1940, and became a B-17 pilot after training at Douglas, Arizona. He went to England in 1943 and had flown twenty-five previous missions.

Four hours out of Chelveston, Northamptonshire, the group came under accurate antiaircraft fire. One shell burst dangerously close, gouging a large hole in *Bertie Lee*'s left wing. The German controllers were expert at their craft by now, and they coordinated flak and fighters extremely well. Michael's crew watched aghast as a Messerschmitt *gruppe* savaged a nearby B-24 formation; a dozen Liberators went down.

Passing south of Berlin, an estimated one hundred Messerschmitts and Focke-Wulfs massed against the Fortresses. Using "P-47 tactics" (the Thunderbolts had been trained in Luftwaffe methods), the Germans attacked head-on from eleven o'clock high. One Fort went down near the initial point and another eventually limped off toward Sweden. Then Michael felt multiple strikes from 20mm shells; the instrument panel was torn apart and he felt a stabbing pain in his right thigh. It was bad: two engines were crippled, the

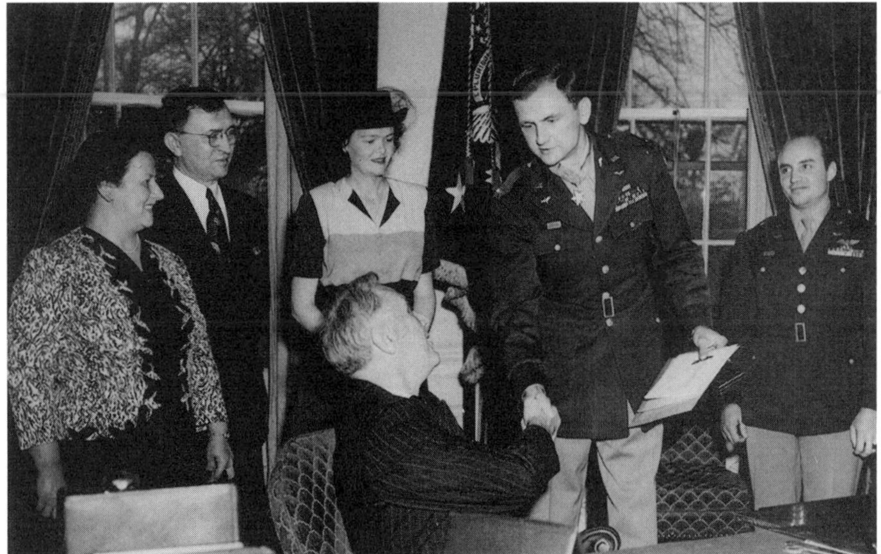

Edward S. Michael with his wife and parents and President Franklin D. Roosevelt

nose turret shot away, top turret damaged, and the windscreen coated in hydraulic fluid. *Bertie Lee* dropped 3,000 feet before Michael regained control. She was completely alone, vulnerable to more fighters.

Then things got worse.

A crewman told Michael that cannon shells had ignited some of the forty-two incendiary bombs, which burned with white-hot intensity in the bomb bay. Even if they did not explode, the searing heat could melt the cables to rudder and elevators or disintegrate part of the airframe.

Out of options, Michael gave the bailout order; six men jumped. However, the wounded copilot, Lieutenant Franklin Westberg, insisted on remaining until Michael applied first aid to the bleeding leg. Michael replied that Westberg should jump before the bombs exploded. The debate was interrupted by more German fighters; Michael shoved forward on the yoke, diving into nearby clouds. He held the descent until the crippled Fort emerged into clear air only 2,500 feet above the ground.

Both pilots were startled when the top turret gunner, Staff Sergeant Jewel Phillips, appeared on the flight deck. His head and shoulders ran crimson with blood and one eye was gouged out. He was unable to attach his parachute to his harness so Michael assisted him forward and watched him leap from the nose hatch.

Michael and Westberg were following Phillips when they heard the nose gun firing. The bombardier, Lieutenant John Lieber, had not known of the drama of the past twenty minutes when his intercom failed. Even worse, a cannon shell had detonated near his chute pack; it was useless.

Another brief dispute arose when Lieber refused to use Michael's parachute. Leaving the bombardier to his fate was unthinkable; the wounded pilot and copilot returned to the flight deck, accepting the growing risk of a midair explosion or crash landing in Occupied France.

Riding an emotional roller coaster, the three airmen experienced a seesaw battle of fortune and impending disaster. When Lieber finally could jettison the incendiaries, he was unable to close the bomb bay doors, which induced additional drag. Furthermore, the fire had burned away part of the fuselage, including the left-hand control cables and wiring.

Then the Luftwaffe reappeared.

Michael shoved up the power on his remaining Wrights and dived for the treetops. At least he could deny the predators a shot at his vulnerable belly. The fighters made five passes, ruining the windscreen and depriving the pilots of any forward view. When the Germans pulled off, light and medium flak opened up. Michael had no rudder movement and only partial elevator control.

At that point a merciful providence yielded the bomber to the North Sea. Michael and his bobtailed crew had survived an agonizing two and a half hours of flak, fire, and fighters. Barely able to maintain altitude, *Bertie Lee* hauled within sight of land.

By then Michael was hemorrhaging again; he fainted from shock and blood loss. Westberg resumed control, intending to set down at the first available field. He came upon Grimsby, Lincolnshire, in the mouth of the Humber, and circled briefly. Lieber was able to rouse Michael, asking whether a landing were feasible.

It did not look good. Michael could try an approach on two engines but he had almost no forward visibility, no airspeed indicator, no flaps, and the landing gear would not lower. He had ailerons but no rudder and only partial elevator control, and the ball turret and bomb bay doors impeded a belly landing. However, with two parachutes for three men, he had to try.

Feeling more than seeing his way down, Michael made a landing approach. He cut the power and settled *Bertie Lee* onto the green turf of England. As the flying wreck slewed to a halt, Michael fainted at the controls. He spent the next seven weeks in hospitals and was recovered enough to return home in late May.

During the ensuing months of recuperation, Michael learned via the Red Cross that six of his seven missing crewmen were reported in captivity. He was ordered to Washington, where President Roosevelt presented the Medal of Honor on 10 January 1945, a day doubly blessed when Michael learned that Sergeant Phillips, the seventh crewman, also survived as a prisoner.

Michael became an instructor and ferry pilot and decided to make the Air Force his career. Subsequently he flew transports and bombers, transitioning to the B-47 in 1957. He served in Guam, Hawaii, and the continental United States, filling reserve affairs, aircrew training, recruiting, and base support roles. He was promoted to lieutenant colonel in 1963.

Edward Michael died in 1994 and is buried in Springfield, Utah. In a letter to future Americans he wrote, "Freedom, my greatest heritage, I bequeath to you. Honor it with your life—for without it, what good is life?"

Crew: 2Lts. Franklin Westberg (CP), John L. Lieber (B), and M. M. Calvert (N); TSgt. R. H. Evans (FE); SSgts. Jewel W. Phillips (TTG), J. W. Phillips, (RO), F. O. Wilkins (RO), A. J. Russo (WG), A. J. Josino (WG), and C. J. Luce (TG).

LIEUTENANT COLONEL LEON ROBERT VANCE JR.

11 AUGUST 1916–26 JULY 1944

BORN: Enid, Oklahoma

DIED: Near Iceland

ACTION: Bombing mission, France; 5 June 1944 (age 27)

UNIT: 489th Bomb Group, 8th Air Force

AIRCRAFT: Consolidated B-24H 41-28690 (QK-I+) 66th BS, 44th BG, *Missouri Sue* "Eye Plus"

OTHER DECORATIONS: Silver Star, Air Medal, Purple Heart

Lieutenant Colonel Leon Robert Vance earned a Medal of Honor on only his second combat mission, leading the 489th Bomb Group against German coastal defenses near Wimereaux, France. It was 5 June 1944, and Vance flew as command pilot in Captain Louis Mazure's aircraft. The 66th Squadron,

Leon R. Vance Jr.

44th Bomb Group, provided lead crews for the Eighth Air Force's Second Division on "D-Minus One," and Mazure's crew was topheavy with talent: six officers besides Vance, including two bombardiers and a radar navigator to assist the 489th bomb through the undercast.

On the run over Wimereaux the Germans were caught by surprise. The radar navigator lined up the formation with the target through the undercast, then relinquished control to the bombardier. However, Lieutenant Milton Segal found that his bombs failed to release; the group overshot the target, requiring a dangerous second approach or an abort. Vance ordered a 360-degree turn, maintaining altitude, which he knew was a risky venture. By the time the group was lined up again, the defenders were fully alerted. They hammered the formation with accurate 88mm fire.

Vance's Liberator was struck by successive antiaircraft shells. The damage was appalling: one propeller windmilling, fuel and hydraulic lines severed, right rudder and most of the elevator destroyed, the pilot dead and crewmen wounded. Vance's right foot was nearly amputated by shell splinters, left dangling by a tendon.

Vance had been standing on the flight deck behind the pilots and, despite his wounds and the aircraft damage, he directed the copilot, Lieutenant Earl Carper, to take over after the formation dropped on target. Then Lieutenant Bernard Bail helped Vance to the radar navigator's seat and applied a tourniquet to stanch the hemorrhage from Vance's right leg. Looking aft and downward, Bail could see that the bomb bay doors remained open with a 500-pounder hung up in the rear bay.

Meanwhile, Lieutenant Carper had turned west over the English Channel, gliding toward Britain. Vance crawled back to the cockpit and relieved

Carper as the crew began preparing to bail out. Amid confusing intercom calls, Vance thought that a wounded man was unable to jump.

"We dropped 5,000 feet in what seemed a second," Carper reported. "A B-24 isn't much of a glider but when we got back over England the colonel told all the crew to bail out."

The crew jumped between Ramsgate and Dover, with Carper landing in the water. Besides Lieutenant Nathaniel Glickman, Sergeant Quentin Skufca also had serious wounds and three men broke bones during parachute landings. The latter included navigator John Kilgore, who broke both legs—and was unable to walk out of the minefield in which he landed!

Concerned about the populated area on the coast, Vance turned the doomed bomber back to the Channel. He was a long way from Enid, Oklahoma.

"Bob" Vance had spent two years at the University of Oklahoma before entering the U.S. Military Academy. He was commissioned in 1939 and completed pilot training a year later. In the expansion of 1941 he commanded a training squadron at Goodfellow field in Texas. By the end of 1942 he was a major and director of flying at Strother field, Kansas. In 1943, during multiengine transition training at Fort Worth, Vance and his wife Georgette played bridge with Major and Mrs. Horace Carswell. That September, Lieutenant Colonel Vance was named deputy commander of the 489th Group at Wendover, Utah, and went to Britain in April 1944. Flying from Halesworth, Suffolk, the group began operations on 30 May with Vance leading the first mission to Oldenburg, Germany, in a B-24H named *The Sharon D.* in honor of his infant daughter.

When the B-24 entered service, Consolidated was uncertain that it could be safely ditched owing to the high wing. Now, over the Channel with his dangling foot caught under the seat, Vance had to stretch himself over the throttle quadrant. Visibility forward was almost nonexistent so he had to rely on peripheral vision out each side, awkwardly holding the copilot's control yoke. The problem was compounded by damage to the elevators, requiring constant pressure on the yoke to prevent a fatal stall.

In an awesome display of airmanship, Vance set the Liberator into the water in a controlled landing. However, the force of impact dislodged the top turret, which smashed onto the flight deck. Though Vance was pinned in a sinking aircraft, he released Mazure's seat belt and pushed the body toward the escape hatch.

Within seconds of drowning, Vance felt a violent explosion. He thought the oxygen bottles had burst; others theorized that the fused bomb let off a low-order detonation. Whatever the cause, the result was miraculous. Vance emerged from the wreckage, not only alive but lucid. He inflated his mae west and looked for the "missing" crewman, then began swimming toward shore. Fifty minutes later he was picked up by a British rescue vessel.

Crew members who visited Vance in hospital found him amazingly optimistic. Despite the loss of his foot he expressed his intention to return to combat following recuperation in the States. He enjoyed a brief reunion with the 489th Group, then boarded a C-54 transport seven weeks after his phenomenal escape.

A kinder deity would have granted Bob Vance a safe return to his family, but between Greenland and Iceland the Globemaster disappeared. Probably not a victim of weather, its fate remains unknown more than half a century later.

Vance's young daughter Sharon received his Medal of Honor at Enid, Oklahoma, on 11 October 1946, and Enid Army Air field became Vance Air Force Base in 1949.

Crew: Capt. Louis A. Mazure (P); 2Lts. Earl L. Carper (CP), John R. Kilgore (N), Nathaniel Glickman (Pilotage Nav), Bernard M. Bail (Radar Nav), and Milton Segal (B); TSgts. Earl L. Hoppie (FE) and Quentin F. Skufca (RO); SSgts. Harry E. Secrist (WG), Davis J. Evans Jr. (WG), and Wiley A. Sallis (TG).

SECOND LIEUTENANT DAVID RICHARD KINGSLEY

27 JUNE 1918–23 JUNE 1944

BORN: Portland, Oregon

DIED: Romania

ACTION: Bombing mission, Ploeşti, Romania; 23 June 1944 (age 25)

UNIT: 341st Bomb Squadron, 97th Bomb Group, 15th Air Force

AIRCRAFT: Boeing B-17F 42-5951 (O) *Opissonya*

OTHER DECORATIONS: Air Medal, Purple Heart

The Fifteenth Air Force was out in strength on Saturday, 23 June 1944: 761 heavy bombers, including all six groups of the Fifth Bomb Wing, targeted against the inevitable petroleum targets of Romania: oil storage at Giurgiu and two refineries near Ploeşti.

Opposition was savage: though escorting Mustangs claimed more than thirty kills, U.S. losses were heavy. Nearing Ploeşti, the 97th Group turned for Giurgiu, seventy miles south. During the bomb run to the Danube, a B-17 irreverently named *Opissonya* was rocked by flak; it dropped behind and began losing altitude. However, the pilot, first Lieutenant Edwin Anderson, was determined to put his bombardier over the target.

David R. Kingsley

Crouched over his Norden sight was Second Lieutenant David R. Kingsley, who would observe his twenty-sixth birthday on Tuesday. He tried to ignore the German fighters that attacked before the group reached Giurgiu and concentrated on the image in his sight: smoke obscuring the target and flak so thick, said one crewman, "you could almost walk on it."

Opissonya took a beating over the target; with damaged controls, Anderson and copilot William Symons eased the battered Boeing away on three engines with one fuel tank ripped loose. Quick to finish a straggler, Messerschmitts pounced on the lone Fortress. The tail gunner, Sergeant Michael Sullivan, was struck by 20mm shell fragments. The same hit destroyed his intercom; he could not call for help.

Barely able to crawl, Sullivan pulled himself forward to the waist position. The two gunners tried to administer first aid but his right shoulder was bleeding badly. They carried him to the radio compartment and called for Kingsley. With the target now astern, the bombardier was best disposed to help. It was for certain that the gunners would be busy.

Kingsley had enlisted at his native Portland, Oregon, in April 1942 and entered the Army aviation cadet program. He failed pilot training but passed the preliminary bombardier-navigator course at Santa Ana, California, in April 1943. Two months later he pinned on his bombardier wings at Kirtland field, New Mexico, but subsequently he became dual qualified as a navigator. He reported to the 97th Group at Amendola, Italy, in April 1944, two years after entering the service.

Since then Kingsley had flown almost continuously: nineteen previous missions in barely two months. Therefore, the mission on 23 June was flown by an experienced crew, though *Opissonya* had a substitute copilot and radioman.

Working in the confined space, Kingsley pulled off Sullivan's damaged parachute harness and jacket, exposing the bleeding shoulder wound. Somehow, he applied a tourniquet and stanched the hemorrhage, but Sullivan was approaching shock. He needed help—soon. Nearly 500 miles from base, with one engine feathered and 8,000-foot mountains ahead, it looked like a long flight to safety. Kingsley told the wounded gunner that two Mustangs had tagged along, but following the combat around Ploeşti the P-51s ran low on fuel and had to depart.

That's when eight Me-109s dived out of the sun. For perhaps fifteen minutes they made repeated gunnery passes, shooting the Boeing to pieces and wounding the ball turret gunner. There was no option but to abandon ship. Lieutenant Anderson rang the bailout bell.

Kingsley helped the wounded men prepare to jump. When Sullivan's damaged harness could not be found, the bombardier shucked his own and wrestled the gunner into it. As Sullivan later explained, "Lieutenant Kingsley took me in his arms and struggled to the bomb bay where he told me to keep my hand on the ripcord and said to pull it when I was clear of the ship. Then he told me to bail out. Before I jumped, I looked up at him and the look he had on his face was firm and solemn. He must have known what was coming because there was no fear in his eyes at all."

Crew members saw their bomber continue its erratic descent, then fall to earth. It burned on the ground, and the captured airmen were shown the singed remains of Kingsley's personal effects. Bulgarian troops told them his body had been found on the flight deck, apparently searching for a spare parachute or vainly trying to make a crash landing.

Other airmen risked or lost their lives trying to save their friends, and several received the Medal of Honor. But David Kingsley knowingly abandoned any hope of survival when he gave away his parachute harness in a doomed aircraft. His action is notable in that it was a decision made with deliberation and reason, with none of the impulsiveness of so many heroic acts. In the history of the aviation Medals of Honor, his action defines "above and beyond the call of duty."

On 9 April 1945 David Kingsley's medal was presented to his brother, Thomas E. Kingsley, in Portland, Oregon.

Crew: 1Lts. Edwin O. Anderson (P) and William C. Symons (CP); 2Lt. Robert L. Newson (N); TSgts. Lloyd E. Kaine (FE) and John Meyer (RO); SSgts. Martin Hettinga Jr. (RO), Harold D. James (WG), Stanley J. Kmiec (WG), and Michael J. Sullivan (TG).

FIRST LIEUTENANT DONALD DALE PUCKET

15 December 1915–9 July 1944

Born: Longmont, Colorado

Died: Romania

Action: Bombing mission; Ploeşti, Romania; 9 July 1944 (age 28)

Unit: 343rd Bomb Squadron, 98th Bomb Group, 15th Air Force

Aircraft: Consolidated B-24G 42-78346 (also listed as 73346)

Other decorations: Distinguished Flying Cross, Air Medal (3), Purple Heart

The policy was called "restrike." Early airpower advocates often were reluctant to adopt it because, being aviators, they were born optimists. But hard experience had proven that striking a target once was seldom adequate. Hermann Goering had failed to absorb the lesson soon enough during the Battle of Britain. American strategic planners had recognized the wisdom and necessity of restrikes against Axis targets after Nazi aircraft and oil production proved surprisingly resilient.

Oil. It always came back to oil.

Perhaps the most "restricken" target in the U.S. air war was the region around Ploeşti, Romania. On VE-Day nearly 60,000 Americans had flown against the refineries, dropping some 13,000 tons of bombs. In 1945 more than 1,000 USAAF fliers were held prisoner in Romania.

Donald D. Pucket

Certainly Ploeşti figured prominently in aviation Medal of Honor actions: by July 1944 six medals had been connected with the city. On 9 July (sixteen days after David Kingsley's mission) the 98th Bomb Group at Lecce, Italy, flew yet another mission against Ploeşti. The targets were familiar to the group: the Xenia and Concordia Vega oil refineries. The 98th had been led by Colonel "Killer" Kane during Tidal Wave in August 1943.

After eleven months of bombing attacks, the Romanians and their German allies were well versed in American operations. The refineries themselves were fairly small for high-altitude bombing, and smoke generators could quickly be activated to complicate bombardiers' tasks. Consequently, the 9 July mission introduced the well-proven pathfinder technique employed by the Eighth Air Force. New M2X radar sets permitted a "drop on lead" technique for the 222 Fortresses and Liberators assigned to the mission.

The Luftwaffe interceptors were kept at bay, and overall U.S. losses were light: a total of six aircraft. But that was small consolation to Lieutenant Donald Pucket and his crew.

Pucket and his bride loved to ski; he insisted that skiing was the next best thing to flying. He had enlisted in the Army at Denver in November 1942 and was selected for bombers. He completed pilot training in October 1943 and was commissioned a second lieutenant. After multiengine transition training he went to Europe, in April 1944, as a B-24 pilot.

In theater only three months, Pucket was nonetheless an aircraft commander with a reputation for mature judgment. However, he could make independent decisions as well; he had proved that two weeks previously when he took his flak-damaged Liberator out of formation to protect a lagging squadronmate. The action was contrary to policy, but Pucket's courage was rewarded with a Distinguished flying Cross.

Now, Pucket's bombardier had barely called "Bombs away" when the Liberator was hammered by flak. The damage was catastrophic: the flight engineer dead, six wounded, two engines shut down, fuel lines punctured, some control cables severed, and an oxygen-fed fire.

Pucket relinquished control to Lieutenant Robert Jenkins and made his way aft to inspect the damage. Finding fuel and hydraulic pooling in the bomb bay, he used a hand crank to open the jammed doors and reduce the fire danger. Then he organized capable crewmen to jettison guns, ammunition, and other equipment.

Despite the efforts to lighten the ship, the crippled bomber steadily lost altitude, descending too fast to reach safety. About 150 miles southwest of the target, Pucket ordered a bailout and five men prepared to jump. However, according to survivors, three fliers either were unable or unwilling to make the leap. With time quickly running out, some of the ambulatory crewmen called on Pucket to join them. Then they jumped.

The pilot who had violated doctrine to stick with a damaged wingmate was not prepared to abandon members of his own crew. He had no time to pull the wounded to the bomb bay so they could jump so he took his final option. As the burning, crippled Liberator dived toward the ground, Pucket returned to the flight deck and attempted to pull the nose into a level attitude. A crash landing offered some prospect for survival, and the crewmen dangling in their parachutes watched intently.

Nearing the ground, still slightly nose down, the B-24 smashed into a mountain slope and exploded on impact. There were no survivors, and one of the men who jumped also died.

Ploeşti had produced its seventh and last Medal of Honor.

The medal was approved in June 1945 and presented to Pucket's widow, Lorene, in Boulder, Colorado, on 12 August. However, she declined to accept the decoration in her husband's name unless a passage in the citation was altered. She felt that allusions to hysterical men reflected poorly on those who died with Donald Pucket on a remote Balkan mountainside. His widow said, "Don's action in staying with his wounded crewmembers and crippled B-24 was what was traditional and expected of the captain of the ship."

Throughout the war at least 350 American bombers were destroyed in attacks on Ploeşti. The complex finally was seized by Soviet forces in September 1944.

Crew: 1Lts. Robert L. Jenkins (CP) and Guy A. Luttrell (N); 2Lt. Leo McElwain (B); TSgt. Frank R. Brunton (RO); SSgts. Lawrence L. Hood (FE), Joseph E. Angeloni (BTG), Ilas B. Dye (WG), James J. Boyle Jr. (WG), Herschel K. Devore (NG), Jack C. Rathbun (TG), and Leon Fourens (photo).

CAPTAIN DARRELL ROBINS LINDSEY

30 December 1919–9 August 1944

Born: Jefferson, Iowa

Died: France

Action: Bombing mission; France; 9 August 1944 (age 24)

Unit: 585th Bomb Squadron, 394th Bomb Group, 9th Air Force

Aircraft: Martin B-26B 42-96101 (4T-N; 4T may not have appeared)

Other decorations: Air Medal (9), Purple Heart

Martin B-26s lived between 10,000 and 12,000 feet, the optimum combination for bombing accuracy and avoiding the worst of the 37 and 40mm flak that the Germans scientifically arrayed across northern Europe. On 9 August 1944 the Marauders of the Ninth Air Force's 394th Bomb Group plunged into a Nazi flak zone over the bitterly contested northern French countryside.

In the two previous days the 394th had attacked bridges and an ammunition depot. The missions were in response to the German counterattack of 7 August, hoping to secure Avranches to establish a defensive line that might contain the Allied ground forces.

The 9 August mission was typical of those the 394th had flown since entering combat five months before: attack on a tactical target, the rail bridge at the bend of the Oise at L'Isle Adam, fifty miles north-northwest of the center of Paris. Conventional wisdom conceded that if it was worth bombing, it was worth defending; the *Wehrmacht* agreed, defending it with batteries of 88mm flak guns.

The bridge at L'Isle Adam was doubly valuable to the Germans since Al-

Darrell R. Lindsey

lied aircraft had dropped most of the spans across the Seine, meandering west of Paris. Consequently, the German army needed the bridge even more in order to channel reinforcements and supplies to the expanding Anglo-American front in Normandy and the Cotentin Peninsula.

Leading the mission was Captain Darrell Lindsey of Jefferson, Iowa. An early member of the group, he had joined as a flight commander almost a year before. Now a twenty-five-year-old veteran, he led the 394th against L'Isle Adam, ending his second year of commissioned service.

After attending Drake University, Lindsey had enlisted in January 1942 and received his lieutenant's bars that August. He was a captain by December 1943 and was regarded as a rare bird since he was trained as a bombardier as well as a pilot. He had flown forty-five previous missions, often at the head of his squadron.

Shortly after crossing the "bomb line" demarking Allied and enemy territory, the Marauders came under sustained gunfire. They avoided significant damage until just before the initial point, when Lindsay's Martin was hit. He nevertheless remained in the lead and took the twenty-nine others on to the target.

During the run Lindsey's right engine was hit hard and he dropped out of formation. It was a major concern in the B-26, as he had learned at McDill Field. "One a day in Tampa Bay" was the watchword, when runaway Curtiss Electric propellers could cause adverse yaw or outright failure that rolled a Marauder inverted without immediate correction. Lindsey wrestled the '26, regained control, and forced the crippled bomber back to the head of the formation.

The flak burst ignited fuel and oil that fed a major blaze spreading across the wing. Lindsey knew that when enough high-octane gasoline burned off, the mixture in his wing tank would reach the critical point when an explosion could occur. "Gas burns; fumes explode," went the mantra. He pressed on, determined to maintain formation integrity before bailing his crew out of the burning aircraft.

Lindsey and his copilot maintained position until the bombardier toggled his load. Only then did the pilot call for his crew to abandon ship. Unable to maintain altitude, the B-26 was descending but the wings remained level.

Last out was the bombardier, Lieutenant Harley Hooper, who called that he intended to lower the landing gear so Lindsey could jump through the nose wheel well. However, Lindsey realized that dropping the gear could result in complete loss of control; with one engine out and the drag imposed by the landing gear, he would never recover from a spin. Therefore, he instructed Hooper to jump through one of the waist windows before the Marauder spun or exploded.

The bombardier scrambled aft and dived overboard. Whether Lindsey had time to leave his seat is unknown, as the blazing wing exploded and the Marauder pitched nose-down, diving into the ground to explode in a fireball.

Lindsey's Medal of Honor was approved in April 1945 and presented to his widow, Evelyn, in Fort Dodge that August. In 1972 Jesse Lindsey donated his son's decorations to the Greene County Historical Society, and in 1993 a monument from Lindsey field near Wiesbaden, Germany, was rededicated during the annual Bell Tower celebration in Jefferson. The 394th Bomb Group memorial at Tucson's Pima Air Museum also contains a tribute to Darrell Lindsey.

Crew: 2Lt. Arthur C. Erbe (CP); 1Lts. William J. Smith (N), Gerald Hyson (Gee-Nav), and Harley R. Hooper (B-N); TSgt. Richard E. Wylie (RO); SSgts. Donald E. Wilson (FE) and Albert P. Lawson (TG); Sgt. Perla Fees Jr. (WG).

MAJOR HORACE SEAVER CARSWELL JR.

16 July 1916–26 October 1944

Born: Ft. Worth, Texas

Died: Kwangtung Province, China

Action: Shipping attack; South China Sea; 26 October 1944 (age 28)

Unit: 374th Bomb Squadron, 308th Bomb Group, 14th Air Force

Aircraft: Consolidated B-24J 44-40825

Other decorations: Distinguished Service Cross, Distinguished Flying Cross, Air Medal, Purple Heart

The target, as usual, was shipping.

On the afternoon of 26 October 1944 the operations officer of the 374th Bomb Squadron at Chengkung, China, briefed another B-24 crew for a nocturnal patrol of the South China Sea. A Japanese convoy of eight ships was reported steaming southwest of Hong Kong, and the Liberator crews were experienced in dealing with such targets.

Flying with Lieutenant James Rinker's crew was Major Horace Carswell, 308th Group operations officer. He would fly in the left seat with Rinker in the right; the regular copilot, Lieutenant James O'Neal, went along as relief pilot.

The Liberator took off at 1715 and, in bright moonlight, found a Japanese convoy southwest of Hong Kong three hours later. Radar showed twelve ships—four more than expected.

Carswell assessed the situation as favorable for an attack. He achieved surprise on his first pass, dropping six 500-pounders from 600 feet to claim a near miss on one escort. Then he shoved up the power to his four Pratt and Whitneys and evaded in the dark.

Carswell circled out of range, assessing the situation. He pulled off nearly twenty miles and waited half an hour before deciding that another run was worth the risk. Though radar showed that the Japanese convoy commander had redeployed his ships in antiaircraft disposition, Carswell selected a large tanker.

Horace Carswell had enlisted as an aviation cadet at Dallas in March 1940 and received his commission late that year. Retained in training command, he instructed at Randolph and Goodfellow fields in Texas before moving to

Horace S. Carswell Jr.

operational training billets in Arizona and back to Texas. By January 1943 he was a captain but he was promoted to major in April. A year later he was in the Far East, flying as operations officer of the 308th Bomb Group. He had bailed out of a B-24 in July but established a reputation for aggressiveness, epitomized by an antishipping mission on 15 October that brought him the Distinguished Service Cross.

Satisfied that he had waited long enough, Carswell made another attack. He ran in from 600 feet again, toggling three bombs. The crew saw one geyser and two explosions.

However, Japanese gunners had no difficulty tracking the big bomber and inflicted lethal damage. Shot out of control, the B-24 careened toward the water but Carswell regained level flight at perhaps 150 feet. Then he took stock of the situation: two engines were shot out and a third damaged; the hydraulic system was holed. It was time to head home, but the battered Liberator could barely make 125 mph.

Carswell advanced power on the remaining engines, slowly climbing toward the China coast. Remaining ordnance and many other items were jettisoned to lighten the load. Once over land it would be safe to bail out.

Lieutenant James O'Neal, the plane's regular copilot, noticed that Lieutenant Rinker was slumped in the right seat. Unknown to anyone, Rinker had taken multiple flak hits; his clothes were covered with blood. He was relieved by O'Neal while the navigator and bombardier applied first aid and revived him.

Subsequently the bombardier, Walter Hillier, reported that his parachute was damaged by flak splinters. He did not want to risk a jump with a questionable chute.

With little option, Carswell and O'Neal nursed the plane up to about 3,500 feet before crossing the coast. It was a tedious process, repeated four or five times owing to faltering power on the left inboard engine. Yet Carswell and O'Neal skillfully used available power and flaps to "stair-step" the big bomber back to altitude.

However, when the damaged engine failed, the Liberator began losing its battle with gravity, and the pilots had trouble maintaining control. At about 2,000 feet the crew, except Carswell, O'Neal, and Hillier, bailed out through the bomb bay. They landed on mountain slopes but under the night sky they watched their aircraft careen between nearly 4,000-foot peaks and disappear from view. Minutes later they glimpsed an explosion as the '24 clipped a mountain, crashed and burned.

The following morning two dead crewmen were found: Lieutenant O'Neal and Sergeant Kemper Steinman. The six survivors trekked back to Chengkung, arriving 9 November.

Carswell was nominated for a posthumous Medal of Honor, which was approved on Valentine's Day 1946. Some crew members felt that Lieutenant O'Neal also merited the award, and though two Eighth Air Force bomber crews received double awards, Carswell remained the only recipient in the 14th Air Force.

The Medal of Honor was presented to Carswell's family in San Angelo, Texas, in April 1946, and two years later Fort Worth's air base was named in his memory. Carswell's body was returned to the United States after the war and was finally laid to rest with his parents in Oakwood Cemetery.

Crew: 2Lts. James H. Rinker (CP), James L. O'Neal (CP), Walter W. Hillier (B), and Charles A. Ulery (N); TSgts. Charles H. Maddox Jr. (FE), Ernest Watras (RO), and Adam J. Hudek (radar); SSgts. Kaemper W. Steinmann (G), Carlton M. Schnepf (NG), and Norman Nunes (TG).

SECOND LIEUTENANT ROBERT EDWARD FEMOYER

31 OCTOBER 1921–2 NOVEMBER 1944

BORN: Huntington, West Virginia

DIED: Rattlesden, Suffolk

ACTION: Bombing mission, Germany; 2 November 1944 (age 23)

UNIT: 711th Bomb Squadron, 447th Bomb Group, 8th Air Force

AIRCRAFT: Boeing B-17G 42-38052 "Hotshot Green" (also listed as 107052)

OTHER DECORATIONS: Air Medal, Purple Heart

The Luftwaffe radar controllers were experienced and skillful. Some 400 German fighters intercepted the Eighth Air Force's mission on 2 November 1944, most of which were tied up by wide-ranging Mustangs. Some made it through the escort, but there was no avoiding the flak.

The 447th Bomb Group was among 500 "heavies" sent on a "restrike" against German petroleum facilities at Merseburg. It was a maximum effort with forty-four B-17s dispatched from Rattlesden, Suffolk, though three aborted. It only got worse: over Germany two Fortresses were shot out of formation in the lead squadron and another fell out of the high squadron.

Two minutes before reaching the control point, two planes of the low squadron collided. One fell apart; the other crashed in Belgium. A third Fortress, badly shot up, ditched in the North Sea. Additionally, an 88mm battery bracketed L-Love with three bursts. Second Lieutenant Jerome Rosenblum's bomber dropped out of formation, proceeding alone without mutual support of its combat box.

Shell fragments had struck the navigator, Second Lieutenant Robert Femoyer, in the back and side. Knocked to the floor of the compartment, he was too badly wounded to be moved but asked his crewmates to prop him upright so he could see outside and check his maps. He refused morphine, concerned that it would effect his mental capacity. Femoyer wanted all his senses if he were to navigate his lone bomber around Germany's myriad flak zones.

Robert E. Femoyer had been in the Army Air Force only two years, having studied for three years at Virginia Polytechnic before enlisting in November 1942. Though accepted for pilot training, he switched to navigator school

Robert E. Femoyer

and was commissioned on 10 June 1944. Three months later he joined the 447th Bomb Group at Rattlesden. His combat career lasted six weeks and seven missions.

Though bleeding and in growing pain, Femoyer continued to direct the bomber's path through the flak zones of Occupied Europe. His ordeal lasted an agonizing two and a half hours, sitting in a growing pool of his own blood, struggling to fight off the pain, nausea, and dimming senses as blood pressure dropped and vision narrowed.

Only after reaching the North Sea did the navigator accept a sedative injection. Rosenblum safely landed the B-17 eight hours after takeoff, and Femoyer was immediately removed from his plane. However, shortly thereafter he died of blood loss and shock. He was two days past his twenty-third birthday.

Robert Femoyer's Medal of Honor was approved 9 May 1945, the day after Nazi Germany surrendered. With Walter Treumper of the 351st Bomb Group, he remains one of two U.S. Air Force navigators to receive his nation's highest award.

Crew: Lts. J. M. Rosenblum (P), G. J. Hecht (CP), S. A. Ferbank (B); SSgt. J. Lonigan (TTG); Sgts. O. R. Pehl (RO), R. R. Hackenberg (BTG), D. M. Douglas (WG), L. E. Neumann (TG).

FIRST LIEUTENANT DONALD JOSEPH GOTT AND SECOND LIEUTENANT WILLIAM EDWARD METZGER JR.

23 JUNE 1923–9 NOVEMBER 1944 (GOTT)

9 FEBRUARY 1922–9 NOVEMBER 1944(METZGER)

BORN: Arnett, Oklahoma (Gott); Lima, Ohio (Metzger)

DIED: Near Hattonville, Meuse, France

ACTION: Bombing mission; France; 9 November 1944 (age 21—Gott; age 22—Metzger)

UNIT: 729th Bomb Squadron, 452nd Bomb Group, 8th Air Force

AIRCRAFT: Boeing B-17G 42-97904 (R) *Lady Jeanette* (not *Janet*)

OTHER DECORATIONS: (Gott) Air Medal (4), Purple Heart; (Metzger) Purple Heart

The mission began and ended in tragedy: the Eighth Air Force lost eight bombers and three fighters in takeoff or landing accidents but the need was urgent, despite the weather. More than 1,100 Fortresses and Liberators supported the Third Army's crossing of the Moselle River, and the "heavies" were assigned to bomb German-held forts at Metz and Thionville.

Worsening weather over the primary targets forced the 452nd Bomb Group to divert forty miles east. Saarbrucken, Germany, was an industrial city and defended accordingly; accurate flak shot two B-17s out of the wintry sky—just part of the forty-plane toll the Mighty Eighth paid while supporting General George Patton this day.

Short of the target, another Fortress was in severe trouble. *Lady Jeanette,* flown by first Lieutenant Donald Gott, was number four in the lead 729th Bomb Squadron, with a veteran crew. Most of the men had more than twenty missions though it was the copilot's third and bombardier's second—a rough introduction to Germany's awesome flak. The damage was catastrophic: one engine was shot off the wing—its severed fuel lines trailing flames to the tail—another was damaged and a propeller refused to feather. Additionally, several bombs were jammed on their racks. There was no hope of returning to Deopham Green, Norfolk; *Lady Jeanette* was going down. Gott would need all his skill and experience. He had won his wings in January 1944 and now, only twenty-one, he had logged twenty-six previous missions.

Donald J. Gott

William E. Metzger Jr.

Farther aft in the shattered bomber the situation only worsened. The radio operator's right arm had nearly been sliced off by a flak splinter and the flight engineer had a serious leg wound. The intercom was useless and punctured hydraulic lines spilled flammable fluid into the fuselage, where a flare had ignited and had to be jettisoned. While Gott struggled to keep *Lady Jeanette* airborne, his copilot left the right seat to help the casualties.

Second Lieutenant William Metzger was more than a year older than Gott but had only joined the group that fall. Originally a flight officer, he was commissioned shortly before going to England. In the radio compartment with the bombardier and waist gunner, he applied a tourniquet to Sergeant Robert Dunlap, who had fainted. Metzger and bombardier Joseph Harms then managed to kick out the bombs that could not be dropped.

Metzger scrambled back to the flight deck and told Gott that it would do little good to have Dunlap bail out; he could not open his own parachute and even if he could, undoubtedly he would bleed to death before any Germans found him. He needed a hospital—now.

The pilots decided to turn westward. There was a chance they could cross the Allied lines before their bomber fell apart or exploded from the flaming fuel leak. With the intercom out, Metzger again headed aft to tell the crew to prepare to bail out before he and Gott tried a landing to save Dunlap. The copilot returned to report that two of the crew had already jumped from the burning Boeing. Metzger did not need to add that he had given away his parachute and the spare to men whose chutes had been damaged. Meanwhile, the tail gunner had accidentally opened his chute in the aircraft and was sucked out the escape hatch, his canopy snagged on the tail.

Gott and Metzger made a controlled descent through the lower cloud layer, emerging near Hattonville, in friendly territory. They spotted a field in a forest that looked large enough for a landing and, relying on the remaining good engine, set up their approach. But the crippled Fortress ran out of altitude, clipping treetops for about 600 feet before slamming into two stout trees that sheared off the wings.

Abruptly *Lady Jeanette* exploded and plunged into the ground; Gott and Metzger lost their lives trying to save Dunlap. The tail gunner, Sergeant Herman Krimminger, also was killed with his parachute caught on the empennage. Medals of Honor for Gott and Metzger were approved on 16 May 1945, shortly after VE-Day.

During the war, segments of the story were altered by U.S. authorities to conceal the fact that a B-24J of the 36th Radio Countermeasures Squadron crashed in the same area the next day. Consequently, researchers had to unravel apparently conflicting French accounts decades later.

An archaeological investigation began in 1991, conducted by Sam Cole of the Battery Corporal Willis S. Cole Military Museum from Washington State. In May 2000 human remains and Gott's dogtag were found, and a memorial was dedicated that November, fifty-six years after *Lady Jeanette*'s last mission.

Crew: 2Lts. John Harland (N) and Joseph F. Harms (B); TSgt. Robert A. Dunlap (RO); SSgts. Russell W. Gustafson (FE), James O. Fross (BTG), William R. Robbins (WG), and Herman B. Krimminger (TG).

MAJOR RICHARD IRA BONG

24 SEPTEMBER 1920–6 AUGUST 1945

BORN: Superior, Wisconsin

DIED: Burbank, California

ACTION: Air combat; Philippine Islands; October–December 1944 (age 24)

UNIT: 5th fighter Command, 5th Air Force

AIRCRAFT: Lockheed P-38J/Ls including J-1LO 44-23964

OTHER DECORATIONS: Distinguished Service Cross, Silver Star (2), Distinguished Flying Cross (7), Air Medal (15)

The hunters were up on 7 December 1944. At Dulag on the west coast of Leyte, four P-38Ls took off at 1430, tucked their tricycle gear in the wells, and banked westward for Ormoc Bay. Leading Daddy Special flight was Major Thomas B. McGuire, operations officer of the 475th fighter Group. His element leader was another young major named Richard I. Bong. Between them they had shot down sixty-four Japanese aircraft in the previous two years. Approximately friends, they were also serious rivals. Bong was America's top gun; McGuire coveted the title. Wingmen to the two aces were Major Jack Rittmayer and Lieutenant floyd Fulkerson of McGuire's old 431st Squadron.

Though a major for eight months, Bong had no leadership responsibility, which suited his taste. With a roving commission from the Fifth Air Force commander, Lieutenant General George Kenney, he could go anywhere, pick his missions, and run up the score. Officially he was a gunnery instructor. In truth he was a freelance hunter—a fighter pilot's dream.

Twenty minutes later the flight was on station over Ormoc Bay, covering the 77th Infantry Division's landing. The hunting was good all day; McGuire had dropped number twenty-nine that morning.

Bong's blue eyes picked up a Mitsubishi Sally low on the water. His Lightning accelerated rapidly in the dive as Bong closed the range. At 1,000 feet he centered the bomber in his reflector sight and pressed the buttons on the yoke. Four .50 calibers and a 20mm cannon set the left engine afire; the Sally crashed on Bohol Island. Bong probably felt no particular elation—he had done the same thing thirty-six times before.

Richard I. Bong, who flew this specially marked P-38J on public relations tours in the United States after his return from combat in 1945

Half an hour later a Kate torpedo plane went after American shipping and Major Rittmayer shot it down amid naval flak. Daddy flight resumed its patrol 3,000 feet over the transports where its patience was rewarded. Five bandits appeared; Nakajima Ki-44s, pugnacious single-engine fighters called Tojos. Attacking from the side and astern, the Lightnings cleared the flak zone and Bong found himself bow-on to the last Nakajima. He fired, saw hits on the cowling, and watched his victim nose into the water. McGuire, Rittmayer, and Fulkerson splashed the other four.

Upon landing, Daddy flight had been airborne three hours. The scoreboard now read Bong thirty-eight, McGuire thirty.

Richard Bong had left Superior, Wisconsin, to enlist in May 1941, being commissioned at Luke Field, Arizona, 9 January 1942. Subsequently he served in three P-38 squadrons, allegedly looped the Golden Gate Bridge, and arrived in New Guinea with 595 hours total time. Flying with the 9th Squadron, 49th fighter Group, he claimed his first two kills over Dobodura on 27 December 1942. Returned to the United States in April 1944, he was acclaimed the American ace of aces with twenty-eight victories.

By his own admission, Bong was a marginal aerial gunner. During his first combat tour he barely hit half of his airborne targets but still claimed twenty-one enemy planes. During his much shorter second and third tours he improved dramatically, recording nearly 90 percent lethality.

Bong was a good pilot who became an excellent shooter and remained an atrocious poker player (he lost $1,500 in one game—serious money in 1944). He was one of a handful of Gen. George Kenney's paladins, professional gunfighters out to carve as many notches as possible for the Fifth Air Force. Unlike Tommy Lynch, Neel Kearby, and Tommy McGuire, Bong was never a leader. In fact, he neither desired nor received squadron command.

Though easygoing and unconcerned on the surface, Bong was as competitive as any of his rivals. His letters home reveal that he kept score on a day-to-day basis, citing who was up and who was down as precisely as any investment manager. The aggressiveness that made him masterkill was tempered by a measured approach to his lethal profession—a keen risk assessment ultimately lacking in contenders such as Kearby, McGuire, Boyington, and Davis.

On 12 December, five days after the Ormoc mission, Bong presented himself before a semicircle of P-38s at Tacloban Airfield, ringed by a dozen veterans of the Ninth Fighter Squadron. Wearing rumpled khakis and a .45 in a shoulder holster, the farmboy was approached by the vainglorious supreme commander. General Douglas MacArthur, who wore the Medal of Honor himself, grasped the fighter ace by both shoulders and intoned, "Major Richard Ira Bong, who has ruled the air from New Guinea to the Philippines, I now induct you into the society of the bravest of the brave, the wearers of the Congressional Medal of Honor of the United States."

Bong's citation stressed that he performed above and beyond his duty as a "gunnery instructor" but that was typical hyperbole. Actually he was Fifth Fighter Command's P-38 standardization officer, evaluating equipment and procedures. It was a convenient method for General Kenney to keep his top shooter on the firing line, ensuring that America's ace of aces was a Fifth Air Force man.

Three days later Bong led Daddy Special flight off Dulag field and dispatched number thirty-nine, an Oscar over Panubulon Island. Two days after that, 17 December, number forty hit the ground on Mindoro. Dick Bong's war was over. Lieutenant General George Kenney grounded McGuire until Bong reached home, lest the ambitious rival surpass the ace of aces too soon. He needn't have worried. On 7 January McGuire was killed while violating almost every combat tenet he ever drilled into his squadron.

Bong returned to the United States on New Year's Eve. He enjoyed a storybook romance with his fiancée, Marge Vattendahl, got married in February, and in April began flying Lockheed's sensational new fighter, the jet-propelled P-80A. Taking off from Burbank, California, on 6 August—the day of the Hiroshima bombing—Bong experienced engine trouble. Trying to bail out from as low as 300 feet, his parachute had no time to open.

He was twenty-four years old.

BRIGADIER GENERAL FREDERICK WALKER CASTLE

14 October 1908–24 December 1944

Born: Manila, Philippine Islands

Died: Belgium

Action: Bombing mission; Germany; 24 December 1944 (age 36)

Unit: 4th Bomb Wing, (487th Bomb Group), 8th Air Force

Aircraft: Boeing B-17G 44-8444 (H8-C)

Other decorations: Silver Star, Legion of Merit, Distinguished Flying Cross (4), Air Medal (5), Purple Heart

In the summer and fall of 1943 the U.S. Army Air Force was in trouble—deep trouble. Precision daylight bombing—the service's doctrinal basis—was at stake. Combat attrition over Occupied Europe was so heavy that analysts (to say nothing of aircrews) computed that it was statistically impossible to complete a twenty-five mission tour. The very future of the self-escorting heavy bomber was in doubt.

Among the Eighth Air Force units suffering at the hands of the Luftwaffe was the 94th Bomb Group, newly moved to Earls Colne, Suffolk. Major General Ira Eaker dipped into his bag of potential leaders and selected Colonel Frederick W. Castle, who had been itching for a combat assignment for almost a year and a half. One of the original eight officers assigned to the Mighty Eighth, he now faced the greatest challenge of his career: turning a dispirited, resentful group of airmen into a fighting machine.

The Castle story is well known to movie fans, as Colonel Beirne Lay's screenplay merely changed Fred Castle to Frank Savage; the 94th to the fictional 918th.

Many men of the 94th resented their new CO, an outsider, a "bean counter," a chairborne airman. His first impression was hardly favorable: quiet and reserved, he told his garrulous, combat-blooded officers that he expected proper dress and gentlemanly behavior. The resentment was palpable.

Frederick W. Castle

The son of a career officer, Fred Castle enlisted in the New Jersey National Guard as a private before his sixteenth birthday and only two years later won entrance to the U.S. Military Academy. He graduated as a lieutenant of engineers in 1930, seventh in a class of 241, and soon applied for flight training. He pinned on his wings in December 1931 and flew "peashooters."

Castle resigned his commission in February 1934 (the time of the Army air mail fiasco) but retained reserve status. For most of the ensuing eight years he remained in the aviation field, working with Sperry Gyroscope Company, which produced aircraft instruments including the Norden bombsight.

Upon returning to uniform six weeks after Pearl Harbor, Castle was shortly bound for England. He had been selected by Major General Eaker for the tiny staff that preceded the Eighth Air Force. Over the next sixteen months Lieutenant Colonel Castle was "A-4" in charge of Eighth Bomber Command's base and service depot planning. As such, he literally built the Mighty Eighth from the ground up. He pinned on his colonel's eagles on New Year's Day 1943.

The day after taking over the 94th, Castle flew his first mission, impressing his pilot by jotting notes as German fighters bored in. Next he scheduled practice missions to improve the B-17s' tactical formations. He knew that Luftwaffe pilots would pass up a tight, alert bomber box in preference of more vulnerable groups. As efficiency increased and losses declined, some crews began to wonder if the methodical bean counter wasn't on to something.

Barely three weeks later, 28 July, the Fourth Combat Bombardment Wing made the deepest penetration of Germany to date: the Focke-Wulf plant at Oschersleben. Fierce opposition was anticipated, but Castle led his Forts through heavy weather and fighters. Some groups became disorganized and aborted but Castle risked all, knowing that success would boost morale.

He was right. Through a break in the undercast the 94th and another group bombed visually with good results. When every Fortress returned to Earls Colne, the 94th realized that its new CO knew his business. Subsequently he led the group to two Distinguished Unit Citations: Regensburg (August 1943) and Brunswick (January 1944).

Having built a winning team, in April 1944 Castle took over the Fourth Wing and was promoted to brigadier general in November. He was then thirty-six—young for a general but old for a fighting airman—yet he continued flying. The following month, poor weather screened Germany's Ardennes offensive but meteorologists predicted clearing on Christmas Eve.

On 23 April, Castle inspected some of the Fourth Wing's bases and returned to learn of a major mission scheduled for the next day. It was a maximum effort—the greatest force yet launched. The Eighth would dispatch more than 2,000 bombers and 1,000 fighters, with the Ninth and RAF also contributing. Castle decided to fly with the 487th Bomb Group; it would be his thirtieth combat mission.

The next morning, 22,000 feet over Belgium, the Luftwaffe unexpectedly intercepted in Allied airspace. Four Lavenham B-17s went down; others dropped out. Castle's Fortress, already suffering engine trouble, fell behind and probably was hit by FW-190s of IV *Gruppe*, JG-3. The *Sturmjaegern* shot out both right-hand engines and wounded two crewmen. Losing altitude, apparently giving no intercom commands, Castle remained seated while the pilot, Lieutenant Robert W. Harriman, grabbed a parachute. During the interim, six men jumped. Subsequent accounts were contradictory or confused, but the Medal of Honor citation credited Castle with keeping the crippled Boeing under control while most of the crew escaped.

At 12,000 feet the FWs attacked again and shot off the bomber's right wing. Castle, Harriman, Lieutenant Claude L. Rowe Jr., and Sergeant Lawrence H. Swain died in the crash near Rotheux-Rimière, Belgium.

Castle was one of the most heavily decorated officers in the history of the Army Air Force. In addition to the posthumous Medal of Honor he received twelve other U.S. decorations plus others from France, Belgium, Poland, and the Soviet Union. His medal was presented to his mother at Mountain Lakes, New Jersey, on 28 February 1946. Additionally, Castle AFB at Merced, California, was named in his honor.

Crew: 1Lt. Robert W. Harriman (P); Capt. Edmund S. Auer (N); Lts. Henry P. McCarty (N), Paul L. Biri (B), Claude L. Rowe Jr. (TG), and Bruno S. Procopio (MO); TSgts. Quentin W. Jeffers (FE) and Lawrence H. Swain (RO); SSgt. Lowell B. Hudson (WG).

MAJOR THOMAS BUCHANAN MCGUIRE

1 August 1920–7 January 1945

Born: Ridgewood, New Jersey

Died: Negros Island, Philippines

Action: Air combat; Philippines; 25-26 December 1944 (age 24)

Unit: 475th Fighter Group, 5th Air Force

Aircraft: Lockheed P-38L 44-24155 (131) *Pudgy V*, and 44-24845

Other decorations: Distinguished Service Cross, Silver Star (3), Distinguished Flying Cross (5), Air Medal (15), Purple Heart

Tommy McGuire was cocky and friendly, talented and egotistical, aggressive and ambitious. He was also a superb fighter pilot. The Fifth Air Force P-38 community was a tight-knit bunch comprised of the 8th, 49th, and 475th Groups. Everybody knew of everyone else, and McGuire was acknowledged as Mr. Lightning. Probably his closest rival as a P-38 virtuoso was Major Cyril Homer of the 8th, "but Cy practiced a lot," said a fellow ace. "Tommy just flew the airplane like it was part of him." McGuire sloughed off the praise but he thrived on the attention.

Reared in a well-off family in New Jersey and Florida, McGuire was slightly

Thomas B. McGuire

built and sustained physical abuse as a football player in an effort to prove himself. Other things came easily to him, including flying.

After three years at Georgia Tech, McGuire applied for the aviation cadets program in 1941. He received his wings in February 1942 and spent most of that year flying P-39s in the Aleutians. Shipped to the Pacific in March 1943, he flew with the 49th Fighter Group until July before transferring to the 475th.

With the Satan's Angels, McGuire became an ace in his first two combats during August 1943. He soon was among the top four shooters in the Fifth Air Force, within reach of Bong, Kearby, and Lynch. His success was not without cost, as he was shot down and seriously wounded on 17 October. However, he recovered and ran his score to sixteen by year's end.

Despite his abrasiveness, McGuire had leadership ability, and he formed a close bond with Charles Lindbergh, who flew with the 475th. McGuire commanded the 431st Squadron from 2 May to 23 December 1944, claiming fifteen of the squadron's sixty-four kills in that period, a tally matched by only one other AAF squadron in the Pacific Theater. Subsequently he gained the plum role of group operations officer. It was exactly the kind of position he craved—he could choose the most lucrative missions.

On Christmas Day 1944 the 475th Group escorted B-24s to Manila. An estimated twenty Mitsubishi Zekes and Jacks hit McGuire's fifteen Lightnings from upsun. Dropping his maneuvering flaps, McGuire hauled *Pudgy V* into a hard turn and burned a Zeke with one of his patented long-range deflection shots. But the Japanese were scoring. McGuire's wingman, Lieutenant Floyd Fulkerson, claimed two Jacks. Then he limped from the combat area on one engine, going down; another pilot called that he was bailing out. Then seven more Zekes arrived.

The scene was chaotic: enemy AA fire bracketed the B-24s beginning their run on Mabalacat Airdrome while Japanese fighters attacked the bombers. Other enemy planes dropped phosphorous bombs amid the Liberators. McGuire intervened, shooting two Zekes off the bombers. A third Lightning pilot radioed that he was going down.

Incredibly, thirty Japanese Army fighters now piled in. The Oscars brought enemy numbers to fifty-seven all told, and McGuire wrenched into another turn to line up his fourth target. When he pressed the buttons his guns chugged out a few rounds, then quit. He had fired with heavy G on the aircraft, preventing feeding. He hit the charging handles repeatedly, to no avail. He was defenseless.

For the next several minutes McGuire made "dry" passes at Japanese fighters. In each instance he forced the bandits to abort their runs on the Liberators, which escaped without loss. It had been an epic fight: in fifty minutes—several eternities in aerial combat—the 431st Squadron claimed sixteen of the enemy. The other fighter squadrons on the mission added twenty-six more. Better yet, it was learned that Lieutenant Fulkerson was safe with filipinos.

The next day, near Clark Field, McGuire did even better. He claimed four of his squadron's seven kills, mostly witnessed by the grateful bomber crews. Upon return to Dulag the exultant ace buzzed the strip and executed four victory rolls. With thirty-eight victories he was well within range of Bong.

The statistics favored McGuire, who averaged 2.00 kills per scoring encounter to Richard Bong's 1.42. All skill and fight, McGuire was determined to displace his arch rival as America's foremost fighter ace.

On 7 January 1945 McGuire led a four-plane sweep over Negros, where an Oscar appeared. Flush with fuel and ambition, McGuire decided to retain his drop tanks and prolong his time on station. He dived at the Ki-43, which evaded while, probably unknown to him, a Ki-84 attacked Major Jack Rittmayer. As McGuire engaged the Frank, number thirty-nine strobed in his brain—only one short of Bong's record. The Frank maneuvered low on the trees; McGuire rolled into a vertical bank and hauled on the yoke. He felt the onset of buffet as the airframe protested the G on the heavy fuel load. The deflection narrowed; McGuire could almost pull lead.

The big Lockheed shuddered, stalled, and fell out of the turn. Too low to recover, it exploded in the trees. The wingmen returned to base telling an eerie tale of a Japanese superman who had killed Tommy McGuire and Jack Rittmayer, shot up a third Lightning, and evaded. Only years later it was learned that there had been two bandits.

On 8 May 1946 the Medal of Honor was presented in Paterson, N.J., where General George Kenney draped the pale-blue ribbon on the neck of McGuire's widow, Marilynn. Sitting alone in the rear of the auditorium was Charles A. Lindbergh.

Fort Dix Airfield was renamed McGuire Air Force Base in 1949 and his crash was found late that year. McGuire's remains were interred at Arlington Cemetery in May 1950.

CAPTAIN WILLIAM ARTHUR SHOMO

30 May 1918–25 June 1990

Born: Jeanette, Pennsylvania

Died: Pittsburgh, Pennsylvania

Action: Air combat; Philippines; 11 January 45 (age 26)

Unit: 82nd Tactical Reconnaissance Squadron, 5th Air Force

Aircraft: North American F-6D 44-14841 (66) *Snooks 5th*

Other decorations: Legion of Merit, Distinguished Flying Cross, Air Medal (5)

Bill Shomo proved that patience counts: he spent a year and a half in the Pacific combat zone and fired at airborne targets on two days. The second occasion brought him the Medal of Honor.

Before the war Shomo graduated from a mortuary college and attended embalming school. However, world events forced a career change. The budding mortician entered the aviation cadet program in August 1941 and was commissioned a second lieutenant ninety days after Pearl Harbor. Assigned to the 71st Observation Group in November 1943, by year's end he had logged 1,015 hours total time.

The group's 82nd Squadron flew Bell P-39Qs and P-40Ns for most of Shomo's tour, operating under Fifth Air Force control on New Guinea. (The other two squadrons flew B-25s and L-5s.) Subsequent bases were Nadzab

William A. Shomo *(right)* with Maj. Gen. Ennis C. Whitehead

and Biak. Redesignated a tactical reconnaissance group in May 1944, the 71st transferred to the Philippines in November. By then Captain Shomo and his fellow pilots yearned for updated equipment. It was not long in coming.

The new year brought sensational change. Shomo had been designated squadron commander on Christmas Eve and warmly greeted the arrival of North American F-6Ds, photo-reconnaissance variants of the P-51D Mustang. However, the 82nd barely had time to acclimate. The F-6s arrived about New Year's Day, and transition was so hurried that Shomo's first Mustang mission, 9 January, was only his sixth flight "in type." It was not unusual for World War II, when the operative philosophy was, "They all have a stick and throttle. Go fly 'em."

Supporting the Mindoro landing off Luzon's southwest coast, Shomo was scouting well north of Manila on the tenth. He spotted an Aichi "Val" dive bomber over the Cagayan River and quickly flamed it. His fourteen-month dry spell had ended.

The next day, 11 January, the twenty-six-year-old squadron commander was back in the same area, south of Tuguegarao Airdrome. Shomo and Lieutenant Paul Lipscomb were flying just off the trees when they spotted several aircraft through intermittent clouds about 2,500 feet above them, on a reciprocal course. Though uncertain of the enemy numbers, Shomo shoved up the power and led his wingman in an Immelmann, rolling out below and behind the bogeys. Closing the distance, the Americans recognized a dozen Kawasaki Ki-61 "Tony" fighters escorting a twin-engine aircraft identified as a Mitsubishi "Betty."

Shomo targeted the leading fighter in the third element, pressed his trigger, and watched the Kawasaki explode. Shifting to the other side of the formation, he flamed another Tony. As the confused Japanese tried to regroup, the Mustangs kept the pressure on—Lipscomb was scoring, too. Shomo's third victim fell in pieces.

The flying undertaker then went after the bomber. He dived beneath it, nosed up and fired a raking burst into the belly. The plane careened into a forced landing, broke up, and burned.

As Shomo pulled off the bomber, regaining altitude, he met another Tony head-on. There was no way to practice that shot, so the Pennsylvanian put his gunsight pipper just above the canopy and fired a telling burst. Then he dived back on the first element and dropped the leader.

With ammunition remaining, Shomo chased down a fleeing Tony and with one more burst sent it flaming from 300 feet altitude. Glancing back, he saw more bandits closing so he disengaged, called Lipscomb for a rendezvous, and reformed. Lipscomb had claimed three Tonys, leaving three survivors.

In the debrief Shomo credited his success to point-blank shooting—mostly fifty yards and closer—at zero deflection. The unlucky Japanese were simply in the wrong place at the wrong time, as only one other Fifth Air Force pilot claimed a kill that day. Japanese records for the period do not identify which of the four Philippines Ki-61 *sentai* the Tonys represented. However, it is known that only one Mitsubishi G4M "Betty" was lost that day south of Formosa. More likely the bomber was an army type.

Occurring just four days after Major Thomas McGuire's death, Shomo's mission created a sensation in Fifth Air Force. He was promoted to major on 14 January and received the Medal of Honor from Major General Ennis Whitehead on 3 April.

Though another AAF pilot and a naval aviator both logged seven-kill sorties, neither received the Medal of Honor. However, the fact that Shomo was a "tac recce" pilot, not expected to engage enemy aircraft, may have figured in the equation.

In any case, Shomo left his squadron in May, completing eighteen months in the Pacific. He retired as a lieutenant colonel in September 1968 and is buried in Greenburg, Pennsylvania.

STAFF SERGEANT HENRY EUGENE ERWIN

8 MAY 1921–

BORN: Adamsville, Alabama

ACTION: Bombing mission; Japan; 12 April 1945 (age 23)

UNIT: 52nd Bomb Squadron, 29th Bomb Group, 20th Air Force

AIRCRAFT: Boeing B-29 42-65302 (37) *The City of Los Angeles*

OTHER DECORATIONS: Air Medal (2), Purple Heart

The B-29 was the most expensive weapon system of the Second World War. It was bigger, faster, longer-ranged, and carried more bombs than any contemporary. It also had the price tag to match. In 1944 the average Superfortress cost $605,000, or nearly three times a B-17 or B-24. Some 4,000 were built from 1942 through 1945, and they burned the heart out of the Japanese Empire.

By the spring of 1945 an awesome fleet of B-29s was based in the Marianas Islands, 1,500 miles south of Tokyo. Major General Curtis LeMay's 20th Air Force had erased hundreds of square miles of Japanese cities, including much of their industrial potential. But the bombing campaign continued.

On April 12, XXI Bomber Command targeted two chemical plants at Koriyama, about 120 miles north of Tokyo. As usual, it would be a low-level mission to optimize the equation of bomb tonnage and accuracy. One of the 130 Superforts assigned to the mission was commanded by Captain George Simeral, a lead pilot with the 52nd Bombardment Squadron of the 29th Group. It was the crew's eleventh mission, flying a plane named *The City of Los Angeles*. The crew was well experienced, having been formed at Dalhart, Texas, in June 1944 and deployed overseas in January 1945.

Simeral's radioman was an unassuming Alabaman, Staff Sergeant Henry E.

Henry E. Erwin

Erwin, called "Red" by his squadronmates. Despite his quiet country boy demeanor, Erwin was regarded among the finest aircrew in the squadron, partly because he was willing to assume extra tasks. One of those chores was dropping phosphorous flares to notify the formation that the lead ship had reached the assembly point before the bomb run.

Approaching the Japanese coast, Erwin prepared to drop a flare through the chute in his compartment. At the low altitude he was dressed for comfort, without a helmet or cap, with his shirt sleeves rolled up. He pulled the pin on the flare and placed the pyrotechnic in the chute.

The world erupted in flames.

A defective fuse prematurely ignited the flare, launching it backward into Erwin's face and setting a hellish blaze in the aircraft. Upon contacting oxygen, the phosphorous flared to its temperature of 1,300 degrees Fahrenheit. Searing heat engulfed Erwin's head, blinding him and destroying his nose and one ear. The aircraft's interior began filling with thick, choking smoke; in moments the pilots were unable to read their instruments.

Unable to see, somehow ignoring the horrible pain, Erwin groped in hellish darkness for the flare. Despite his horrible injuries, he was thinking clearly. Unless jettisoned, the flare would burn through the deck into the bomb bay where the *City*'s ordnance would detonate.

Erwin found the flare and, completely without protective clothing, scooped it up. He felt his way forward, hoping to toss the device out the copilot's window. Making his way around the forward turret with his arms and face afire, he was blocked by the navigator's table, which hinged down off the bulkhead. The navigator had been taking a landfall sighting and could offer no help. Nevertheless, Erwin tucked the blazing flare under his right arm, used both charred hands to unlatch the table, and staggered onto the flight deck. Though unable to see, he made a desperate toss and flung the device overboard. By then his right arm had burned down to the bone; he fainted between the pilots.

During the confused, choking moments of terror the *City* had dropped almost to the wavetops. Captain Simeral, finally able to see, recovered from a steep dive about 300 feet over the water and immediately turned south for Iwo Jima. The porkchop-shaped island, purchased with the lives of 5,000 marines barely a month before, offered Red Erwin a slim chance.

Other airmen extinguished the fire in Erwin's clothes and applied what first aid they could. But whenever Erwin's burns were exposed the phosphorous reignited, smoldering with agonizing intensity. Yet despite his agony, Erwin remained alert; his only words were about the condition of his fellow crewmen.

Doctors on Iwo Jima saw almost no chance of Erwin's survival. He was treated to the extent possible, then flown to Guam's superior facilities. Meanwhile, in a matter of hours Major General LeMay submitted a Medal of Honor recommendation, hoping that the critically burned noncom could receive the award before he died. With no medal on hand—it had never been presented to a 20th Air Force man—one was stolen from a display case in Hawaii, flown to Guam, and presented to Erwin in the fleet hospital on 18 April. General Henry H. Arnold wrote Erwin a personal letter accompanying the medal, saying, "I regard your act as one of the bravest in the records of this war."

The devoutly religious Alabaman not only clung to life but slowly improved. He was returned stateside where his condition stabilized enough to begin reconstructive surgery. Over an agonizing thirty months he regained his vision and the use of one arm. Promoted to master sergeant, he received a disability discharge in October 1947, the month the U.S. Air Force became an independent service.

Red Erwin not only recovered, but he pursued a career in the Veterans' Administration. He served as a benefit counselor at the VA hospital in Birmingham, Alabama, for thirty-seven years.

Crew: Capt. George A. Simeral (P); 2Lts. Leroy C. Stabler (CP) and Lee Conner (Radar); 1Lt. William T. Loesch (B); Capt. Pershing I. Youngkin (N); Sgts. Howard Stubstad (TTG), Herbert Schnipper (G), Vernon G. Widemayer (G), and Kenneth E. Young (TG).

FIRST LIEUTENANT RAYMOND LARRY KNIGHT

15 JUNE 1922–25 APRIL 1945

BORN: Timpson, Texas

DIED: Italy

ACTION: Ground attack, northern Italy; 24–25 April 1945 (age 22)

UNIT: 346th Fighter Squadron, 350th Fighter Group, 12th Air Force

AIRCRAFT: Republic P-47D 42-26785 (6D5) *Oh Johnnie* "Ivory Lead"

OTHER DECORATIONS: Distinguished Flying Cross, Air Medal (6), Purple Heart (3)

The last aviation Medal of Honor of World War II went to first Lieutenant Raymond Knight, a P-47 pilot of the 350th Fighter Group, Twelfth Air Force. Despite some notable leaders (Doolittle, Spaatz, and Vandenberg), as the tactical air force of the Mediterranean Theater, the Twelfth received little wartime coverage though it logged 430,681 sorties and dropped 217,000 tons of bombs while losing 2,667 aircraft.

During 1944–45 the Twelfth's seven fighter groups had almost no opportunity for aerial combat. Operating in Italy and southern France, they claimed 113 shootdowns, with no aces. The 350th Group had the best of the shooting with fifty-three credited victories in that period, but only nineteen group pilots scored aerial victories, two of whom notched three each.

Low on the priority list for new equipment, the 350th Group had slowly converted from P-39s, transitioning by squadrons between June and September 1944. The 346th was well adapted to the Thunderbolt by the time Knight joined the unit, and he soon proved that he knew his way around a P-47.

On 5 April the allied armies began an offensive intended to drive German forces northward, across the Po River. The Twelfth Air Force targeted bridges and communications routes in an effort to trap the *Wehrmacht* troops remaining in northern Italy.

By late April, Knight was a first lieutenant with eighty missions and two Purple Hearts. Known as an aggressive flight leader, on the morning of 24 April he volunteered to take Ivory Flight against the strongly defended enemy airdrome at Ghedi, near Lake di Garda. When one pilot aborted, Knight continued with Lieutenants William E. Hosey and Alva D. Henehan.

Overhead Ghedi Airfield, Knight kept his wingmen "topside" while he made an exploratory pass. It was a dangerous procedure, as his solo run alerted the German gunners of his presence without other planes to divide the fire. Nevertheless, he spotted eight enemy aircraft beneath camouflage nets. He climbed back to altitude, briefed Hosey and Henehan on targets and defenses, then nosed down to attack. In successive passes through German flak he claimed five planes destroyed while his wingmen notched two more. Low on ammunition, Knight led his bobtailed flight back to base. There he immediately offered to take three more pilots to Bergamo-Orio al Serio Airfield, twenty-five miles northeast of Milan, where he felt other Luftwaffe planes would be found. His instincts were good; he spotted several camouflaged aircraft and, ignoring the AA fire, he attacked.

Raymond L. Knight

One pass at a Luftwaffe airdrome in 1945 was a roll of the dice; the guns were scientifically sited for maximum coverage. Yet Knight ignored the odds and rolled the dice ten times. Though his Jug was hit by light flak, he reported burning six twin-engine aircraft and two single-engine fighters. His wingman and second element claimed five more destroyed. The Jug pilots left the remnants of two Luftwaffe reconnaissance squadrons, 4. and 6.(F)/122. With few spare parts and little fuel, the Germans had stood on hangar roofs watching the Thunderbolts shoot up their dozen Ju-88 and 188s, plus a lone Italian Bf-109. Knight returned to Pisa, thinking ahead to the next day's mission.

Raymond Knight was Texas born and bred and served most of his military career in his home state. He graduated from Houston's John Reagan High School in 1940 and enlisted in the Air Corps in October 1942. Following flight training at Stamford, Sherman, and Foster Fields, he was commissioned in May 1944. Subsequently he served at Matagorda and Abilene, and according to some AAF sources he was not slated for overseas service. However, he volunteered for combat and arrived in Italy in November 1944, joining the 350th Fighter Group's 346th Squadron on 7 December. He named his Thunderbolt *Oh Johnnie* in honor of his high school sweetheart and wife, Johnnie Lee Kincheloe.

Knight led Ivory flight away from Pisa at 0925 on 25 April with first Lieutenant Roger E. Clement as his wingman; Second Lieutenants William T. Rogers and Clinton J. Webber were in the second section. Heading outbound the flight received word from a ground controller regarding enemy transportation targets in the Milan area, with heavy flak. Knight rogered the call but maintained course for Bergamo Airfield.

Arriving near the target, the Americans noted aircraft still in revetments and Knight called for a company-front attack. However, the attack axis was changed at the last moment resulting in two sections attacking in trail, north to south. "The flak was terrific," Lieutenant Rogers reported, but Knight attacked a Bf-109 and the other pilots claimed ten more. Almost certainly their targets were the same planes they had strafed the day before, as the AAF's last air-air claims over Italy had occurred on the nineteenth. The Luftwaffe was doing very little flying; many of the Bergamo contingent walked to Austria.

Pulling off target, Knight called for a damage check. *Oh Johnnie* was the only Jug hit, and Weber eased alongside for a visual check. "There was a huge hole in the left wing at the root and his elevators also were shot up badly. The wing and stabilizers were vibrating badly, and 150 m.p.h. was the maximum airspeed he could get." Unable to climb, Knight needed both hands on the stick to maintain level flight but he turned homeward with Rogers alongside to warn of impending structural failure.

Despite the obvious danger, Knight remained on his return course. He might have made it except for violent currents over the Apennines. The rugged Republic airframe finally was overstressed, and *Oh Johnnie* came apart, victim of battle damage and mountain turbulence.

Axis forces in Italy surrendered seven days later, on 2 May. Nazi Germany capitulated on the eighth.

The Mediterranean air forces received relatively little press during the war. Apart from the Ploeşti mission of August 1943, only two MTO airmen received the Medal of Honor before Knight, and some veterans see his medal as compensation. The citation stated that he declined to bail out because of a shortage of aircraft, but the facts speak otherwise. Despite nine losses during April, the 346th Squadron maintained a full allotment of twenty-five to thirty P-47Ds, as replacements were readily available. More likely Raymond Knight stayed with *Oh Johnnie* because he was an extremely courageous pilot. In any case, the final month of combat sorely tested the 350th Group, which lost nearly one-fourth of its wartime attrition in those thirty days.

In September, the month the war ended, Knight's Medal of Honor was presented to his widow, Johnnie Lee, and her two-and-a-half-year-old son at Reagan High School. Knight's body was recovered and buried in Woodlawn Garden of Memories in 1949 but was reinterred at Houston National Cemetery in 1992, sharing his native soil with other Medal of Honor recipients.

Raymond Knight's medals were presented for display at Davis-Monthan Air Force Base near Tucson, Arizona, in 1995, when his name was bestowed upon the 12th Air Force administration and operations building.

Army Air Force Aviation Related (2)

Colonel Demas T. Craw and Major Pierpont M. Hamilton; French Morocco; 8 November 1942. During the Anglo-American invasion of North Africa, the two Army Air Force officers volunteered to contact Vichy French officials in hope of inducing a surrender that would prevent casualties on both sides. They went ashore with a driver in a vehicle bearing U.S. and French flags but Craw was killed by suspicious Vichy troops and Hamilton was briefly captured. Craw and Hamilton received Medals of Honor; it is unknown if their driver, Private First Class Orris Carey, was decorated.

MARINE CORPS (11)

CAPTAIN HENRY TALMAGE ELROD

27 SEPTEMBER 1905–23 DECEMBER 1941

BORN: Rebecca, Georgia

DIED: Wake Island

ACTION: Air and ground combat; Wake Island; 8–23 December 1941 (age 36)

UNIT: Marine Fighting Squadron 211

AIRCRAFT: Grumman F4F-3 BuNo 4019 (211-MF-11)

OTHER DECORATIONS: Purple Heart

Pearl Harbor had been attacked that morning, back across the International Date Line, where it was still Sunday, 7 December. On Wake Island, nearly 2,400 miles farther west, it was the eighth, but whatever the calendar said, Wake was due for some unwelcome attention. The marines of the First Defense Battalion could only stand by and prepare to repel boarders.

Fortunately, the garrison was reinforced by a dozen Grumman Wildcats of Major Paul Putnam's VMF-211 which had flown in from the carrier USS *Enterprise* (CV-6) on 4 December. The F4F-3s were a welcome addition, as patrols were flown in anticipation of Japanese bombers from the Marshall Islands, nearly 600 nautical miles to the south.

Captain Henry Elrod's four-plane division was up during the noon hour but as luck would have it, the Grummans zigged when the enemy zagged.

The Chitose Air Group's Mitsubishi G3Ms (later called Nells) attacked out of a rain squall that shielded them from the Wildcats. Bombing unopposed, thirty-four G3Ms destroyed seven of eight fighters on the ground and damaged the other. Only the four airborne F4Fs remained operational, and one of those was damaged when the pilot struck his propeller on some debris. However, innovative maintenance men salvaged a prop from one of the wrecks.

Henry Elrod was a long, long way from Rebecca, Georgia.

Elrod had attended the University of Georgia and Yale, then enlisted in the Marine Corps in 1927. He was commissioned in 1931 and became an aviator in February 1935. At thirty-six he was somewhat old for a captain, but that was typical of the service. Wartime had a way of catching up with the career lags of peacetime. Very soon, men a decade younger than Elrod would

Henry T. Elrod

wear "railroad tracks," and in the Army Air Force officers of Elrod's vintage could be colonels. However, on Wake Island rank meant little—courage and competence meant everything. Hank Elrod had both.

The Japanese bombed almost daily, and on 10 December Elrod got his chance. In repeated runs he claimed two of twenty-six attacking bombers though apparently only one Mitsubishi was lost. Nevertheless, the victory boosted Wake's morale.

However, the next day lookouts spotted Japanese ships. In response, Major Putnam led Elrod with Captains Herb Freuler and Frank Tharin against the Japanese ships. The aviators found three light cruisers, six destroyers, two transports, and two patrol craft. Armed only with machine guns, 100-pound bombs, and a generous helping of optimism, the Wildcats attacked. Elrod and Tharin strafed and bombed what they tentatively identified as two light cruisers; Elrod scored a near-miraculous hit with his two 100-pounders. The explosion detonated depth charges stowed on the deck of the 1,770-ton destroyer *Kisaragi,* which exploded and immediately sank with all 167 crewmen.

Elated, Hank Elrod turned for home. However, return fire had holed his oil line, and he barely managed a gear-up landing on the beach. "Mike Foxtrot Eleven" was a writeoff, but the Japanese had sustained a drubbing. The destroyer *Hayate* had been sunk by the Marine shore batteries; the cruiser *Yubari* was damaged, as were two destroyers and a transport. The Imperial Navy pulled off to lick its wounds, regroup, and rethink the operation.

With magnificent impudence, Wake radioed, "Send us more Japs." Though inserted as "padding" in the message, it spoke volumes of the marines' spirit.

Realistically, however, there was little hope of holding Wake. The Pacific fleet was unable to mount a suitable relief effort in time to offset the Japanese advantage, and as bombing continued, Putnam's remaining Wildcats were whittled down until only two remained. On 22 December they intercepted Japanese carrier planes and one F4F was shot down, the other damaged. The renewed assault came before dawn on the twenty-third. The last thing America heard was, "Enemy on island."

Japan did not have an independent marine corps, but it did possess well-trained naval landing troops. The Battle for Wake Island pitted U.S. Marines against the emperor's Special Naval Infantry.

Out of aircraft, VMF-211 reverted to the traditional Marine Corps role of riflemen, and Putnam placed Elrod in command of the squadron's flank near one of the three-inch guns sited to engage landing craft. With fourteen years in the corps, Elrod was a capable infantryman. During prolonged contact with the Japanese, he seized a light machine gun and passed his own weapon to another man. In confused fighting shortly before dawn, Elrod repeatedly rallied his men until killed by a gunshot from one of the Special Naval Infantrymen lying among the Japanese dead.

When Wake's survivors returned home in 1945 the full story was learned and Elrod retroactively became the first Marine aviator awarded the Medal of Honor in World War II. The medal was presented to his widow on 8 November 1946, further confirming a Japanese analyst's assessment that "Wake Island was one of the most humiliating defeats our navy ever suffered."

CAPTAIN RICHARD EUGENE FLEMING

2 November 1917–5 June 1942

Born: St. Paul, Minnesota

Died: Off Midway

Action: Ship attacks; Battle of Midway; 4–5 June 1942 (age 24)

Unit: Marine Scout Bombing Squadron 241, Marine Air Group 22

Aircraft: Douglas SBD-2 BuNo 2011 (2) 4 June; Vought SB2U-3 BuNo 2088 (2) 5 June

Other decorations: Purple Heart

The mid-Pacific sky was a blue palette superimposed with nature's white clouds and man-made dirty brown puffs. Nearly 10,000 feet above the ocean, sixteen Marine Corps dive bombers approached *Kido Butai,* the Japanese carrier striking force northwest of Midway Atoll. The leathernecks belonged to

Richard E. Fleming

Scout Bombing Squadron 241, which had barely tucked its wheels in the well before 107 Imperial Navy planes had begun wrecking the American outpost 1,100 miles northwest of Honolulu.

Midway's garrison air force was a cobbled-together assortment of Navy, Marine, and Army Air Force squadrons. Advance intelligence had given them the precious knowledge of Japanese intentions—seizure of Midway—but none of the units had trained together. VMSB-241 had been on Midway for months but still was not fully up to speed: the skipper, Major Lofton "Joe" Henderson, led sixteen Douglas SBD-2s, while Major Benjamin Norris took eleven antiquated Vought SB2U-3s. Nevertheless, they represented the major share of Midway's airpower. Greater strength reposed on the flight decks of three Pacific fleet carriers farther east.

Flying Henderson's wing was a twenty-four-year-old captain, Richard E. Fleming. His radioman-gunner was Corporal Eugene T. Card, and they faced a rough introduction to combat.

Henderson selected the nearest Japanese carrier, the HIJMS *Hiryu,* and led his hodge-podge squadron into a slanting descent. Some of the pilots were so green that they had insufficient dive bombing experience, requiring an easier but more vulnerable glide attack. The HIJMS *Hiryu*'s fighter unit quickly took advantage of the situation. Mitsubishi A6M2 Zeros shot the lead Dauntless out of formation, putting Dick Fleming in charge. He possessed, in his own words, "a keen desire to finish one Jap carrier" and continued his attack on the rakish 20,000-ton flattop.

The Zeros made successive gunnery runs, pressing as close as they dared. Their 20mm cannon and 7.7mm machine guns scored repeatedly: six SBDs were shot down. Marine back-seaters returned fire with their single .30 calibers.

Nevertheless, Fleming grimly hung on, pressing through jarring AA fire, trying to ignore the gray fighters with their astonishing performance. He held his drop as long as possible, toggled his 500-pound bomb over the *Hiryu,* and recovered at 400 feet. He shoved the throttle and prop controls full ahead, dived to the deck, and made for home.

Zeros chased the lonely Dauntless almost twenty miles but fleming's evasive maneuvers and Card's return fire kept the tormenters at bay. When they broke off, Card was wounded and fleming's instrument panel was shot to pieces. So was his compass; he told Card, "We may have to sniff our way home."

Actually, Midway was not hard to find: burning fuel tanks sent a smoky signal into the clear air. When Fleming plunked down on the runway, his SBD had a flat left tire but he kept the Dauntless tracking straight. He cleared the runway, shut down, and exclaimed to onlookers, "Boys, there is one ride I'm glad is over." Then he shook hands with Card. They counted 179 holes in the SBD's tough hide.

Twenty-seven Marine dive bombers had taken off that morning. Sixteen returned. And the battle was far from over.

Dick Fleming had received his gold wings and gold bars in November 1940. In January 1941 he joined Scouting Two in San Diego, proceeding to Hawaii in May. Two months later the squadron was redesignated VMSB-231. On 17 December, Fleming flew 1,137 nautical miles from Oahu to Midway, probably the longest overwater flight by a single-engine aircraft at that time. The Vought Vindicators had no plane guard ships along the route, but all made it.

In March 1942 Fleming joined VMSB-241 as navigation officer. He was appointed a first lieutenant in April and, as of 16 May, he made captain. Shortly thereafter the squadron began frantic preparation for the Battle of Midway. Fleming's letters home hinted at his mindset. Perhaps with a premonition he wrote, "I've been prepared for this rendezvous for some time. . . . this is something that comes once for all of us."

That night nobody got much sleep on Midway. Word arrived that Navy carrier planes had sunk three, maybe four, Japanese carriers, but there were still powerful enemy ships beyond the horizon. The remnants of 241 reshuffled the flight schedule and prepared to launch six SBDs at 0700 with six SB2Us. With his Dauntless out of action, Fleming reverted to his previous Vindicator and his regular gunner, Private First Class George A. Thoms.

The marines' target on the morning of the fifth was a Japanese cruiser reported badly damaged. She was the HIJMS *Mikuma,* which had collided with her sister the *Mogami* during the night. She was not hard to track—aircrews picked up her oil slick from ruptured fuel tanks almost forty miles out. Since Major Norris had been lost the night before, 241's third CO, Captain Zack Tyler, led the attack. Barely an hour after takeoff the marines were overhead the handsome 8,000-ton cruisers and dived into fierce AA fire. Fleming, flying his second combat mission in a second type of aircraft in two days, learned fast. He took his section in a glide-bomb run initiated from 4,000 feet with the sun behind him.

Japanese gunnery remained accurate; Fleming's SB2U began streaming smoke almost immediately. Smoke quickly turned to flames but Fleming continued his attack and released his bomb at about 500 feet—a near miss close astern. The gunner in another SB2U thought he saw two parachutes; others felt that Fleming's plane dived into an aft turret. Still others said that he went into the water close aboard. None of the bombs struck the target but the HIJMS *Mikuma* was doomed; Navy planes sank her the next day.

Eleven Marine aviators received the Medal of Honor in World War II; Fleming was the only bomber pilot. The USS *Fleming* (DE-32), an 1,140-ton Evarts-class destroyer escort, was launched in June 1943. Two months later an auxiliary field to NAS Minneapolis also was named in Fleming's honor.

Crew: Corp. Eugene T. Card (G) 4 June; PFC George A. Thoms (G) 5 June.

MAJOR JOHN LUCIAN SMITH

26 December 1914–10 June 1972

Born: Lexington, Oklahoma

Died: Encino, California

Action: Air combat; Guadalcanal; August–October 1942 (age 27)

Unit: Marine Fighting Squadron 223

Aircraft: Various Grumman F4F-4s including 02127 (16)

Other decorations: Navy Cross, Legion of Merit, Distinguished Flying Cross, Bronze Star Medal, Air Medal (3)

During a wartime interview, John L. Smith reportedly described himself as "a rifleman commanding a fighter squadron." If so, it was a departure from his later unabashed advocacy of aviation in America's *corps d'élite.*

John L. Smith, CO of VMF-223 on Guadalcanal

Following graduation from the University of Oklahoma in 1936, Smith was commissioned an Army second lieutenant via the university's ROTC program. However, he was drawn to the Marine Corps and resigned from the Army to enter Navy flight training. Upon winning his wings of gold in 1939, he embarked on one of the most significant Marine aviation careers of the Second World War.

Smith was promoted to captain in March 1941 and in May 1942 he received his first command: Marine Fighting Squadron 223. He had barely three months to prepare VMF-223 for a crucial mission: the first fighter squadron on Guadalcanal in the Solomon Islands.

Launched from the escort carrier USS *Long Island* (CVE-1) on 20 August 1942, Smith's nineteen F4F-4s and Lieutenant Colonel Richard Mangrum's dozen SBD-3s were "plankowners" in the "Cactus Air Force." Over the next fifty-three days, 223 was usually short of everything but disease, fatigue, Japanese—and leadership. Smith's forceful personality and innate ability were evident from the start, as he claimed the squadron's first victory when he engaged an A6M2 Zero the next day.

With the benefit of a handful of experienced pilots, including Captain Marion E. Carl, the squadron kept "Cactus" (Guadalcanal's radio call sign) operating until reinforcements arrived. Smith was promoted to major on 1 September, by which time his personal score stood at nine. His best day was 30 August, when he claimed four kills. Ironically, in view of his entire tour at Guadalcanal, his medal citation only referred to the three weeks from 21 August to 15 September. He was credited with eight kills during September and took the lead in his approximately friendly rivalry with Carl, who was shot down on the ninth and needed five days to reach safety. According to Marine Corps legend, when Carl learned that his CO had passed him in Zero hunting, the lanky Oregonian told Brigadier General Roy Geiger, "Damn it, General, ground Smitty for five days!"

On 2 October, in a dogfight near Henderson Field, Smith bagged a Zero (his eighteenth victory), then was shot down but bailed out and immediately returned to base. On the tenth he led VMF-223's last interception and splashed a floatplane during an escort mission up the "Slot," the stretch of open water leading northwest of Guadalcanal. Two days later VMF-223 was relieved by Major Duke Davis's VMF-121; Smith's squadron claimed 126.5 victories while on Guadalcanal.

The initiative for Smith's Medal of Honor appears to have arisen from Washington rather than Vice Admiral William F. Halsey, Commander South Pacific Forces (ComSoPac). On 22 September the secretary of the Navy requested details of citations for Smith, Carl, and Lieutenant Colonel Richard C. Mangrum, commanding VMSB-232. ComSoPac replied on 7 November, stating that Smith and Carl had received Navy Crosses and Mangrum a DFC—a puzzling development considering Mangrum's important contribution to the defense of "Cactus." Then on 19 November Admiral Chester Nimitz's CinCPac headquarters passed the buck to Halsey, stating, "no further recommendations received from ComSoPac as to conduct of subject men."

When Smith returned to the States in October, his Medal of Honor recommendation was rejuvenated, evidently from the office of Navy Secretary Frank Knox. Although sympathy existed for Carl's nomination, it was shortstopped by service politics, as the Army objected to the large number of medals going to the Marine Corps. Smith's award began a long string of Medals of Honor to leatherneck Wildcat pilots: Bob Galer, Joe Foss, Joe Bauer, Jeff DeBlanc, and Jim Swett, plus three leading Corsair aces: Ken Walsh, Greg Boyington, and Bob Hanson. No Army fighter pilot received the Medal of Honor until 1943.

As the first major American ace of the war, Smith's fame not only rivaled Foss's but preceded it. "John L." appeared on the cover of *Life*'s 7 December 1942 issue, and in February 1943 he received the medal from President Roosevelt. Almost unheard of for a marine, he also received Britain's Distinguished Service Order (second only to the Victoria Cross), and subsequently he was the only leatherneck ace awarded the Legion of Merit.

Smith returned to the Pacific and commanded a group before the war ended. He was promoted to colonel in 1951 and led MAG-33 during 1953–54. His last two and a half years on active duty were spent as assistant director of Marine Corps Aviation. An unrepentant advocate of "the air" in a service that resented artillerymen, Smith made few friends with "the ground." His outspoken demeanor assured that he would not achieve general officer rank, and he was retired in September 1960.

For the next decade Smith worked for aerospace firms in Europe and California, but the industry's economic ills spelled the end of his civilian career. Increasingly despondent over his seeming unsuitability for employment, John L. Smith took his own life at age fifty-seven.

MAJOR ROBERT EDWARD GALER

24 October 1913–

Born: Seattle, Washington

Action: Air combat; Guadalcanal; September–October 1942 (age 29)

Unit: Marine Fighting Squadron 224

Aircraft: Various Grumman F4F-4s including 02109 and 02118

Other decorations: Navy Cross, Legion of Merit, Distinguished Flying Cross (2), Air Medal (5)

Major Bob Galer was in deep trouble.

The skipper of VMF-224 had scrambled with three of his own pilots and nine others, belatedly warned of Japanese bombers approaching Guadal-

Robert E. Galer

canal. It was familiar routine to the "Cactus Air Force": Wildcats clawing for altitude in time to meet the raiders.

Major John L. Smith's VMF-223 division was first to engage thirty-six Zeros with nine Mitsubishi G4M (later Betty) bombers as decoys. The marines had been lured into an enemy fighter sweep and now, badly outnumbered, they fought for their lives.

Galer's four-plane division collided with ten or twelve Zeros at 23,000 feet. While six Zeros executed professional high-side attacks, the remainder perched overhead, ready to cut off any survivors.

With no other option, Galer wracked his Wildcat hard to starboard, meeting the nearest threat head-on. The sudden turn pitched his second section out of position, and as Galer triggered a hopeful burst, he and his wingman were on their own, riding a tiger they dared not dismount.

Seattle native Bob Galer had been a standout college basketball player and graduated with an engineering degree in 1935. Attracted to the Marine Corps, he received a commission the next year and was designated a naval aviator in April 1937. As a fighter pilot he flew Grumman F3F biplanes before conversion to F4Fs in 1941. While assigned to VMF-211 in Hawaii he became one of a handful of Marine landing signal officers. That happy coincidence prevented him from sailing to Wake Island with Major Paul Putnam just before Pearl Harbor was attacked. Promoted to captain, in May 1942 Galer established VMF-224 at MCAS Ewa.

Galer was an enigma to some, as he did not behave the way many people—including some marines—expected of a Marine squadron commander. Pleasant and soft-spoken almost to the point of shyness, he was fully capable of leatherneck initiative. He not only helped his troops "requisition" some rare F4F tailwheels before deploying to Guadalcanal but also later confessed, "Stole the officer of the day's jeep, too."

With barely enough time to stand up a new squadron, he took it to Guadalcanal on 30 August. Before the interception of 2 October he had been credited with nine kills.

Galer and Second Lieutenant Dean Hartley began scissoring with one another, taking snap shots at the Zeros making individual passes at each Grumman's tail. It worked for a few reverses, then Hartley's plane was struck by cannon shells. The youngster had to poke his nose down and head for the fighter strip. Deprived of a wingman, Galer was now purely defensive.

In the mind-blurring series of hard turns, Galer fired at several Zeros and felt that he hit two. However, the odds were telling. A particularly aggressive Japanese pilot rode up behind him, firing 7.7 and 20mm rounds into the Grumman's wings, cockpit, and engine. Miraculously, Galer was not hit even though one rudder pedal was shot away. He gratefully watched his assailants turn in search of other prey as he glided his powerless Wildcat to a water landing off Florida Island. The former Washington varsity athlete needed all his strength, swimming to shore in more than an hour.

Not only the Japanese felt they had killed Robert E. Galer (Zeros claimed eleven Wildcats in that dogfight). When he returned to Guadalcanal the next morning, Galer was just in time for the memorial service being held in his honor!

Galer continued leading 224 until the squadron was evacuated on 16 October, claiming fifty-five enemy aircraft, thirteen by the CO. Recommended for the Medal of Honor, Galer received the award from President Roosevelt on 24 March 1943. Promoted to lieutenant colonel that year, he returned to the Pacific in 1944 as operations officer of the Third Marine Air Wing.

Galer remained in the corps and again flew combat in Korea. As commander of Marine Air Group Twelve in August 1952 he survived being shot down and wounded to became the principal in one of the most daring helicopter rescues of the war. Unable to land in the rugged terrain, the Sikorski pilot tossed Galer a line and, as the group commander related, "away we went down the valley, everybody shooting at us." It was a narrow getaway, but it worked.

After Korea, Galer graduated from the Air War College at Maxwell AFB,

Alabama. Subsequently he reported to Headquarters Marine Corps in Washington, D.C., where he served as director of the Navy's guided missile division.

Upon retirement in 1957 Galer received a "tombstone" promotion to brigadier general, based on combat decorations. Settling in Dallas, he became vice president for engineering with Ling Temco Vought, working to develop the F8U Crusader, the Navy's first supersonic aircraft. Later he worked for the owners of the Dallas Cowboys football team.

In summarizing his combat career, Bob Galer wrote, "I've been shot up and shot down four times. God always had someone there to help. I never met an atheist when under fire!"

CAPTAIN JOSEPH JACOB FOSS

17 April 1915–

Born: Sioux Falls, South Dakota

Action: Air combat; Solomon Islands; October 1942–January 1943 (age 27)

Unit: Marine Fighting Squadron 121

Aircraft: Various Grumman F4F-4s including 03444 and 03533

Other decorations: Distinguished Flying Cross

Raised on the family farm, Joe Foss worked his way through school and graduated from the University of South Dakota in 1940. Though his degree was in business administration, he was determined to fly and earned a private pilot's license. He had logged about 100 hours by the time he graduated, and applied for the Naval Aviation Cadet program. Upon completion in March 1941 he was designated a naval aviator and commissioned a lieutenant of Marines.

Foss was retained as a flight instructor at NAS Pensacola, Florida, where he was officer of the day on 7 December 1941. He immediately applied for combat duty, first for the ill-fated Marine glider program, then for a photographic squadron at NAS San Diego, California—the only slot available. He struggled through the photo curriculum, describing it as "one of the hardest things I've ever done." Upon arrival at North Island he wrangled his way into

Joseph J. Foss

the Aircraft Carrier Training Group, being accepted based on his willingness to do "all the dirty work" from sweeping the hangar to commanding burial details. He was promoted to first lieutenant in April, and over a six-week period Foss logged 156 hours, learning gunnery and tactics. His hard work paid off, as he was promoted to captain in August and joined VMF-121 as executive officer to Major Leonard K. "Duke" Davis, previously an Annapolis football star.

The squadron arrived in the Southwest Pacific that fall, being launched from the escort carrier USS *Copahee* (ACV-12) on 9 October to reinforce Guadalcanal. By then Foss had logged nearly 1,100 hours flight time and was an accomplished aerial marksman. He lost no time making his presence felt, being credited with his first Zero four days later.

From that point on, Foss led his half of the squadron in a series of spectacular combats. "Joe's flying Circus" was composed of two four-plane divisions that produced five aces under Foss's leadership. Between 13 and 25 October he was personally credited with sixteen victories, including five in two missions on the twenty-fifth. He thus became the Marine Corps's first "ace in a day."

With sixteen kills in thirteen days the cigar-chewing exec appeared untouchable—until 7 November. That afternoon he splashed three floatplanes but was himself shot down. He bailed out, reached safety with a coast watcher, and returned to Guadalcanal three days later. He was soon back in harness, claiming four more shootdowns before VMF-121 rotated to Australia on 19 November. He was the clear leader among American fighter pilots with twenty-three victories.

Upon return to Guadalcanal on New Year's Day 1943, Foss resumed flying despite advanced malaria. On 15 January he claimed his last three kills in a combat off Vella Lavella. Two weeks later he left "Cactus" to begin the long trek home, where a hero's welcome awaited him.

Credited with twenty-six victories, Foss was hailed as America's ace of aces, matching the tally credited to Eddie Rickenbacker a quarter century earlier. Foss received the Medal of Honor from President Roosevelt on 18 May 1943. The Dakota farmboy became an immediate celebrity; he appeared on the cover of *Life* magazine and conducted a national tour that he called "the dancing bear act." However, he was always emphatic that he was a member of a team—a team that sustained painful losses with its success.

Foss was eager to return to combat and, upon promotion to major, he established VMF-115 at Santa Barbara, California, on 17 July. "Joe's Jokers" flew new F4U-1A Corsairs and took them to the Pacific in early 1944. Flying from Emireau and Green Islands in the Solomons, Foss had no opportunity to increase his score and eventually succumbed to another bout of malaria. He reluctantly left his squadron in September and returned to the United States for a lengthy treatment.

Foss wanted to remain in the Marine Corps but fell afoul of bureaucracy. In early 1946 he learned that he was two weeks too old for a regular commission even though the commandant, General Archer Vandegrift, endorsed Foss's request. It was a blow to Foss and to marine aviation, as he was one of a handful of aviators being groomed as possible commandants, a revolutionary concept in the corps, which has always been ruled by "the ground."

Undaunted, Foss returned home and helped establish the South Dakota Air National Guard. With the rank of lieutenant colonel he soon was leading a P-51 aerobatic team. Increasingly interested in politics, he was elected to the state legislature in 1948 while continuing his air guard duty. He was promoted to colonel in 1950 and was recalled to stateside active duty during the Korean War. Promoted to brigadier general, he was sworn in as governor in 1954 and remarked that his first executive decision was to sell the state's twin-engine aircraft, saying, "If there's any flying to be done, the governor will do it in a fighter." Eventually he led a sixteen-plane jet aerobatic team, unheard of today, when regulations limit formations to six aircraft. When he stopped flying in the 1980s, he had logged more than 10,000 hours.

Over the next four decades Foss maintained a rigorous schedule. In 1959 he became first commissioner of the American Football League and between 1962 and 1974 he produced two television sports programs. Additionally he was active in the Air Force Association, the National Society of Crippled Children and Adults, Campus Crusade for Christ, and the Congressional Medal of Honor Society. He was also president of the National Rifle Association and the American Fighter Aces Association and worked with KLM Airlines. He was inducted into the National Aviation Hall of Fame in 1984.

Foss has produced three books: *Joe Foss, Flying Marine* (with Walter Simmons, 1943), *Top Guns* (with Matthew Brennan, 1991), and *A Proud American* (with Donna "Didi" Foss, 1992).

Ironically, Foss's only other military decoration is the Distinguished Flying Cross. He was nominated for the Navy Cross while on Guadalcanal, but there were too few medals on hand, and because of poor record keeping Foss's recommendation was not pursued.

LIEUTENANT COLONEL HAROLD WILLIAM BAUER

20 NOVEMBER 1918–14 NOVEMBER 1942

BORN: Woodruff, Kansas

DIED: Guadalcanal

ACTION: Air combat; Guadalcanal; 16 October 1942 (age 33)

UNIT: Marine Fighting Squadron 212

AIRCRAFT: Grumman F4F-4s BuNos 02122 and 03491

OTHER DECORATIONS: Purple Heart

The nineteen Wildcats were at the end of their tether. Following a five-hour flight from Espiritu Santo in the New Hebrides, they approached Guadalcanal low on fuel.

Leading the F4Fs was Lieutenant Colonel Joe Bauer, skipper of Marine Fighting Squadron 212. He was no stranger to the Canal. On 28 September he had hopped an R4D up to Cactus and cadged a Wildcat from Major Bob Galer, skipper of VMF-224. In that "guest appearance," Bauer shot down a Mitsubishi G4M bomber. He returned on 1 October and two days later persuaded Major John L. Smith of 223 to let him fly with Captain Marion Carl's division. Carl, who had fought Bauer to a draw in a prewar contest, was delighted to have him. Skillful and aggressive, Bauer's motto was, "When you see Zeroes, dogfight 'em." It worked: the five marines tangled with nine Zeros and bagged five; Bauer claimed four.

Harold W. Bauer

Now, on 16 October, the climax was approaching at Guadalcanal. Bauer's squadron was badly needed, as was the precious cargo being unloaded off the island's north coast. Perennially short of aircraft and pilots, the Cactus Air Force also thirsted for aviation fuel.

Bauer's reinforcements arrived to find a Japanese air raid in progress as Val dive bombers attacked the USS *McFarland* (AVD-14) at an inopportune moment. The converted tender had arrived with 200 drums of aviation fuel and a dozen aerial torpedoes—supplies that Cactus badly needed. Only half the cargo had been offloaded when an air raid alert sounded at 1700. The tender shoved off, still with a fuel barge and lighter secured alongside.

Nine Aichi D3As of the Imperial Navy's 31st Air Group spotted the lucrative target and dived on it. Though the barge and lighter were cut adrift as the USS *McFarland* tried to accelerate eastward, the Japanese were accurate. One bomb struck the fantail, detonating depth charges that blew off the stern. On the barge, 20,000 gallons of gasoline erupted with volcanic force. Twenty-seven men were dead or missing as the rudderless ship canted to port. However, her gunners splashed one attacker. The eight survivors raced away westward.

Bauer orbited while most of the other marines landed. His prudence paid dividends: he spotted the Aichis withdrawing from their attack on the USS *McFarland* and, despite his low fuel state he gave chase. Diving from 3,000 to 200 feet, his Wildcat was impeded by a drop tank that refused to transfer fuel, but Bauer had bandits in front of him and a full ammo loadout. He shoved throttle, mixture, and prop controls to the firewall, overhauled the dive bombers from astern and methodically sent three careening into the water near Savo Island. (He claimed four, the figure credited, but one in fact crashed on landing.) Meanwhile, Bauer landed on fumes. The aggressive squadron commander was delighted with the situation—a base where it was necessary to shoot down enemy planes before landing!

Joe Bauer was a popular figure in Marine Corps aviation. Hailing from Nebraska, he was appointed to the Naval Academy and became known as "Injun Joe" for his dark complexion and enthusiastic war whoops at Annapolis football games. Upon graduation in 1930 he was commissioned a Marine lieutenant, subsequently applied for aviation, and was designated an aviator in February 1936. His first squadron was VO-7M, but in April 1940 he went to VF-1M, which became VMF-2, then 211. In the latter part of 1941 he became executive officer of VMF-221. By then Joe Bauer was widely regarded as the finest fighter pilot in the Marine Corps. The talent he cultivated in VMF-221 and -212 yielded incalculable benefits over the Solomon Islands. Meanwhile, Bauer and his wife, Harriette, provided a comfortable atmosphere in 221 at San Diego.

Bauer was promoted to major immediately after Pearl Harbor and briefly led VMF-221. However, he formed 212 on 1 March 1942 and traded gold oak leaves for silver on 7 August. By the end of the month he had logged 1,800 hours, mostly in fighters. To the pilots he had trained from pups, he was the Coach.

On the morning after avenging the USS *McFarland,* Bauer became "ComfitCactus," in charge of all Guadalcanal fighter operations. As usual, he continued leading from the front. On 14 November the Japanese sent a major reinforcement convoy down the Slot, intent on landing at Guadalcanal. Despite his supervisory role, Bauer wanted "to see for myself what the convoy looks like." There was much to see: the Japanese dispatched eleven transports screened by eleven destroyers.

Bauer led the escort for dive and torpedo bombers against the ships, and a low-level dogfight developed. Bauer splashed two Zeros, then was shot down and parachuted into the water. Floating in his mae west, he was seen to motion toward Guadal for help. Joe Foss and Major Joe Renner leapt into a J2F Duck and flew to the scene of the shootdown, guided by the fires of burning Japanese ships. No trace was found of the Coach. In only four combats he was credited with eleven kills and a probable.

On 6 December, Major General Louis E. Woods of the first Marine Air Wing recommended Bauer for the Medal of Honor. A five-month battle ensued: originally denied, the recommendation was revived by Major General Roy Geiger, and Secretary of the Navy Frank Knox approved the award in May 1943. Lacking conclusive proof of his death, Bauer's medal was not presented until 11 May 1946, when his widow and son, Billy, accepted the award from General field Harris.

In June 1943 the airfield at Vila, Efate, was named in Bauer's honor. Much later, in 1957, a Dealey-class destroyer escort (DE-1025) bore his name. The class was named for Bauer's Annapolis classmate Commander Sam Dealey, who received a posthumous Medal of Honor as a submarine skipper.

However, perhaps the finest tribute came from Joe Foss, who wrote Bauer's parents, "Marine Corps Aviation's greatest loss in this war was that of your son Joe. I am certain that wherever Joe is today, he is doing things the best way—the Bauer way."

FIRST LIEUTENANT JEFFERSON JOSEPH DEBLANC

15 FEBRUARY 1921–

BORN: Lockport, Louisiana

ACTION: Air combat; Solomon Islands; 31 January 1943 (age 21)

UNIT: Marine Fighting Squadron 112

AIRCRAFT: Grumman F4F-4 BuNo 03446 (29)

OTHER DECORATIONS: Distinguished Flying Cross, Air Medal (4)

On the afternoon of 31 January 1943 a twenty-one-year-old Louisianan led an eight-plane escort for Marine Corps bombers to Kolombangara Island in the Solomons. Japanese fighters intercepted at 14,000 feet as the SBDs and TBFs egressed from the target area; the Wildcats tied into the Zeroes and a spirited dogfight erupted. First Lieutenant Jeff DeBlanc already had three planes to his credit and tangled with the Mitsubishis as the Dauntlesses and Avengers scooted for Guadalcanal.

However, while outbound on the deck the SBDs were attacked by Mitsubishi F1M "Petes," biplane float fighters. Supported by three seaplane tenders at

Jefferson J. DeBlanc

Gizo Bay, New Georgia, the Petes were a perennial threat to AirSols bombers. Hearing the SBDs' calls for help, DeBlanc abandoned the A6Ms and bent his throttle southward. He arrived in time to break up the Petes, allowing the SBDs to complete their getaway.

With his escort duty completed, DeBlanc could have disengaged as two of his pilots had done earlier. However, he remained to shoot it out with the Petes despite running dangerously low on fuel.

"I had to shoot over the head of Lieutenant Poole's SBD in order to shoot a biplane off his tail since they were both heading directly at me," DeBlanc recalls. "In order to save Poole and his gunner, I fired directly over his cockpit and burned the floatplane. Another floatplane's rear gunner put a few arrows in my aircraft that day. So although it would seem that a float biplane is no match for a Wildcat, they are still dangerous with the rear gunner shooting at you, hence I made my run on another floatplane by coming in below the sight of the rear gunner."

The young marine had barely turned southwesterly when he noticed Zeroes diving on him from six o'clock high. Outnumbered and alone, he was forced to fight. He turned into the threat and resigned himself to swimming home.

DeBlanc graduated from high school in 1938 and attended college for three years before becoming a naval aviation cadet in 1941. Commissioned in April 1942, he entered combat in November as an infant aviator, let alone fighter pilot. With merely 290 hours flight time, he possessed rudimentary experience, but DeBlanc joined VMF-112 only days before deploying to the Pacific. However, what he lacked in experience he more than offset in determination. He scored two kills and a probable in his first combat, 12 November, and added a floatplane five weeks later.

The combat degenerated into a descending spiral over Kolombangara. DeBlanc gunned three of his assailants, who in turn perforated the Grumman airframe further. He caught sight of the withdrawing Dauntlesses as his Wildcat seemed to collapse beneath him. He rang up the "for sale" sign and went over the side, parachuting into the water just offshore.

Fortunately, the efficient coastwatcher network quickly learned of the situation. Friendly natives found DeBlanc and a squadronmate, Staff Sergeant James Feliton, but they were by no means safe. On a February morning DeBlanc feared he was about to be captured by Japanese patrols, as he awoke to the realization that the jungle birds were silent. "I knew that from when I was living in the swamp back home."

Upon return on 12 February (he was exchanged for a bag of rice), DeBlanc learned that his skipper, Major Paul Fontana, had recommended him for the Navy Cross. There were rumors that Colonel Toby Munn of the First Marine Air Wing had nominated DeBlanc for the Medal of Honor, since no marine had previously claimed five kills in one mission. Years later DeBlanc learned that Admirals Halsey (SoPac) and King (CNO) had referred the recommendation for later consideration.

DeBlanc returned to the United States and was promoted to captain. In early 1945 he fetched up on Okinawa with VMF-422, where he notched another kill, his ninth of the war.

In 1946 DeBlanc was unexpectedly recalled to active duty. "The Navy Cross I wore during the war years was rescinded and the Medal of Honor was presented by Harry Truman," he recalls of the December 1946 ceremony. "I was glad to get the Medal, and in good faith I could easily have turned back like two other fighter pilots did (and I resented this bitterly) because we needed all the guns we could get up there to protect the dive bombers. This left us only six fighters to do the job of eight."

Listening to the military aide reading his citation, DeBlanc realized that errors had crept in. "My citation isn't correct. I shot down two floatplanes going after our bombers and three Zeros and a possible fourth. Since I had no control over the details of my citation, they have me bailing out over the trees of Kolombangara. That was Jim Feliton, my wingman. I was seen by Jack Maas as bailing out over the ocean and had to swim in. My kills were confirmed by the dive bombers and by Missionary Silvester on Vella Lavella.

"However, one does not correct the President of the U.S. During the Civil War Medals of Honor were handed out for almost zilch and some to promote careers. After all, the 'CMH' was a Yankee medal in those days!"

After the war, DeBlanc led an extraordinarily varied life. He gained four college degrees between 1947 and 1973, including a doctorate in education. He taught mathematics and physics in the United States and in DOD schools in Holland and worked in the telecommunications industry. Remaining an active aviator, he served with a reserve fighter squadron in New Orleans and commanded the Marine Reserve air group there. When he hung up his helmet, he had logged some 3,000 hours total time.

DeBlanc made a national reputation in the Senior Olympics, winning medals in track and field events. An extraordinary raconteur, he has been in frequent demand for public appearances. Apart from his academic publishing, he also wrote a family history titled, *Once They Lived by the Sword.* Writing of the influences in his life, DeBlanc said, "I was fortunate to be reared in the Roman Catholic faith and in a community reflecting the Cajun culture of South Louisiana. The depression years helped me set my values at an early age."

FIRST LIEUTENANT JAMES ELMS SWETT

15 June 1920–

Born: Seattle, Washington

Action: Air combat; Guadalcanal area; 7 April 1943 (age 22)

Unit: Marine Fighting Squadron 221

Aircraft: Grumman F4F-4 BuNo 12036 (77) *Melvin Massacre*

Other decorations: Distinguished Flying Cross (2), Air Medal (4), Purple Heart

James E. Swett was commissioned a lieutenant of Marines on 16 April 1942; twelve months later he was famous. He became a role model for a generation of wartime fighter pilots who wanted nothing so much as to "do a Jimmy Swett."

Swett arrived at Guadalcanal on 16 March 1943, and by early April he had logged 458 hours flight time, including 125 in Wildcats. Almost brashly extroverted with a breezy sense of humor, he chafed for the opportunity to start shooting "meatballs."

At first there were only sightings of Japanese aircraft, and the trend continued during the first week of April. On the seventh Swett flew two uneventful patrols but upon landing the second time he was ordered to stand by: coastwatchers reported "a huge enemy force" winging south, headed for U.S. shipping at the Tulagi anchorage forty miles away.

James E. Swett

Swett led his division into the afternoon sky, part of just sixty-seven U.S. Fighters to oppose sixty-seven Aichi D3A dive bombers escorted by more than 160 Zero fighters. Cactus Radio described the condition as "very red!"

Fighting 221 took the brunt of the attack: eleven pilots claimed kills in the ensuing shootout but only Swett's division seriously challenged the Aichis of the 582nd *Kokutai* and the carrier HIJMS *Zuikaku*'s beached air group. Lining up the "Vals," Swett mentally licked his chops—he had been on the Canal six weeks and had yet to fire his guns. He was flying a pool aircraft unaccountably named *Melvin Massacre;* it proved appropriate.

The Wildcats caught the Aichis just as the bombers nosed over from 15,000 feet, aiming at American transport ships off Tulagi. U.S. gunners already were putting a flak screen but it deterred no one, American or Japanese.

Flying in close, Swett flamed his first two Vals without trouble. He dived after the third into the increasing AA fire and exploded it low on the water. Then a U.S. gunner put a 40mm round through his port wing. Swett pulled away, checked his Wildcat, and determined that he could still fly and fight. Spotting five Vals retiring northward, he shoved up the power and gave chase.

Swett reeled in the fleeing D3As and stalked them from six o'clock low. They were flying line astern, and Swett executed the two tail end bombers without receiving a shot in return. Though he gave it no thought at the time, he had just tied Jeff DeBlanc's Marine record with five kills in one mission.

With ammunition remaining, Swett continued the chase. He had the sixth Val in sight about three-quarters of a mile ahead and closed the range. This time he got so close that his F4F was caught in the victim's slipstream. He eased back, settled his gunsight on the fuselage, and pressed the trigger. Like the others, it fell to the concentrated firepower of six .50 calibers.

Until now, most of Swett's shooting had been from dead astern, but the next Val crossed his nose. He tracked the target in his sight, applied the textbook deflection, and fired. One burst sent the bomber burning into the water. That made seven.

By now the last Aichi crew was fully alerted to the lethal Grumman. The Japanese gunner was fast and accurate; he expertly placed a burst of 7.7mm rounds across *Melvin*'s engine and cockpit. Swett's face was cut by glass shards and his windscreen was coated with a film of engine oil. Without firing, he wracked the Wildcat into a turn for another approach.

Zeke Swett was determined to finish the last target but he knew he was nearly out of ammunition. Ignoring the pain, coping with reduced vision, he bored in. His first burst killed the sharpshooting gunner; his next burst got strikes on the Val. Then he was empty. Ruefully, Swett watched Number Eight plunge into a cloud, trailing smoke.

En route to Cactus, Swett realized he would not make base. Finally out of oil, the Pratt and Whitney seized over Tulagi and Swett glided toward a water landing. His mood was not improved when more trigger-happy gunners shot at him.

Though a fine airplane, the Grumman F4F made a poor boat. *Melvin* sank almost immediately, pulling Swett down with it. He bobbed to the surface, tried to wipe the blood, oil, and saltwater from his eyes, then struggled into his raft. A PT boat investigated and a sailor asked if the downed flier were an American. Swett's English monosyllables removed any doubt.

During the shootout over Tulagi the Americans claimed thirty-nine shootdowns for the loss of seven F4Fs. Japanese records conceded loss of nine Aichis plus two damaged, which closely matched the U.S. claims for twelve D3As.

While Swett recovered in sick bay, a Navy friend, Lieutenant (jg) Pete Lewis, sought the eighth Val. He found a D3A on Malaita Island and returned with the data plate, telling Swett that the gunner died in the aircraft "and the natives got the pilot." Recent research indicates that the Val came from the carrier HIJMS *Junyo*'s air group, which attacked another group of ships than Swett defended.

Still recuperating, Swett was shown a dispatch from Vice Admiral Marc Mitscher, commander of allied aircraft in the Solomons. "AirSols" had nominated the instant ace for the Medal of Honor. Six months later Swett was decorated by Major General Ralph Mitchell, commanding marine aviation in the South Pacific.

Meanwhile, Swett was promoted to captain effective 31 May and the squadron converted to F4Us in June. He became a Corsair ace with seven and a half kills between then and early November. He was shot down a second time on 11 July—this time by the Japanese.

In 1945 VMF-221 returned to combat in vastly different condition—flying F4Us from the carrier USS *Bunker Hill* (CV-17). Swett scored his last kill, another dive bomber, near Okinawa on 11 May, the day his ship was critically damaged in an air attack.

Swett left the service in 1945 but retained a reserve commission, retiring as a colonel in 1970.

FIRST LIEUTENANT KENNETH AMBROSE WALSH

24 November 1916–30 July 1998

Born: Brooklyn, New York

Died: Santa Ana, California

Action: Air combat; Solomon Islands; 15 and 30 August 1943 (age 26)

Unit: Marine Fighting Squadron 124

Aircraft: Vought F4U-1/1As including BuNo 02486

Other decorations: Distinguished Flying Cross (6), Air Medal (10)

The ailing Corsair flew a tight pattern over New Georgia, dropped onto Munda's hard-packed runway, and taxied to the flight line. Before the prop whirled to a stop, the pilot unstrapped and climbed down from the high cockpit. He was met by the operations officer, Major Jim Neefus, who immediately recognized him. "Ken, what the hell are you doing here?"

Kenneth A. Walsh

First Lieutenant Ken Walsh had known Neefus before the war, when flying as an enlisted marine. "My supercharger quit," Walsh explained. "I can still catch the bombers."

Neefus told his former squadronmate to climb in a jeep and they raced to the dispersal area where four Corsairs were parked. "Take your pick," Neefus grinned.

Ten minutes after landing, Walsh tucked his wheels in the well and bent the throttle northward. The attack on Kahili Airfield, Bougainville, was bound to draw Japanese fighters into the air, and Walsh wanted a piece of the action. Two weeks previously he had a good day over Vella Lavella, responding to a fighter director's call for help. Japanese planes were threatening the amphibious shipping, and Walsh tied into them with five Corsairs against thirty bandits. Walsh gunned two Vals and a Zeke before another A6M jumped him and shot his Corsair to pieces. Walsh had barely managed a landing at base; the F4U never flew again.

Walsh had enlisted in 1933, barely seventeen, expecting to become a pilot as a private. He attended aircraft mechanic and radio schools for two years before entering flight training, receiving his wings as a private first class in April 1937. As a noncommissioned aviation pilot he flew in scout and observation squadrons including deployments in the carriers USS *Yorktown* (CV-5), *Wasp* (CV-7), and *Ranger* (CV-4).

Technical Sergeant Walsh was assigned to VMF-121 at New Bern, North Carolina in December 1941, learning the intricacies of the new Grumman F4F Wildcat. Upon promotion to warrant officer in May 1942, he became one of a handful of Marine landing signal officers, though he never put the skill to use aboard ship. That September he was assigned to VMF-124, which he considered "the best thing that happened to me in the Marine Corps."

Commissioned shortly thereafter, he featured prominently in developing the Vought F4U as a fighter airplane. Major Bill Gise's squadron inaugurated the Corsair to combat at Guadalcanal in February 1943, escorting a PBY to fetch back Lieutenant Jeff DeBlanc, who had been shot down 31 January. Walsh already had put one Corsair in the water with engine failure and subsequently survived two crash landings and a shootdown. No wonder he described himself as "Vought's best customer." Meanwhile, he claimed ten kills in four combats between 1 April and 12 August 1943, becoming the first Corsair ace on 13 May.

Knowing the objective, Walsh calculated the geometry of the 30 August mission. Twenty-four Liberators were to overfly Kahili Airdrome on Bougainville's south coast, then turn southeasterly to bomb on a homeward heading. By cutting the corners, Walsh arrived alone at 30,000 feet as the B-24s began their run. He estimated that fifty Mitsubishi Zeros intercepted (there were fifty-five from the 201st, 204th, and 251st Naval Air Groups). The Japanese initiated stern passes at the bombers, leaving some of the Zekes vulnerable. Walsh wasted no time: closing to boresight range, he pressed his trigger in short, controlled bursts and flamed two bandits almost before they knew he was there.

Seventy miles southeast of the target, Walsh tangled with another flock of Zekes. In a running battle he claimed two more but the unequal odds accumulated. Other allied fighters were hard pressed to offset the Japanese numerical advantage; Walsh saw a Liberator shot down with no parachutes visible, and a Bell P-39 went down aflame. The pilot bailed out.

Lacking a wingman, Walsh became the lone bogey in a Mitsubishi "furball." He jousted with several Zekes but his F4U was repeatedly hit by machine gun and cannon fire. Finally he managed a water landing off Vella Lavella, close enough to shore for the Seabees to observe his dilemma. They fetched him in a Higgins boat, and he was returned to Guadalcanal the next day. Beside him in the LST was the Army pilot he had seen jump from the burning P-39.

The mission was costly—seven U.S. Fighters and two bombers downed—but the results were considered good. Three Corsair squadrons claimed fourteen kills, and two Army units accounted for five more. For once the Japanese claims were conservative: one U.S. bomber and four fighters plus three probables were credited; the defenders actually lost five Zeros and four damaged. Walsh had run his string to twenty, including twelve victories during August alone.

Fighting 124 completed its tour a week later and returned to the United States. For the missions of 15 and 30 August, Walsh, newly promoted to captain, received the Medal of Honor from President Roosevelt on 8 February 1944.

Walsh was an operational instructor at NAS Jacksonville, Florida, before joining VMF-222. The flying Deuces served in the Philippines from April to June 1945, proceeding to Okinawa where Walsh scored his twenty-first victory 22 June, apparently a suicide Zeke. During the Korean War, Walsh flew R5Ds (C-54s) with Marine Transport Squadron 152. In October 1958 he was promoted to lieutenant colonel (usually the highest possible for a "mustang") while assigned to the Third Marine Air Wing at MCAS El Toro, California. He retired on 1 February 1962.

"The Medal has never gone to my head," Walsh later wrote. "I look back on everything that happened with all humility. On both the missions for which I was awarded the Medal of Honor, we lost pilots. I always remember that."

MAJOR GREGORY BOYINGTON

4 DECEMBER 1912–11 JANUARY 1988

BORN: Coeur d'Alene, Idaho

DIED: Fresno, California

ACTION: Air combat; Solomon Islands; August 1943–January 1944 (age 30)

UNIT: Marine Fighting Squadron 214

AIRCRAFT: Various Vought F4U-Is including BuNo 17915

OTHER DECORATIONS: Navy Cross, Purple Heart

The voice on the radio had a raspy, boozy quality, but the message was clear enough. English-speaking Japanese on Bougainville not only understood the words—they knew the speaker.

It was Boyington again.

"Come up and fight," the marine challenged. Whatever his sense of invulnerability, he was not complacent—he had two squadrons of Corsairs to back up his bravado. As further inducement to the Zero pilots on the ground, Boyington taunted them as "yellow bellies" and "yellow bastards."

They took the bait. Zeros of the 201st and 204th *Kokutai* lifted off from Kahili and foolishly climbed directly toward the insolent F4Us. Completely vulnerable, they were jumped from overhead and suffered the consequences. Boyington claimed one of eight credited to his increasingly successful Black Sheep squadron.

Gregory Boyington

Thirty-year-old Greg Boyington became famous as "Pappy" but his Marine Corps associates knew him as "Rats" for his resemblance to movie actor Gregory Ratoff. Graduating with an engineering degree from the University of Washington in 1934, he was also a regional wrestling champion. Two years later Boyington entered the naval aviation cadet program and nearly washed out of Pensacola. However, he steadily improved his flying skills and earned his wings in July 1937, subsequently flying fighters and scouts. Assigned to VMF-2 in 1940, he was surrounded by talent, including future Medal of Honor pilots Joe Bauer, Hank Elrod, and Bob Galer.

In August 1941 Boyington became the only officer with a regular commission to enroll in the American Volunteer Group. By then he had largely worn out his welcome in the corps owing to drinking, gambling, and generally undignified conduct. His family life was a shambles and, deeply in debt, he was lured by the prospect of high pay as a mercenary pilot in China.

Boyington made even fewer friends in the Flying Tigers than he had in the Marine Corps. Unlike another future Medal of Honor recipient, Jim Howard, Boyington left the AVG in April 1942, forfeiting an honorable discharge from the Tigers. He returned to the United States claiming six aerial victories (AVG records show two air, two and a half ground) and rejoined the Marines in September; by year's end he was a major.

Upon deploying to the Solomons, Boyington led two fighter squadrons without much notoriety except a broken leg in a drunken brawl. Then on 7 September he assumed command of the inactive VMF-214, which he led to fame over the next four months. He made a sensational start, claiming five kills in his first combat only nine days after taking the helm.

Eager to become the top Marine ace, Boyington pulled within reach of that goal on the basis of his claim for six kills in China. Actually, Joe Foss remained the premier leatherneck fighter pilot because all of his twenty-six victories were in Marine service. Nevertheless, the Corps and the press accepted Boyington's statistics as he neared the magical twenty-six mark. He pushed the Black Sheep and himself until the odds caught up with him. Separated from his squadron near Rabaul on 3 January 1944, Boyington was shot down and captured; his wingman was killed. "Pappy" spent the rest of the war as a POW in Japan.

Popular legend—abetted by Boyington—held that his Medal of Honor was authorized because he was thought dead. In fact, the Marine Corps had been caught short when reporters asked why the current top gun had received no decorations. Anxious to cover the lapse, the Corps nominated its black sheep for the Medal of Honor in November 1943, a fact known to Boyington. Realizing that months would pass before the medal could be approved, the secretary of the Navy authorized a Navy Cross to fill the breach. President Roosevelt signed the Medal of Honor authorization on 15 March 1944, presumably posthumously. Consequently, when Boyington returned from captivity in 1945, he received both decorations. The Marines willingly accepted his claim of twenty-eight victories, despite the inflated China score and lack of witnesses for two on the day he was captured. Joe Foss was too much of a gentleman to make an issue of it.

Actually, Boyington's POW status was learned as early as February 1944, when a decoded message was read from the Japanese admiral commanding the Caroline Islands. He requested permission of Naval General Headquarters to execute a troublesome field grade officer named Boyington. However, the fact that Boyington was alive remained a secret to protect U.S. intelligence sources.

Boyington's memoir, *Baa Baa Black Sheep,* was published in 1958. Its sardonic, self-deprecating tone found a popular audience for the next thirty years, although the text was often inaccurate. The 1970s television series was widely condemned by Black Sheep veterans and knowledgeable viewers, as it perpetuated Boyington's assertion that VMF-214 was composed of "screwballs and misfits" who nonetheless became "the terrors of the South Pacific." Despite the second-season injection of "Pappy's Lambs" (beautiful young women in form-fitting jumpsuits whose role was tacitly obvious), the series deservedly flopped. However, it rebounded in the 1990s with support from some 214 pilots willing to lend credence to cable TV reruns. The genuine stars of the program were—and are—half a dozen flying Corsairs.

A string of failed marriages and public scandals characterized most of Boyington's postwar life. He refereed wrestling matches, sold various products, and ran for Congress. Ultimately he settled in Fresno with his fourth wife, Josephine, and found solace in painting. He was also supported by a cadre of kind-hearted friends, including fellow Marine ace Bruce Porter. Boyington became a familiar figure at air shows, signing copies of *Baa Baa Black Sheep,* extending the legend of "Pappy." He died in 1988 and was buried in dress blues at Arlington National Cemetery.

Author Bruce Gamble has produced two definitive accounts of the Boyington saga: *The Black Sheep,* a history of VMF-214; and *Black Sheep One,* an extremely objective biography.

FIRST LIEUTENANT ROBERT MURRAY HANSON

4 FEBRUARY 1920–3 FEBRUARY 1944

BORN: Lucknow, India

DIED: New Ireland

ACTION: Air combat; Solomon Islands; November 1943–January 1944 (age 23)

UNIT: Marine Fighting Squadron 215

AIRCRAFT: Various Vought F4U-1s including 17472 and 56039?

OTHER DECORATIONS: Navy Cross, Air Medal, Purple Heart

On 1 November 1943 the U.S. Navy destroyer USS *Sigourney* (DD-643) hove to in Empress Augusta Bay on the west coast of Bougainville Island. Lookouts had sighted a yellow life raft, and the ship stopped to investigate an odd

Robert M. Hanson

scene. Paddling toward them was a well-built young aviator lustily singing "You'd Be So Good to Come Home To." He was first Lieutenant Robert M. Hanson, who had shot down three Japanese planes earlier that day to become an ace. In turn, an enemy rear gunner had brought down Hanson's F4U. The Corsair pilot was eager to get on with the war.

"Butcher Bob" was an odd nickname for the son of Methodist missionaries. Largely educated in India, where he was a champion boxer and wrestler, young Hanson returned to America in 1938, bicycled in Europe, and graduated from Hamline University in 1942. When he became a Marine aviator in February 1943, he had one year to live.

Hanson had joined the original (pre-Blacksheep) VMF-214 and first drew blood on 4 August 1943. Having completed his first of three required combat tours, he went to VMF-215 when his original squadron stood down.

fighting 215 was an intensely competitive organization. The CO, Major Robert G. Owens, apparently gave wide latitude to his top shooters, especially Hanson and Captains Donald Aldrich and Harold Spears. Operating successively from Guadalcanal, Munda, and Vella Lavella, the fighting Corsairs completed their tour while based at Torokina on Bougainville.

On an 18 January bomber escort to Rabaul, the marines were met by an estimated sixty Zekes over New Ireland. A running battle ensued all the way to the target.

With Second Lieutenant Richard V. Bowman, Hanson stayed with the TBFs through the attack, recovering low over Simpson Harbor. "There were lots of Zekes cruising around low, and their speed did not seem to exceed 180 knots," Hanson observed. The two Corsairs stalked a brace of Zekes and surprised them at 1,500 feet. Hanson and Bowman each dropped one burning into the water.

Glimpsing two more Mitsubishis, Hanson chased one into clouds and exploded it. Back above the cloud layer he noticed two Zekes dogging a section of Corsairs and discouraged their pursuit.

With an estimated thirty bandits still in the area, Hanson began cloud hopping, seeking additional opportunity. He found it at 3,000 feet when a pair of Zekes crossed his nose about 500 feet lower. He nosed down, closing fast, when he was spotted. The leader banked toward some cloud cover, affording Hanson a quarter deflection shot. He pressed the trigger and reported his target flamed immediately.

Content for the moment, Hanson climbed for more altitude, recovering at 2,500 feet. "I looked out of the clouds again and saw I was right on the tail of a Zero and just a little below him. I ran right up on him and fired. My tracers went into his belly and he burst immediately into flame." Later he wrote, "I think this is the best way to shoot them: from astern and below."

After some inconclusive passes at occasional Zekes, Hanson turned for the rendezvous point. En route, he spied a single Mitsubishi, which he attacked from behind and reported falling in flames. Finally he noticed two more Zekes astern so he poked his nose into a cloud "and beat it for home." He landed at Torokina twenty minutes behind his squadronmates with only twenty gallons of fuel remaining. He had run his score from five to ten.

Hanson had a habit of breaking away from his division; despite the well-known fate of lone wolves, he thrived in the target-rich environment. In his next five fights he claimed fifteen more kills, and almost every time he fired his guns he returned with multiple claims: five on 18 January; four on the twenty-fourth; four more on the thirtieth. By then he had claimed twenty-five kills including twenty in just six missions over thirteen days. The Marine Corps never established independent victory credit boards, so claims were mostly accepted on the honor system. Many of Hanson's victories were unwitnessed but credited as allowed by regulations. At month's end he was only one short of the twenty-six credited to Foss and (erroneously) Boyington.

On 3 February VMF-215 swept the Rabaul area and claimed three kills but Hanson did not score. Returning from his only unsuccessful combat, he called the flight leader, Captain Harold Spears, asking to strafe Japanese positions at Cape St. George, New Ireland. Spears, having just run his score to fourteen, perhaps felt generous toward his rival and granted permission. The lone Corsair dived on the area, which included a radar station, drawing ground fire. Hanson cleared the target but continued a shallow descent until impacting the water offshore. He would have been twenty-four the next day. Equally sad, he was due to rotate home a week later.

Hanson's Medal of Honor was presented to his mother in August 1944 and he received a posthumous promotion to captain. The USS *Hanson* (DD-832), a Gearing-class destroyer of 2,425 tons, was launched in March 1945.

Marine Corps Aviation Related (1)

Lieutenant Colonel Merritt A. Edson, first Marine Raider Battalion, Guadalcanal, September 1942. Though designated a naval aviator in 1922, Edson left flying, reportedly for vision problems. Aviation's loss was the infantry's gain, as his raiders defended Edson's ("Bloody") Ridge the night of 13–14 September. Continually exposing himself to enemy fire while conducting a desperate defense of the last high ground overlooking Henderson Field, "Red Mike" Edson became an icon of the Old Corps.

NAVY (6)

LIEUTENANT (JG) EDWARD HENRY O'HARE

13 MARCH 1914–26 NOVEMBER 1943

BORN: St. Louis, Missouri

DIED: Off the Gilbert Islands

ACTION: Air combat off New Britain; 20 February 1942 (age 27)

UNIT: Fighting Squadron 3, USS *Lexington* (CV-2)

AIRCRAFT: Grumman F4F-3, BuNo 4031 (F-15)

OTHER DECORATIONS: Navy Cross, Distinguished Flying Cross (2), Purple Heart

The Type One land attack bombers came out of Rabaul, New Britain—fast, olive-drab shapes making a dual-axis attack. Seventeen of the Mitsubishi G4Ms approached at 1630, belonging to the Fourth Naval Air Group. Each carried a pair of 550-pound bombs, not the best weapons for attacking an aircraft carrier, but thirty-four chances to hit the USS *Lexington* (CV-2). Her radar only detected them twenty-five miles out: nine minutes away at 170 knots.

Lieutenant Commander John Thach's Fighting Three was extremely professional, but this was still the Felix Squadron's first day in combat. Never-

Edward H. O'Hare

theless, in the initial interception on nine bombers at 11,000 feet, the Wildcats splashed three and forced another away, spoiling the survivors' accuracy. Lex was temporarily safe. The skipper's division chased down two more but the G4Ms' return fire also took a toll. Two Wildcats were downed; one pilot was killed.

The second wave of eight Mitsubishis got much closer. Approaching from the opposite beam, they had a clear shot at Lady Lex except for the two Grummans retained as a reserve near the ship. There was precious little time to spare. The section leader was a stocky, dark-haired "trade school" professional from the Annapolis class of 1937. With his wingman's guns jammed, Edward H. "Butch" O'Hare was on his own.

It was a race. The bombers nosed down, accelerating to reach their drop point before the Grummans intercepted. With the experience of more than 900 hours flight time, O'Hare made a textbook high-side pass from starboard, holding his fire until he had the deflection he wanted. At one hundred yards he opened up; his four .50 calibers torched the engine of the nearest G4M. Closing fast, O'Hare continued his run and shifted his gunsight to the next bomber. He got hits, dived out below the formation, and saw his second target peel off to starboard. O'Hare recovered to port, pulled around and prepared for another pass.

Attacking from the left side of the formation, O'Hare did even better on his second pass. Triggering his Brownings in short, disciplined bursts, he flamed one bomber that dropped out of position. As before, he continued his run, selected the next target in line, and shredded a wing with his gunfire. The engine flared and raw fuel ignited. The Mitsubishi exploded in midair.

This time O'Hare wracked around in a tight turn, remaining on the bombers' port side. By now the task force's antiaircraft guns had opened up; flak bursts erupted near the raiders, whose gunners hosed tracers at the persistent Grumman. Nevertheless, O'Hare dived again for a third time, concentrating on the leader. As before, he blew the bomber apart.

Then the G4Ms were in their runs. The four remaining in formation dropped their bombs from astern, producing a cluster of geysers perhaps only one hundred feet in the USS *Lexington*'s churning wake. As the bombers cleared the flak zone, O'Hare went after them again, firing his remaining ammunition at the trailing Mitsubishi. In his first combat, lasting just four minutes, he shot five enemy bombers out of formation. Japanese records show that one of his targets returned to Rabaul, but Butch O'Hare's courage and marksmanship possibly saved one-third of the Pacific Fleet's operational carriers.

Back aboard ship, O'Hare asked for a glass of water and examined his plane. Fox fifteen had taken just one 7.7mm bullet through the fuselage, but American steel had punched two holes in its wings.

O'Hare was recommended for a Navy Cross but his instant celebrity as the first Navy ace of the war ensured more. He received the Medal of Honor on 21 April, and perhaps even more heartfelt in war-rationed America, patriotic citizens sent him 5,000 cigarettes.

Promoted to lieutenant commander, O'Hare was on the fast track. He took over VF-3, later redesignated VF-6, and began imparting the fighter pilot wisdom he received from Thach. By the summer of 1943 O'Hare was back in combat, flying new F6F-3 Hellcats from the new light carrier USS *Independence* (CVL-22). He downed two more planes in his second and last battle—Wake Island on 5 October. The next month he was aboard the USS *Enterprise* (CV-6) as air group commander, supporting the invasion of the Gilberts.

An early advocate of night operations, O'Hare had trained specially formed "bat teams" in Hawaii. Leading another Hellcat directed by airborne radar in a Grumman TBF Avenger, O'Hare proved the concept off Tarawa on the night of 27 November 1943. In the darkness and confusion he and his wingman became separated from their aerial eyes, but the concept was validated as the torpedo pilot shot down two Bettys. Calling for a rendezvous, O'Hare approached the Avenger and apparently crossed the nose of an unseen Betty. The anonymous Japanese gunner glimpsed a ghosting shape, fired a short burst, and thought little of it since he made no claim.

Ensign Warren Skon, O'Hare's wingman, watched the CAG's F6F fly into the water. A search revealed nothing of O'Hare or his aircraft.

OHare's memory was preserved in DD-889, a Gearing-class destroyer launched in January 1945. The airfield on Abemama, Gilbert Islands, was a short-lived tribute, but the main airport at Chicago was renamed O'Hare Field in 1949. It remains one of the busiest airports in the world, and one terminal displays a fully restored F4F-3 Wildcat as a permanent tribute to one of America's earliest heroes of World War II.

LIEUTENANT (JG) WILLIAM EDWARD HALL

31 OCTOBER 1913–15 NOVEMBER 1996

BORN: Storrs, Utah

DIED: Kansas City, Missouri

ACTION: Air defense; Battle of the Coral Sea; 7–8 May 1942 (age 28)

UNIT: Scouting Squadron 2, USS *Lexington* (CV-2)

AIRCRAFT: Douglas SBD-3 BuNo 4537 (S-8)

OTHER DECORATIONS: Purple Heart

Aboard the carrier USS *Lexington* (CV-2), twenty-eight-year-old Bill Hall was called "Pappy" not only because of his "advanced" age but because of his previous experience aboard the USS *Yorktown* (CV-5) and *Enterprise* (CV-6). At that time he was probably the most experienced combat aviator in the U.S. Navy, owing to circumstances that had placed him aboard three carriers in the first five months of the war.

Hall had graduated from college as a professional musician in 1936. Two years later he entered the Naval Aviation Cadet program and received his wings of gold in September 1939. He joined the fleet as a scout-bomber pilot, and by May 1942 he had twenty months experience.

On 6 May, the eve of the world's first aircraft carrier duel, Hall was in exactly the right place at the right time. Flying with Scouting Squadron Two in the USS *Lexington,* he was poised on the brink of two days that would propel him to fame.

Radio intelligence had provided the U.S. Pacific Fleet with detailed knowledge of Japanese intentions to occupy Port Moresby, New Guinea. Seizure of

Lt. (jg) William E. Hall *(left)* receiving the Medal of Honor for his defense of the USS *Lexington* in the battle of the Coral Sea

the port would position Japan to strike at Northern Australia, further limiting allied mobility in the Southwest Pacific. Consequently, the USS *Lexington* and *Yorktown* were dispatched to intercept the invasion force in the Coral Sea.

On the morning of the seventh the U.S. flattops launched a ninety-three-plane strike against the Japanese covering force including the light carrier HIJMS *Shoho.* The Dauntlesses, Devastators, and Wildcats found their prey steaming under clear skies and made the only fully coordinated attack on an enemy surface unit in 1942. Hall, flying with Radioman Doyle Phillips, followed Lieutenant Commander Robert E. Dixon toward the target. Approaching downwind and downsun, Scouting Two dived from 12,500 feet.

With Zeros snapping at the rear of the formation, the Dauntlesses tracked the HIJMS *Shoho* through a port turn. Of ten 500-pound bombs dropped, three were claimed as hits. One SBD was shot down during the attack and another pulled off with battle damage, limping away to ditch safely.

Then Bombing Two rolled in with fifteen half-ton bombs that took the 12,000-ton carrier apart. Combined with torpedo planes and the USS *Yorktown*'s dive bombers, the U.S. attack sank the HIJMS *Shoho* in about twenty minutes. Dixon radioed the USS *Lexington,* "Scratch one flattop!"

The next morning brought more carrier combat. The large carriers HIJMS

Shokaku and *Zuikaku* exchanged strikes with the Americans, resulting in casualties on both sides. Ten Scouting Two planes were among twenty-three SBDs expected to intercept inbound enemy torpedo planes. In Hall's rear seat Seaman first Class John A. Moore replaced Phillips, wounded the day before.

The SBDs deployed below 3,000 feet within a nautical mile of the destroyer screen—just beyond effective range of AA fire. Hall led his wingman, Ensign Robert E. Smith, on the USS *Lexington*'s port side. The task force steamed southeasterly with all but three of the defensive Dauntlesses deployed on the engaged (northern) side. Between them the HIJMS *Shokaku* and *Zuikaku* air groups deployed fourteen Nakamima B5Ns with nine Zero escorts.

Beneath a low cloud layer, fighting their own local action, Hall and Smith necessarily split the section to engage two prongs of the Japanese torpedo squadrons. Smith had "only" four Nakajimas to contend with and did well, dropping two in the limited time available. The other pair broke free and launched their torpedoes at Lady Lex.

Meanwhile, Bill Hall had his hands full. When he broke port, he tackled six HIJMS *Shokaku* planes that dropped out of the overcast at 600 feet, making knots for the USS *Lexington*. Hall latched onto the nearest Nakajima and opened up with his forward-firing .50 calibers. He had nearly washed out of Pensacola for poor gunnery, but now he got hits as the B5N penetrated the destroyer screen. Despite a serious fire, the valiant Japanese crew held on long enough to drop its torpedo before crashing off the starboard bow. Meanwhile, two more VS-2 SBDs tied into the other Nakajimas.

The Japanese dive bombing attack was well coordinated with the torpedo planes. As Hall assessed the situation, he was jumped by three Zeroes, two of which stayed with him. Scissoring at low level, Hall took snap shots as the fighters crossed his nose, relying on Moore to protect his tail. In the wavetop melee, Hall claimed two Mitsubishis shot down and Moore claimed a third. As it developed, none of the fighters were destroyed, and they gave as good as they got. One landed a 20mm hit on the starboard side of the cockpit; the explosion nearly severed Hall's right foot. With steel splinters in his leg and the hydraulic system inoperable, Pappy Hall had every reason to disengage. However, despite being unable to place his right foot on the rudder pedal, he compensated with his other foot and the aileron trim tabs. He remained in the fight, continuing to shoot at the slashing Zeroes as long as his .50 caliber ammunition lasted.

As the Japanese attack spent itself, the USS *Lexington* seemed invulnerable. She had taken two bombs and two torpedoes but steamed a steady course into the wind, ready to recover aircraft. Though partly dazed and in serious pain, Hall retained presence of mind to fire a distress flare indicating a need for immediate landing. However, jittery gunners misinterpreted the signal and opened fire. Incredibly, a destroyer's five-inch shell smashed through Hall's cockpit, probably too close to arm the fuse. Despite a severe wound and a damaged aircraft, Hall flew a decent approach, snagging the last arresting wire. He was helped from the cockpit and taken to sick bay while deckhands gaped at the riddled remains of Sail Eight. It was pushed overboard with another severely damaged SBD; six more never returned at all.

Roughly an hour after Hall landed, the USS *Lexington* was stricken by a massive internal explosion. Fuel-fed fires raged out of control, forcing the crew to abandon ship. She sank that evening.

Hall became the USS *Lexington*'s second Medal of Honor recipient, ten weeks after Butch O'Hare. After return to the United States, Hall underwent hospital treatment for his wounds and met his future wife among the attending nurses. Once recovered he was assigned to a training command base at Daytona, Florida, and later he qualified as a landing signal officer. Following release from the Navy, Hall studied for the ministry, serving in Oklahoma and Missouri.

Crew: RM2c Doyle Phillips (G) 7 May; S1c John A. Moore (G) 8 May.

LIEUTENANT JOHN JOSEPH POWERS

13 July 1912–8 May 1942

Born: New York City

Died: Coral Sea

Action: Ship attacks; Battle of the Coral Sea; 7–8 May 1942 (age 29)

Unit: Bombing Squadron 5, USS *Yorktown* (CV-5)

Aircraft: Douglas SBD-3, BuNo unknown

Other decorations: Purple Heart

Lieutenant John Powers stood at the head of Bombing Five's ready room aboard the USS *Yorktown* (CV-5). Dark and slender, the squadron gunnery officer reviewed the attack against the Japanese carrier HIJMS *Shoho* that morning. The light carrier had succumbed to a massive strike from the USS *Yorktown* and *Lexington* (CV-2), and spirits were high. Powers had been one of four VB-5 pilots credited with hits on the HIJMS *Shoho*. But now the realization set in—tomorrow the Americans would face veterans of Pearl Harbor flying from big-deck carriers. The HIJMS *Shoho* had been an execution; the HIJMS *Shokaku* and *Zuikaku* would be a battle. In that knowledge, Powers reviewed dive angle and aimpoint, stressing the basics of dive bombing.

Lt. John J. Powers of Bombing Five, who posthumously received the Medal of Honor for his point-blank attack on the Japanese carrier *Shokaku* in the Coral Sea, 8 May 1942

Powers spoke calmly, with obvious conviction. He concluded saying, "Remember what the Japs did to us at Pearl Harbor. The folks back home are counting on us." He glanced around the gray-painted compartment, taking in the faces of his friends and shipmates. "As for me, I'm going to get a hit tomorrow if I have to lay one right on the flight deck." Bombing Five would remember his words.

Powers had entered the Naval Academy in 1931 and made a name as an intercollegiate boxer. He graduated in 1935, assigned to the battleship USS *West Virginia* (BB-48) for the next two years. That duty was followed by service in the cruiser USS *Augusta* (CA-31), flagship of the Asiatic fleet. She called at Shanghai in 1937 and was twice attacked in error by Chinese forces. Then-Ensign Powers organized an entertainment program with proceeds going toward relief funds for refugees. Subsequently he served aboard the USS *Utah* (BB-31).

"Jojo" Powers had applied for flight training and went to Pensacola in 1940. He had joined Bombing five in January 1941 and by year's end he had more reason to sink Japanese ships than most Americans: both his battlewagons were victims at Pearl Harbor; his cruiser had been hit by Chinese fighting the Japanese.

Powers already was a mature naval officer. As a division leader he took personal interest in the professional education of his men, including the reservists who were in only "for the duration." Before the war, Annapolis men were required to serve two years in surface ships before applying for aviation or submarines. Powers had spent five years in the "blackshoe navy." He took his new pilots on extensive tours of the USS *Yorktown,* explaining the intricacies of engineering, navigation, and even gunnery. He also arranged for them to stand bridge watches—a rarity for aviators, who proclaimed their identity with sporty brown shoes.

Leading his division on 8 May, Powers flew with Radioman Second Class Everett C. Hill as his radioman-gunner. Clouds obscured the Japanese task force, preventing another coordinated air group attack, but Lieutenant Wally Short led Bombing Five down on the nearest carrier, the 20,000-ton HIJMS *Shokaku.* She was ably defended by A6M2 Zeros and heavy flak.

However, Powers's third division would not be deterred. He advocated extreme low release and recovery, placing his faith in the SBD's rugged airframe. As he nosed over to draw a bead on the HIJMS *Shokaku,* one of her fighters scored a telling burst of 7.7 and 20mm fire. Pilot and gunner were wounded and one fuel tank was holed. The high-octane vapor ignited in the slipstream but Powers persisted in his dive, aligning his optical sight with the big carrier's flight deck. Accounts of his wingmen varied, but clearly he held his drop until below 1,000 feet, streaming flames behind his battered Dauntless throughout the dive. Powers hauled the stick back, regaining level flight at only about 200 feet, then was lost from sight as his bomb struck home.

The armor-piercing 1,000-pounder apparently penetrated the flight deck and exploded to starboard, aft of the island. The detonation set off secondary explosions on the flight and hangar decks—a decisive hit. Bombing Five got another hit as well.

Powers crashed in flames close aboard his target. Another USS *Yorktown* SBD also was missing, but the HIJMS *Shokaku* was out of action. The USS *Lexington* was sunk; the *Yorktown* damaged.

Jojo Powers was sorely missed by his squadronmates, but they were extremely proud of him. When the USS *Yorktown* returned to Pearl Harbor Bombing five went ashore, expecting to be relieved as the USS *Saratoga*'s (CV-3) air group was slated to replace "Yorky's" exhausted squadrons. However, during the seventy-two hours allotted to repair the ship's Coral Sea bomb damage, Lieutenant Short's pilots were alerted for redeployment. Something big was in the air, and VB-5 worked round the clock to absorb new SBDs and replacement crews.

On the afternoon of 29 May, Short and company availed themselves of the Ford Island Officers' Club. After working round the clock for two days, they felt entitled. The bartender, overwhelmed by thirsty aviators, retreated in dismay. When he returned with the officer of the day, Short was pouring drinks for his pilots. The three-stripe commander took in the situation—never contemplated in the *Watch Officer's Guide*—and pulled rank. Aside from boisterous behavior, he cited the officers for improper dress: wrinkled, oil-stained khakis, no ties, etc.

The commander braced the junior officers, condemning their appearance and behavior. Wally Short never flinched. When the tirade ended, he evenly replied, "Well, Commander, one of my pilots has just been recommended for a posthumous Medal of Honor. Will that even things up?"

Subsequently VB-5 reboarded the USS *Yorktown* and helped win the Battle of Midway. Short's was the only squadron engaged in the world's first two carrier battles.

The USS *Powers* (DE-528) was commissioned in February 1944, an 1,140-ton Evarts-class destroyer escort sponsored by Powers's mother. The ship was decommissioned in October 1945 and scrapped in 1946. Powers also is memorialized in the Naval Academy's Medal of Honor Rooms program. The room he occupied during his Annapolis days is dedicated with a plaque, as are the rooms of other aviators Joe Bauer, Butch O'Hare, and Bruce Van Voorhis.

Crew: RM2c Everett C. Hill (G).

LIEUTENANT COMMANDER BRUCE AVERY VAN VOORHIS

29 January 1908–6 July 1943

Born: Aberdeen, Washington

Died: Caroline Islands

Action: Bombing mission; Caroline Islands; 6 July 1943 (age 35)

Unit: Patrol Bombing Squadron 102

Aircraft: Consolidated PB4Y-1 BuNo 31992

Other decorations: Purple Heart

The war was over, but Admiral Marc Mitscher still wanted a Medal of Honor for one of his boys. Of the two combat commands Mitscher held in 1942–43, neither produced a medal under his leadership. Jimmy Doolittle received it for the Tokyo raid, launched from then-Captain Mitscher's USS *Hornet* (CV-8), but that was an AAF award. Less than two months later the ship was badly mishandled during the crucial Battle of Midway, and Mitscher felt that his career was ruined. However, he recommended Medals of Honor for all fifteen pilots of Torpedo Squadron Eight, fourteen of whom were killed. It was an outlandish concept, especially since every naval aviator airborne at Midway already had received a Navy Cross. The task force commander, Rear Admiral Raymond Spruance, declined the nomination, noting that two other "torprons" also had been destroyed.

Mitscher's next combat assignment was Commander Aircraft Solomon Islands in 1943. Based on sensitive code breaking, "AirSols" executed the flawless interception of Admiral Isoroku Yamamoto on the anniversary of the Tokyo raid, and Mitscher recommended Medals of Honor for the leading AAF pilots on the mission. However, one of the pilots bragged to a reporter and word leaked out. Admiral William F. Halsey, the South Pacific theater commander, was apoplectic; he canceled the recommendations.

Through most of 1944–45 "Pete" Mitscher commanded the Fast Carrier Task Force, and he justified the confidence shown in him. However, among his thousands of aviators throughout the war, only Commander David McCampbell received the Medal of Honor. Therefore, after Japan's surrender Mitscher pursued the medal for Lieutenant Commander Bruce Van Voorhis.

Van Voorhis's credentials were profound: he was appointed to the Naval

Bruce A. Van Voorhis

Academy from Nevada, and following graduation in 1929, he served in battleships before winning his wings in 1931. Subsequently he returned to battlewagons as an observation pilot.

In 1934 Van Voorhis transferred to carriers, flying scout-bombers from the USS *Ranger* (CV-4) and *Saratoga* (CV-3). However, that idyll was short lived as he became a patrol plane pilot in Panama. In 1938 he returned to carriers, flying from the USS *Enterprise* (CV-6) and *Yorktown* (CV-5). He resumed observation work in 1940, aboard the cruiser USS *Honolulu* (CL-48), before a year and a half of instructing at Pensacola.

In December 1942 Van Voorhis, then a lieutenant commander, assumed command of VP-14, which was redesignated VB-102 with transition to PB4Y Liberators in February 1943. The squadron arrived at Carney Field, Guadalcanal, in April. There Van Voorhis quickly earned a reputation for aggressiveness but in doing so he consolidated many of the most experienced men into his own crew.

From Guadalcanal PB4Y squadrons flew a dozen searches per day, one aircraft in each of twelve sectors. The typical pattern was 700 nautical miles outbound, an 80-mile crossleg, and return. It could amount to twelve or more hours in the air, primarily searching for Japanese fleet units.

According to squadron personnel, Lieutenant Gordon Miller's Liberator drew fire over Kapingamarangi Atoll, southernmost of the Eastern Carolines, on or about 4 July. Japanese aircraft were observed, and Miller evaded into clouds. Reportedly, upon hearing of the event, "the skipper decided to go out for a looksee."

On 6 July Van Voorhis chose Sector Three, which from Guadalcanal was a straight line north-northwest toward Truk Atoll, the major Japanese base in the Carolines.

Van Voorhis and his crew were killed at Hare (Greenwich) Island of

Kapingamarangi Atoll. His citation said in part, "Abandoning all chance of a safe return, he executed six bold, ground-level attacks to demolish the enemy's vital radio station, installations, antiaircraft guns, and to destroy one fighter plane in the air and three on the water." The narrative also asserted that his Liberator was destroyed by its own bombs.

Records of the Greenwich Island Observation Station and 902nd Naval Air Group indicate otherwise. Japanese documents mention some "B-24" attacks in 1943, but despite occasional heavy bombing, evidently little damage was inflicted on "Station PG."

The postwar investigation was conducted by Commander Thomas "Chick" Hayward, a respected aviator who was well acquainted with the Van Voorhis family. With no American witnesses, and apparently no consultation of Japanese records or personnel, the citation relied upon the testimony of Caroline Islanders. Not surprisingly, errors occurred—especially given multiple bombing attacks, the confusion of war, and passage of time. A consensus was reached, and formed the basis of Hayward's text. Only decades later were enemy records compared to the citation.

Japanese and American researchers have concluded that Van Voorhis's plane was downed by the rear gunners of three Mitsubishi F1M floatplanes taking off while he made his low-level approach. The "Petes" had arrived the day before, anticipating their tender's arrival in a day or so. The rear gunners fired only 160 rounds to splash the Liberator into the lagoon.

The PB4Y crew was buried in a common grave, which was uncovered by Hayward. On his recommendation the copilot, Lieutenant (jg) Herschel Oehlert, received a Navy Cross; the rest of the crew received Distinguished Flying Crosses. The Medal of Honor was presented to Van Voorhis's family in 1948; his son became a Navy aircraft mechanic.

The USS *Van Voorhis* (DE-1028) was launched in July 1956. The Courtney-class destroyer escort was decommissioned in 1972.

Van Voorhis Field, NAAS Fallon, Nevada, was dedicated in November 1959. Today NAS Fallon is locale of the Naval Strike Air Warfare Center, training aircrews for the twenty-first-century equivalent of Bruce Van Voorhis's profession.

Crew: Lts. (jg) Herschel A. Oehlert Jr. (CP) and Jack O. Traub (N); ACOM Charles D. Linzmeyer; ACRM Johnny A. Renner; AMM1c George C. Stephens; AOM2c Donald B. Clogston; AMM2c Charles A. Martinelli; AMM2c Henry F. Watson; AMM2c Frederick C. Barker Jr.; and ARM3c Richard W. Roscoe.

LIEUTENANT (JG) NATHAN GREEN GORDON

4 SEPTEMBER 1916–

BORN: Morrilton, Arkansas

ACTION: Combat rescue; Bismarck Sea; 15 February 1944 (age 27)

UNIT: Patrol Squadron 34

AIRCRAFT: Consolidated PBY-5 BuNo 08434 (71) (called *Arkansas Traveler*)

OTHER DECORATIONS: Distinguished Flying Cross(2), Air Medal (6)

The mission had turned to hash. On 11 February 1944 the Fifth Air Force launched eighty-seven heavy and medium bombers against Japanese targets in the Bismarck Sea, but things went wrong from the start. One B-25 crashed on takeoff and seven were shot down in the target area around Kavieng Harbor, New Ireland, as were three A-20s.

Three army planes had made water landings within 1,000 yards of shore, within easy range of enemy artillery. If the crews were to be saved, somebody had to get them out quickly. The nearest air-sea rescue aircraft was orbiting more than 100 miles away, but Lieutenant (jg) Nathan Gordon responded to the call of an A-20 down in Kavieng Harbor. He was already some 400 miles north of his squadron's base at New Guinea but Gordon immediately turned north, escorted by a flight of P-47 Thunderbolts of the 348th Fighter Group. Their original CO, Colonel Neel Kearby, had been the first USAAF fighter pilot awarded the Medal of Honor for a mission four months before.

Gordon knew something about Kavieng, a notoriously well-defended Japanese base. The harbor was almost fully encircled by land with no breakers or seawall. Consequently, waves inside the harbor could reach fifteen feet or more. It was going to be hard on the Catalina—and Gordon's nine-man crew.

About 3,000 yards offshore, the Navy men spotted debris, including dye marker at the reported shootdown site. After dropping smoke markers to

Nathan G. Gordon

gauge the wind, Gordon executed a jarring, full-stall landing between the troughs of the waves but found no sign of the A-20 crew. However, his men reported that the landing had popped rivets; water was entering one of the pontoons. Gordon shoved up the power and took off through the waves, knowing that other Americans were down in the water.

Nate Gordon had attended Columbia (Tennessee) Military Academy, Arkansas Tech, and the University of Arkansas at Fayetteville, graduating in 1939 with a J.D. degree. He returned to his hometown, Morrilton, to practice law but enlisted as a naval aviation cadet in May 1941, receiving his wings in February 1942. Assigned to the globe-trotting Patrol Squadron 34, he flew in the Caribbean and the central and southwest Pacific, including Australia and New Guinea. By January 1944 the "Black Cat" PBYs were based at Samarai Island, near Milne Bay at the east tip of New Guinea. Nocturnal shipping strikes were their stock in trade, and Gordon had damaged a destroyer and sunk a dozen or more barges. However, the Catalinas also performed rescues, operating under the call sign beloved of downed fliers everywhere: Dumbo.

Airborne over Kavieng Harbor, Gordon heard from a B-25 squadron commander operating as rescue coordinator. With another position report, Gordon turned his Catalina to the heading and was rewarded with the sight of a full bomber crew: all six men of a 345th Bomb Group B-25D named *Gremlin's Holiday.* The crew was close enough to shore for the Japanese to launch a boat toward them but it was deterred by strafers.

However, rough seas made it dangerous for the downed fliers to approach the PBY with engines idling. Therefore, Gordon asked his plane captain if the port engine would restart and AMM Wiley Routon answered affirmative—a vital consideration with Japanese small arms and mortar fire beginning to range in. An aircrewman tossed the Army men a line and hauled them up to the portside waist blister.

With the B-25 crew safely aboard, Gordon started the engine and lost no time taking off. The strafing Thunderbolts had suppressed much of the Japanese gunfire, but two "Jugs" now departed, low on fuel. It looked like a good job all round.

Twenty miles outbound, the B-25 leader was back on the radio. Another downed crew had been spotted, even closer to shore. Nonetheless, Gordon repeated the previous evolution, performing a safe landing and shutting down the port engine while three extremely grateful AAF men scrambled aboard. The Catalina cranked up and took off with nearly a full load: a ten-man crew and nine passengers.

By now the last two Thunderbolts had also turned southward. However, again twenty miles outbound Gordon heard from the senior Army officer: a third crew had been spotted closer to shore than the previous two. Gordon did not feel there was time to consult with his crew: he merely asked the P-47s if they could stay, then turned the yoke and headed back to Kavieng.

This approach was worst of all—necessarily over the town with a landing between 600 and 800 yards from shore. The dogged Thunderbolts stretched their fuel and luck, but Japanese resistance was heaviest yet. Nevertheless, the high waves partially hid the PBY from view and no damage was incurred. The final B-25 crew was pulled aboard through the waist hatch and Gordon executed a jarring, pounding takeoff despite an overload consisting of twenty-five men.

Many of the rescued fliers were badly injured or burned, and the PBY crew applied what first aid was possible. With barely enough fuel to show on the gauges, Gordon decided to land at Finschafen, which was 200 miles closer than Samarai and boasted a hospital ship besides. After refueling, the Catalina returned to base, landing after eleven hours flight time that day.

PatRon 34 continued its routine for the next several months before Gordon and his crew were ordered to Brisbane. Gordon received the Medal of Honor and his men received Silver Stars.

Released from active duty in 1945, Gordon resumed his law practice and soon became active in state politics, becoming a cofounder of Arkansas

Young Democrats. In 1946 he was elected lieutenant governor and retained the office for twenty years.

Crew: Ensigns Leu R. Fulmer Jr. (CP), Walter L. Patrick (CP), John A. Kelly (CP); AMM1c Wiley R. Routon Jr. (PC); AMM2c Joseph P. Germeau; AMM3c John Brately; ARM1c Aleck G. Alexander (RO); ARM2c Robert Murch (RO); AOM2c Paul J. Wodnick.

COMMANDER DAVID MCCAMPBELL

16 January 1910–30 June 1996

Born: Bessemer, Alabama

Died: Riviera Beach, Florida

Action: Air combat; Marianas and Philippines; June–October 1944 (age 34)

Unit: Carrier Air Group 15, USS *Essex* (CV-9)

Aircraft: Grumman F6F-3s and F6F-5 BuNo 70143 Minsi III

Other decorations: Navy Cross, Legion of Merit, Silver Star, Distinguished Flying Cross (3), Air Medal

When Commander David McCampbell deployed to combat in the spring of 1944, he felt supremely confident. "We flew so much gunnery that I simply got to the point that I couldn't get any better," he recalled years later. "On my last hop I shot the tow cable off the target sleeve. When I saw my first Zero I knew I would shoot him down, and I did."

Thirty-three more followed over the next five months. McCampbell not only remained the top U.S. Navy fighter ace but also holds the American record for most enemy aircraft shot down in a single tour of duty, during one day of combat, and in one mission. He is also the only two-time American "ace in a day."

McCampbell attended military school with a young Arizonan named Goldwater, then entered Annapolis in 1929. He excelled at aquatics, winning an NCAA regional diving championship. Graduating in the lower half of the class of 1933, he was released from active duty for a year as a budgetary measure.

Upon recall to service McCampbell became a gunfire spotter aboard the new cruiser USS *Portland* (CA-33), including a year in Curtiss SOC floatplanes. Enamored with aviation, he applied for flight training and received his wings of gold in April 1938. For the next two years he learned the fighter trade in VF-4 aboard the USS *Ranger* (CV-4) and cut a wide swath. Said a squadronmate, "Dave and I were asked to leave most of the good restaurants in New York City."

David McCampbell. Leading *Essex*'s Air Group 15, Cdr. David McCampbell shot down seven Japanese aircraft in two sorties on 19 June 1944. He added nine in one mission on 24 October. McCampbell's final score was thiry-four confirmed victories.

McCampbell transferred to the new USS *Wasp* (CV-7) in May 1940 and became the senior landing signal officer. The USS *Wasp* made two Mediterranean runs in early 1942, delivering RAF fighters to Malta, and on one of those trips McCampbell made LSO history. One of the Spitfires lost its belly tank on launch and the Canadian pilot elected to try a landing rather than bail out. His first approach was too fast, and McCampbell waved him off. On the next try the LSO "cut him long," anticipating a touchdown faster than normal. Flight Sergeant Jerry Smith hit the deck, stood on the brakes, and lurched to a halt six paces from the bow. That night the "hookless" pilot received a set of naval aviator wings.

McCampbell remained aboard when the USS *Wasp* deployed to the Pacific and swam away from her when she was sunk by a Japanese submarine in September. The former collegiate diver said, "I always thought that if my ship was sunk I'd do a layout and maybe a one and a half gainer. But when I looked over the side, I held my nose with one hand, myself with the other, and went in like a kid in a pond!"

Promoted to lieutenant commander, McCampbell established VF-15 in September 1943 and "fleeted up" to air group commander in February 1944. Riding the USS *Essex* (CV-9), "Fabled Fifteen" entered combat in May with "warmup" strikes at Marcus and Wake Islands, but in June the Marianas campaign began in earnest. McCampbell's first kill was a Zeke over Saipan on the eleventh, followed by a confirmed and a probable during the next four days.

On 19 June, "The Great Marianas Turkey Shoot," Task Force 58 repelled successive attacks by Japanese land- and carrier-based aircraft. In two sorties McCampbell ran his score from two to nine, splashing five Judy dive bombers in the morning and two Zekes that evening. Fighting fifteen notched sixty-eight and a half victories, a record at the time.

Four months later Air Group 15 was still aboard the USS *Essex,* supporting the Philippine landings. During the Battle of Leyte Gulf—the largest naval engagement of the war—McCampbell led a scramble with the last seven Hellcats aboard the USS *Essex.* The fighter director, Lieutenant Commander John Connolly (a future secretary of the Navy), vectored McCampbell and his wingman, Lieutenant (jg) Roy Rushing, onto a formation of some sixty Japanese Army and Navy fighters. For ninety minutes the two F6Fs harried the aerial armada, making repeated gunnery runs. At the end of the mission, McCampbell claimed nine kills and two probables; Rushing six destroyed and three damaged. McCampbell recovered aboard the USS *Langley* (CVL-27) with barely enough fuel to taxi up the deck. Upon return to the USS *Essex* his plane captain rounded out the scoreboard on *Minsi III,* now sporting thirty rising suns.

McCampbell was accused of ignoring his command duties to chase "meatballs" but the record indicates otherwise. Air Group 15 was credited with destroying more enemy aircraft (318 air, 348 ground) and more shipping (296,500 tons sunk; 500,000 tons damaged) than any other unit in the Fast Carrier Task Force. When Fabled Fifteen completed its deployment in November, McCampbell's tally had increased to thirty-four. Ashore, Major Tommy McGuire had twenty-eight kills; Major Dick Bong thirty-six.

McCampbell remained the only pilot of the Fast Carrier Task Force to receive the Medal of Honor. He also remains the only recipient to command an aircraft carrier, as he conned the USS *Bon Homme Richard* (CV-31) during 1959–60. He retired to Florida in 1964.

"Dashing Dave" (as he called himself) was a chain-smoking, confessed chocaholic who quipped, "If I'd known I was going to live this long, I'd have taken better care of myself." He enjoyed telling of his appearance at a

Thunderbolt reunion, circa 1980: "There weren't any living P-47 Medal of Honor pilots so I was invited. When the emcee introduced me he said, 'Now we come to Dave McCampbell. He's seventy years old, he shot down thirty-four airplanes, he's been married five times—and he still has more torque than a P-47.'"

America's all-time naval fighter ace was honored with the USS *McCampbell* (DDG-85), an *Arleigh Burke* (DDG-51)–class guided-missile destroyer, christened in July 2000.

Navy Aviation Related (5)

Chief Petty Officer John W. Finn; Hawaii; 7 December 1941. On duty at NAS Kaneohe, Finn responded to the Japanese air attack by manning a heavy machine gun. Despite numerous wounds he continued firing and, after treatment of his injuries, he helped arm VP-14 PBYs for search missions.

Lieutenant Richard N. Antrim; Dutch East Indies; April 1942. As a prisoner of the Japanese, Antrim intervened on behalf of another POW being beaten to death and offered to take the balance of the punishment upon himself. Inspired by his example, the 2,700 other allied personnel rallied to Antrim's defense, leading to an improvement in camp conditions.

Lieutenant Milton Ricketts; USS *Yorktown* (CV-5), Coral Sea; 8 May 1942. In command of a repair party, Ricketts was blown into a bulkhead by a bomb explosion that killed or stunned all his men. Despite a mortal injury, he regained his feet and opened a fire main by himself before collapsing at his station.

Lieutenant Commander Joseph T. O'Callahan and Lieutenant (jg) Donald A. Gary; USS *Franklin* (CV-13), off Japan, 19 March 1945. A Catholic chaplain, O'Callahan was a significant leader in efforts to save the ship from severe damage. He led rescue parties, directed salvage operations and fire fighting, and ministered to the wounded and dying throughout the ordeal. As an engineering officer, Gary led rescue teams that freed hundreds of sailors from trapped spaces where otherwise they may have died.

5

THE KOREAN WAR

AIR FORCE: 4
NAVY: 2

TOTAL: 6

At the end of World War II, Korea was divided along the 38th Parallel with conflicting ideologies on either side. The north was backed by China and the Soviet Union, whereas the south possessed a nominally democratic government recognized by the United States and most western powers. However, the Stalinist regime in Pyongyang needed only five years to assemble, train, and indoctrinate a powerful army focused upon a single-minded goal: to "reunify" the nation under communist rule.

The Korean "police action" lasted three years, producing some 34,000 American fatalities to preserve the prewar division of the peninsula. From the night of 25 June 1950, when North Korean troops swarmed southward, to the morning of 27 July 1953, when the armistice took effect, 131 Medals of Honor were awarded, including six for airmen: four Air Force and two Navy. Five of the six aviation medals were posthumous, including all four Air Force men—a fatality rate far beyond any other war.

Korea was a tactical air war, largely because North Korea possessed no significant industry and because Communist China enjoyed immunity from allied attack. Consequently, though four of the six Medal of Honor recipients flew fighters, only one engaged in aerial combat. The aircraft types included three World War II "retreads": the F-51 Mustang, B-26 (originally

A-26) Invader, and F4U Corsair. However, the Korean War also was notable for introduction of the helicopter on a routine basis. The Army Air Force had briefly employed Sikorski R-4s in Burma during World War II, but in Korea the "chopper" became a proven, viable system. Both of the Navy actions involved Sikorski HO3S "eggbeaters," though only one of the "rotorheads" was awarded the Medal of Honor.

Like the Mustang, Invader, and Corsair, their pilots also were mostly combat veterans. All four Air Force recipients and one Navy pilot had flown in World War II, though two had not been sent to combat. Majors George Davis and Charles Loring were fighter pilots in both wars; Major Lou Sebille had flown Martin B-26s in Europe and Captain John Walmsley had been a wartime instructor.

Lieutenant (jg) John Koelsch had been a fixed-wing pilot in World War II but transitioned to helicopters between the wars. Lieutenant (jg) Tom Hudner was a fighter pilot before and after Korea.

Perhaps no other example so well illustrates the essential nature of the Korean War: with a mortality rate of 83 percent among the aviation Medals of Honor, the only victory was in surviving.

AIR FORCE (4)

MAJOR LOUIS JOSEPH SEBILLE

21 NOVEMBER 1915–5 AUGUST 1950

BORN: Harbor Beach, Michigan

DIED: Near H'amchang, South Korea

ACTION: Ground attack; near H'amchang, South Korea; 5 August 1950 (age 34)

UNIT: 67th Fighter-Bomber Squadron, 18th Fighter-Bomber Wing, 5th Air Force

AIRCRAFT: North American F-51D 44-74394

OTHER DECORATIONS: Distinguished Flying Cross (2), Air Medal (12), Purple Heart

The Korean War was six weeks old—and going badly for the South Koreans and their American allies. The North Korean army, supported by massive Soviet and Chinese assistance, had launched a blitzkrieg across the 38th Parallel on 25 June, driving the ill-prepared, poorly trained allies southward. If

Louis J. Sebille

not for tactical airpower, the U.S. and R.O.K. forces would have faced an even greater disaster.

With friendly ground forces hemmed into the shrinking Pusan Pocket, American airmen flew multiple sorties every day, trying to dent the communist juggernaut. Even with outright air supremacy it was a rugged task, as the reds rolled southward behind T-34 tanks and powerful artillery.

On 5 August, Major Louis Sebille led a flight of four F-51D Mustangs off Taegu Airfield. Like himself, the aircraft were World War II "retreads." He had led the 67th Fighter-Bomber Squadron through a complex period since November 1948, transitioning to F-80 Shooting Stars and back to Mustangs. Though the Lockheed jets were substantially faster than the "'stangs," they lacked the range and loiter time of the '51s and could not operate from rough fields. With the rest of the 18th Fighter-Bomber Group at Clark Field in the Philippines, the 67th had wrestled with absorbing "new" planes and pilots while deploying to Japan. But the CO was equal to the task.

Sebille had entered pilot training in January 1942, already "over the hill" at twenty-six. However, the need was such that his age was not held against him, and he became an accomplished airman. Lou Sebille did most things well, including a stint as an entertainer following graduation from Wayne State College in Detroit. Assigned to medium bombers, he mastered the tricky Martin B-26 and went to Britain with the 450th Squadron, 322nd Bomb Group, which arrived in January 1943. The 322nd was the original Marauder unit in the United Kingdom and flew its first mission on 14 May, a low-level attack on a Dutch electrical plant. Opposition was heavy with one plane lost and ten damaged, but Sebille had logged his first sortie. Three days later he was off the schedule when a restrike went after the same target. It was catastrophic: one plane aborted; none of the others returned.

Sebille survived sixty-eight missions and 245 combat hours. By the end of his tour in March 1945 he was a major with considerable leadership experience as well as two DFCs and twelve Air Medals.

Though he left active duty in late 1945, Sebille was recalled in July 1946. He worked at Headquarters Ninth Air Force and attended the Air Tactical School. Subsequently he became a fighter transition instructor and assumed command of the 18th Fighter Bomber Group's 67th Squadron in the Philippines. In July 1950 he deployed the squadron to Ashiya, Kyushu, Japan, flying long-range tactical support missions across the 120-mile wide Korean Strait.

On the afternoon of 5 August, Sebille checked in with the Joint Operations Center at Taegu, about seventy miles north of Pusan. His wingman had aborted but Sebille reported his flight's remaining ordnance loadout of 500-pound bombs plus .50 caliber and rockets. The CO's flight was handed off to a "Mosquito," an airborne controller in an AT-6 orbiting near H'amchang to the north. The FAC had spotted communist troops crossing the Naktong River, headed southward.

Upon locating the grid coordinates, Sebille identified the targets and led his Mustangs in a dive bombing attack. He was first to roll in, but upon recovering from his dive, he found that he was burdened with "hung ordnance." One of his 500-pound bombs was stuck on the rack. Captain Martin Johnson and Lieutenant Charles Morehouse safely dropped their bombs and joined Sebille in rocket and strafing runs against troops and vehicles partially hidden beneath the trees.

On a subsequent pass Sebille's Mustang was tagged by ground fire and pulled off, streaming glycol from the punctured coolant system. Captain Johnson eased alongside, confirmed the damage, and radioed the suggestion that Sebille turn for K-2, as he could possibly stretch the coolant long enough to reach Taegu, a few miles east. At worst, the CO could reach the allied lines and bail out or perhaps manage a crash landing.

As Johnson related it, Sebille called, "I'll never be able to make it back. I'm going back and get that bastard." He turned his faltering fighter, drew a bead on a truck, and made a thirty-degree strafing run, firing all the way down. He continued shooting until he dived into the target, exploding on impact.

Johnson and Morehouse felt that Sebille probably had been mortally wounded but did not say so. In any case, the CO's attitude clearly was "above and beyond," even though Fifth Air Force balked at the sentiment. Lieutenant Don Bolt, the squadron's assistant awards officer, felt so strongly that he overcame initial reluctance from headquarters and got the Medal of Honor citation forwarded to Washington.

Loss of a dedicated commander was bad enough, but within minutes the 67th Squadron also lost its operations officer, Captain Robert Howells.

One year later the Air Force chief of staff, General Hoyt Vandenberg, presented the Medal of Honor to Sebille's widow and son at March Air Force Base, California. In sublime understatement the citation referred to Sebille's "selfless devotion to duty." Shortly afterward, Captain Johnson concluded, "We had lost a remarkable friend, a fine commander, and a very brave man."

On 2 October 1950, Lieutenant Don Bolt was shot down, captured, and executed by the North Koreans.

CAPTAIN JOHN SPRINGER WALMSLEY JR.

7 January 1920–14 September 1951

Born: Baltimore, Maryland

Died: Near Yangdok, North Korea

Action: Night bombing mission; near Yangdok, North Korea; 14 September 1951 (age 31)

Unit: 8th Bomb Squadron, 3rd Bomb Wing, 5th Air Force

Aircraft: Douglas B-26C 44-34314 (Z) "Skillful 13"

Other decorations: Distinguished Flying Cross, Air Medal (2), Purple Heart

Kunsan was in the night-flying business. "K-8" was home of the Third Bomb Wing, which, with affiliated units, worked at shutting down communist nocturnal logistics. Both sides were committed, innovative, and industrious. Neither completely solved its problem, but the advantage lay with the Chinese and North Koreans, who benefited from huge manpower pools and any adverse weather.

The Third Wing's three squadrons flew Douglas B-26 Invaders, not to be confused with "Martin's Maligned Madam" of World War II fame. The Martin Marauder was long gone from the inventory, but the Douglas (originally A-26) soldiered on. With twin Pratt and Whitney engines, a robust airframe, and an awesome ordnance loadout, it was well adapted to the night intruder role.

In August 1951, fourteen months into the war, the Far East Air Force began

Operation Strangle, named for the similar campaign conducted in the Mediterranean during 1943–44. The goal was identical: to choke off enemy supply lines and impede their war effort by denying logistic support.

John S. Walmsley Jr.

Among the leading pilots of Lieutenant Colonel Edward L. Wilson's Eighth Bomb (Night Interdiction) Squadron was Captain John Walmsley. He had served mainly as an instructor in World War II, then flew bombers in Japan from 1946 to 1949. He attended the Air Tactical School, graduating in July 1949, eleven months before the start of the Korean War.

Cheerful and popular, Jack Walmsley had helped initiate the latest tactic in night attack. Although 260-pound fragmentation bombs and .50 caliber gunfire could rip a truck to pieces, the trick was first to find the elusive enemy transport, which devoutly did not wish to be found. Consequently, the Third Wing installed former U.S. Navy carbon arclights beneath the Invaders' wings. The 80 million candlepower lights had been mounted on blimps during the U-boat campaign of 1943–44 and promised a huge increase in night vision along the western supply routes of North Korea. The lights were so intense that they could only be illuminated for less than one minute at a time.

Fliers also noted, however, that the lights would remove any doubt of their own position for enemy gunners. The supply routes were heavily defended with automatic weapons: 12.7, 20, and 40mm. It was bad enough flying against alerted, capable defenders; doing so at night, in mountainous terrain, was off the scale. Yet the aircrews stuck at it, frequently flying fifteen missions per month, each lasting four hours or more. Walmsley had survived more than twenty nerve-wrenching missions en route to a complete tour of fifty-five or sixty.

On the night of 12 September, Walmsley spotted a communist truck convoy and attacked with 500-pound bombs. With the lead trucks disabled, he lit up the carbon light and made repeat passes over the immobile vehicles. It was a turkey shoot: between "frags" and gunfire he destroyed or damaged at least sixteen trucks. There was also a residual benefit: from the nose of the plane the bombardier saw Chinese drivers, apparently blinded by the immense light output, run off the road, ram into trees, or collide with each other.

Two nights later Walmsley was again trolling for trucks in the night sky. Unexpectedly he found a locomotive near Yangdok, nearly 100 miles into North Korea. He attacked and though he damaged the engine, he was out of bombs and ammunition. Calling in another Kunsan B-26, Walmsley offered to provide illumination while the newcomer attacked. Despite taking battle damage from ground fire, Walmsley made three passes over the target. Each time the brilliant light provided a solid aim point for the antiaircraft gunners, who scored repeatedly. Yet still Walmsley persisted, not only illuminating the target for his partner but drawing most of the heavy ack-ack onto himself.

On the third pass his wings streamed fuel which ignited. Blazing low across the dark void, Walmsley's Invader fought to maintain altitude. After flying approximately two miles it smashed into the ground. Walmsley was killed with his bombardier and photographer, but his gunner, badly injured, was captured and survived the war.

Four weeks later the Third Wing took the lights off its Invaders. The penalties offset the advantage: more weight, increased drag, greater fuel consumption, shorter range and endurance.

Walmsley's Medal of Honor was presented to his widow at Bolling Air Force Base, D.C., on 12 June 1954. His was the second medal for the squadron and the wing: Raymond Wilkins had received a posthumous award for his Rabaul mission in November 1943.

Crew: 2Lt. William D. Mulkins (B-N); Capt. Philip W. Browning (photo); MSgt. George Moror (G).

MAJOR GEORGE ANDREW DAVIS JR.

1 DECEMBER 1920–10 FEBRUARY 1952

BORN: Dublin, Texas

DIED: North Korea

ACTION: Air combat; North Korea; October 1951–February 1952 (age 31)

UNIT: 334th Fighter Squadron, 4th Fighter Wing

AIRCRAFT: North American F-86E 51-2752

OTHER DECORATIONS: Silver Star (3), Distinguished Flying Cross (4), Air Medal (10), Purple Heart

Though not well known to the public, George Davis remains one of the finest fighter pilots the United States ever produced. After nearly a year of training as an army aviation cadet, he pinned on his second lieutenant's gold bars and silver wings in February 1943. That August he joined the 348th Fighter Group with 314 hours total time, flying Republic P-47 Thunderbolts under Colonel Neel Kearby, who set an example for his pilots, including the Medal of Honor. (See World War II, Army Air Force.)

Davis's first war brought him success and a taste for combat. Flying with the New Guinea–based Fifth Air Force, the 348th introduced the Thunderbolt to the Southwest Pacific Theater. From December 1943 to December 1944 Davis scored seven aerial victories, including five during a two-week period in the Philippines. He departed the group in April 1945 as a captain, having logged 705 hours in 266 missions.

When he began his second war in October 1951 Davis had more than 2,200 hours of first pilot time, most in fighters. He set a fast pace in the fast company of the MiG killers. His first fight in MiG Alley resulted in a probable on 4 November; thereafter he returned with kills every time he made a claim. Skilled, confident, and aggressive, Davis scored in multiples when doubles were rare.

Davis became America's fifth jet ace on 30 November by dropping three Tu-2 bombers and a MiG-15 in one sortie, a feat unequalled throughout the war.

In June the Air Force had issued a policy ostensibly requiring jet aces to be returned stateside to impart their knowledge—and promote the Air Force.

George A. Davis Jr.

Davis would have none of it. Like most of the Sabre tigers, he preferred to remain in combat and exerted "command influence" from the bottom up. Consequently, FEAF was permitted to keep those aces who had not completed their tours. Davis was happy: he considered fighter piloting "the best profession in the world."

Doris Davis did not share her husband's enthusiasm.

Two weeks later Davis flamed two MiGs in the morning and another brace that afternoon. He had become a double ace in merely seventeen days—the next best record was fifty-one days—and at year's end he had twelve kills when nobody else claimed more than six. By early February 1952 Davis was barely halfway through his tour but he was averaging one kill every four or five takeoffs.

On 10 February, Davis led eighteen Sabres of the 334th Squadron off Kimpo Airfield, screening F-84s attacking rail targets near Kunu-ri. En route his wingman and element leader aborted, but Davis continued with his number four, Lieutenant W. W. "Skosh" Littlefield. Patrolling on the south side of the river at 38,000 feet, Davis spotted contrails to the northwest and took Littlefield to investigate. They found three flights of MiGs southbound.

Unconcerned about the odds of two against twelve, Davis used his altitude advantage. Attacking from five o'clock high, he closed on the last MiG in the third flight. Once in range, the Sabre ace opened fire and the batwinged jet fell away, smoking.

Davis pulled off to the right, using his energy to pitch up into a vertical reverse. While repositioning, he overshot the two trailing flights and went for the leading four MiGs, now slightly below 30,000 feet. Still aggressive, Davis pressed ahead, ignoring the seven bandits behind him. He hammered the last MiG in the formation, which also went down.

Still hungry, Davis pressed his position—and his luck. He selected a third target when the trailing Chinese pilots opened fire. Comrade Zhang Jihui of the 12th Division, People's Liberation Army Air Force, fired on the Sabre, supported by his wingman, Comrade Xien Ziyu. Zhang Jihui (also spelled Chang Chi-Wei) was credited with the victory, one of at least four attributed to him.

Littlefield saw Davis's landing gear extend—evidence of hydraulic failure. Then the crippled F-86 rolled inverted and pulled through into a split-S. It plummeted out of control with Littlefield gallantly trying to cover his leader from continued attack. He traded gunfire with several MiGs, then saw Davis's jet strike the ground thirty miles south of the Yalu.

Heartsick, Skosh Littlefield headed south.

Well above the contrail level, perhaps the shade of Neel Kearby chided his star pupil for committing the same lapse that ended the Thunderbolt ace's career eight years previously.

Doris Davis was understandably grieved at her loss, but unlike many military widows she was vocal about it. She was quoted as saying, "If I could feel that he lost his life for some good reason, I could feel better about it." The Air Force began seeking ways to alleviate the situation.

Sensitive to the PR aspects, Davis's Medal of Honor citation credited him with protecting F-84s that might have been attacked by the dozen MiGs. However, there was a strong Sabre formation in the area for the specific purpose of securing that airspace for the fighter-bombers.

Meanwhile, even in death, Davis retained a lofty position among the MiG killers. When the fighting ended in July 1953, he still ranked fourth among the 800 F-86 pilots who flew counterair missions. By then two squadronmates from the 334th edged past him: Jim Jabara and Manuel Fernandez with fifteen and fourteen and a half, respectively. One of only seven American aces in each of two wars, Davis destroyed twenty-one enemy aircraft.

Davis received a posthumous promotion to lieutenant colonel in April 1953, and thirteen months later Air Force Chief of Staff Nathan F. Twining presented the Medal of Honor to Mrs. Davis at Reese Air Force Base, Texas.

Major William Whisner, another of the two-war aces, said, "George Davis was the best fighter pilot I ever knew. The only thing he didn't have was concern for his own life."

MAJOR CHARLES JOSEPH LORING JR.

2 October 1918–22 November 1952

Born: Portland, Maine

Died: Near Kunhwa, North Korea

Action: Ground attack; near Kunhwa, North Korea; 22 November 1952 (age 34)

Unit: 80th Fighter-Bomber Squadron, 8th Fighter-Bomber Wing, 5th Air Force

Aircraft: Lockheed F-80C 49-1830

Other decorations: Distinguished Flying Cross, Air Medal (12), Purple Heart (2)

It was Major Charles Loring's second war, but there were nearly as many similarities as differences. Now he flew Lockheed F-80 Shooting Stars instead of Republic P-47 Thunderbolts, and the locale was Korea rather than northwest Europe. But the job was the same—fighter-bomber operations against a determined, well-organized enemy. Communist Chinese supply lines were vulnerable to daylight airpower, but like their Nazi counterparts eight years previously, they had learned how to exact a toll from their aerial tormentors.

For the previous five weeks U.S. and South Korean forces had waged a relentless battle for the mountainous terrain, which often changed hands. Operation Showdown focused on two promontories, Triangle Hill and Sniper Ridge, both northeast of Kunhwa, some twenty miles north of the 38th Parallel. Enemy artillery was particularly dangerous to allied forces, and Fifth Air Force fighter-bombers regarded it as a priority target. Because the artillery was valuable to the communists, it was defended accordingly. The commanding general of the Second Infantry Division knew the value of tactical airpower, and he appreciated the risks the fliers took in ground attack by noting, "It takes real guts to go in and do that job."

Leading his flight of Shooting Stars, Loring sized up the situation. He was an old hand now, having flown fifty missions in Korea—nearly as many as he had completed in Europe. As a thirty-one-year-old, two-war pilot, he was typical of many of the professionals flying in Korea. He had enlisted in the Army Air Force in March 1942 and began pilot training in May. Seven months later he was on his way to the Caribbean, flying P-39s and P-40s before returning to the United States for transition to the "Jug." He went to Europe in March 1944, where, flying P-47s with the 36th Fighter Group of the Ninth Air Force, he logged fifty-five missions before his Thunderbolt was hit by flak while strafing Belgian targets on Christmas Eve 1944. Loring was captured and remained a POW until VE-Day.

Charles J. Loring Jr.

Upon return to the United States, Loring was promoted to captain and held various staff assignments while attending Army and Air Force schools through 1949. He was out of the cockpit most of that time, but in May 1952 he entered his second war, flying F-80s with the 8th Fighter-Bomber Group at K-13 on Korea's west coast. He provided theater checkout for new pilots while flying with the group's 36th and 80th Squadrons, and he was promoted to major in September, serving as the 36th's operations officer.

That morning in late November 1952, Loring checked in with an airborne forward air controller. The AT-6 "Mosquito" pilot provided a map reference for enemy artillery that had pinned down friendly forces near Sniper Ridge. As usual, the artillery was ringed by automatic weapons for air defense.

Loring checked his map, identified the position, and prepared for a dive bombing attack. His jet was spotted almost immediately, and AA fire came up in volume. By now there were plenty of seven- and eight-level gunners in the Communist Chinese forces.

Loring's Shooting Star nosed over and his wingmen noted that he took several hits. Rather than abort the attack—the main line of resistance was not far south—Loring pressed his run. At roughly 4,000 feet he pulled off his initial dive heading about forty-five degrees in what appeared to be an intentional, controlled maneuver, and lined up the enemy batteries. Evidently he made no radio calls indicating he had been wounded. Instead, he tracked straight down the "chute" he had selected. The other pilots watched awestruck as their leader's F-80 impacted into the enemy guns, ending the threat to friendly troops at the cost of his own life.

The Medal of Honor citation said, "Major Loring's noble spirit, superlative courage, and conspicuous self-sacrifice in inflicting maximum damage on the enemy exemplified valor of the highest degree and his actions were in keeping with the finest traditions of the U.S. Air Force."

Loring's widow received the medal from President Eisenhower on 5 May 1954. As a further memorial, Loring Air Force Base was named in his home state.

NAVY (2)

LIEUTENANT (JG) THOMAS JEROME HUDNER

31 AUGUST 1924–

BORN: Fall River, Massachusetts

ACTION: Attempted rescue; North Korea; 4 December 1950 (age 26)

UNIT: Fighter Squadron 32, Air Group Three, USS *Leyte* (CV-32)

AIRCRAFT: Vought F4U-4 BuNo 82050 (K-205)

For American airmen flying in Korea during late 1950, the news was as bad as the weather. In late November at least 120,000 Chinese troops swarmed south, shoving back 15,000 Americans of the First Marine Division and Seventh Infantry Division. Conditions could hardly have been worse, with temperatures dropping as low as −35 degrees Fahrenheit. In such extremes, guns could fail to fire, rockets became erratic, and even napalm did not always burn. Still, with most Air Force units forced back to Japan, on-call tactical airpower was the province of carrier aviation; this day was no different.

Shadows were already lengthening as four Corsairs of Fighter Squadron 32 swept the barren, snow-covered terrain fifty miles inland, west of the Chosin Reservoir. Lieutenant Commander Richard Cevoli's division had launched from the USS *Leyte* (CV-32) to provide much-needed support to the marines fighting their way southward, and the Chinese were alert to the aerial threat; the F4Us drew fire while flying up the valley to the briefed area.

Cevoli had barely assigned targets when his section leader reported battle damage. Ensign Jesse Brown, a Mississippian, would have to force land. His wingman was Lieutenant (jg) Tom Hudner, a Yankee from Massachusetts.

Thomas J. Hudner

Quickly, Cevoli spotted a clearing near the reservoir and directed Brown toward it. Brown managed a crash landing on the slope but was trapped in his plane owing to a buckled fuselage. Worse yet, smoke from inside the cowling indicated there was fire that could engulf the cockpit.

Lieutenant (jg) William Koenig, Cevoli's wingman, climbed to make a mayday call but the news was discouraging. With a helicopter at least thirty minutes away, Tom Hudner made a tough choice: he called Cevoli and announced his intention to make a belly landing near Brown's Corsair. There was no discussion; somebody radioed, "Good luck, Tom," as Hudner set up his approach.

Tom Hudner was a "trade school" product, a member of the Annapolis class of 1947. Originally a communications officer, he won his wings in the summer of 1949 and joined VF-32 October. The USS *Leyte* deployed for a Mediterranean cruise in May 1950, and by early August she was in port at Beirut when the USS *Midway* (CV-41) arrived to assume the duty in Sixth Fleet. "Leading Leyte" was badly needed off Korea: she was rated combat ready and there were too few carriers in Task Force 77. She steamed 20,000 miles to Norfolk, Panama, Hawaii, and Japan to arrive off Korea. The first strikes were flown sixty days after leaving Beirut.

In his 408 hours of Corsair time, Hudner had mastered the art of landing an F4U on a straight-deck carrier. But landing gear-up on a snow-covered slope at 6,000 feet elevation was a one-time evolution—there was no way to practice it. However, he executed a safe "belly flop" only fifty yards from Brown's plane, scrambled out, and ran to his friend's assistance.

Brown was in pain but mainly suffered from the intense cold; the threat of burning was an unnecessary subject. Hudner tried piling snow into the cowling but it had no apparent effect, as magnesium components fed the flames.

Returning to the buckled cockpit, Hudner gave Brown a woolen watch cap and wrapped a scarf around his frozen hands. Throughout the ordeal, Hudner was impressed with his friend's composure.

Forty-five minutes after Brown's landing, a Sikorski HO3S arrived from Hagaru-ri, flown by First Lieutenant Charles Ward of Marine Observation Squadron Six. The helo was marginal at that altitude, forcing Ward to leave his crewman behind, but the marine was willing to try a rescue. Said Hudner, "He responded to a call for help for a downed pilot he didn't know despite the fact that another pilot from his squadron had been killed in a similar rescue mission only a few days before."

Hudner and Ward conferred, sorting their limited options. Ward brought a small fire extinguisher and an axe, neither of which were helpful. One of Brown's legs was pinned in the wreckage, and an effort to free him proved painfully futile; Brown asked them to stop. Finally they were forced into a bitter decision: running out of daylight with their top cover departed low on fuel and enemy forces in the area, they had to leave.

Again Hudner climbed the fuselage to speak with his friend. Apparently lapsing in and out of shock, Brown remained eerily calm and composed, speaking of his wife and how much he loved her. Increasingly Brown failed to respond, so when Hudner told him they were going for more help, he didn't know whether Brown heard him or not.

Ward took off from the snowy slope and managed a return through the mountains to Hagaru-ri, where Ward reported to his superiors. Next they flew to Koto-ri, fifteen miles farther down the valley, where they stayed for the night in a small tent with eight marines, with Chinese troops in the vicinity. Ward flew to Wonsan the next day, with Hudner rejoining VF-32 on 7 December.

The USS *Leyte* departed Korean waters in January 1951, returning to the Mediterranean. Meanwhile, the *Leyte*'s Captain Thomas Sisson recommended Hudner for the Medal of Honor, which was presented by President Truman on 13 April 1951. Of the six carrier aviators ever awarded the medal for combat, Hudner remains the only one honored for attempting to save the life of a shipmate.

Tom Hudner continued flying fighters, including Vought's sensational F8U Crusader, and logged an Air Force exchange tour. He commanded a training squadron and was executive officer of the USS *Kitty Hawk* (CVA-63). When he retired as a captain in 1973, he had logged 4,120 hours and 243 carrier landings. Subsequently he entered a second career administering veterans' affairs in his native Massachusetts.

Forty years after the Korean War, Hudner met with marines who had survived the "Frozen Chosin." He said, "Every night they prayed that daylight would bring good weather so the planes would come to help offset the eight to one odds they were fighting against. 'Gullwings in sight' meant Navy and Marine close air support was inbound, giving them new hope every day." Hudner attended commissioning of the USS *Jesse L. Brown* (DE-1089) in March 1972.

LIEUTENANT (JG) JOHN KELVIN KOELSCH

22 December 1923–16 October 1951

Born: London, England

Died: Chiang-Song, North Korea

Action: Attempted rescue; North Korea; 3 July 1951 (age 27)

Unit: Helicopter Squadron One

Aircraft: Sikorski HO3S-1 BuNo 122715 (UP 34)

In *The Bridges at Toko-Ri,* James Michener's Korean War novel, a beleaguered task force commander tries to persuade a cynical aviator to remain in the Navy. "Whatever progress this world has made has always been because of the efforts and sacrifice of the few," Rear Admiral George Tarrant tells Lieutenant Harry Brubaker.

John Koelsch was one of the few.

Born in London, where his father headed the National City Bank office, Johnny Koelsch was primed for success. He entered Princeton University in 1941 but his higher education was cut short by the war. He left the Ivy League

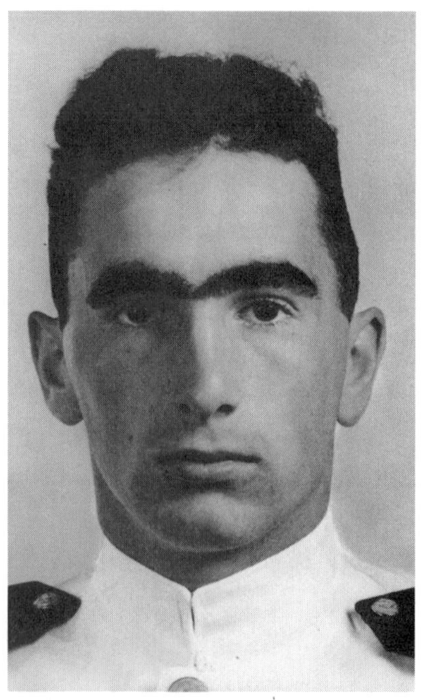
John K. Koelsch

to become a naval aviation cadet and received his gold wings and ensign's bar in November 1944, still not twenty-one. He was assigned to torpedo planes and proceeded through operational training with a fleet squadron but the war ended before he reached combat. Subsequently he made two deployments in the USS *Leyte* (CV-32).

Remaining on active duty, Koelsch returned to Princeton in 1948 and graduated in February 1949. Later that year he was designated a helicopter pilot flying Sikorski HO3S machines.

The '3S was the guardian angel of carrier aviators. It had entered service in 1946, immediately valued for its rescue capability. Only ninety-one were procured but every aircraft carrier deploying to Korea embarked at least one chopper. Though nominally a four-place machine, it typically flew with a pilot and crew chief who doubled as rescue swimmer.

Koelsch turned his considerable talent to improving means of air-sea rescue. Quiet and reflective, he invented a floating sling that simplified the task of hoisting downed aviators from the water, and he experimented with methods of improving helicopter performance in cold weather. Both projects paid dividends downstream.

When the Korean War broke out in 1950, Koelsch volunteered for sea duty. By then he was senior enough to lead a detachment bound for West-Pac. He willed one of his brothers "one case of excellent whiskey" and sailed as officer in charge of the helo "det" in the USS *Princeton* (CV-37) at year's end. "Sweep P" returned from combat in June 1951, but Koelsch immediately volunteered for a second cruise. In the words of a shipmate, he shunned the relatively easy life at NAS Miramar "because his conscience would not permit him to do so."

Koelsch deployed again in October and was scheduled for rotation home after a six-month tour. However, in April he decided to extend his second combat cruise. He was assigned to an LST in Wonsan Harbor, joined by his aircrewman, Aviation Machinist Mate Third Class George M. Neal, who shared the pilot's sense of duty.

On the evening of 3 July 1951, the "scow" at Wonsan received word of an aviator down twelve miles west of Kosong, thirty-five miles southward on Korea's east coast. In less than ten minutes Koelsch and Neal were on their way, chugging inland at eighty knots. Though Koelsch was assigned a fighter escort, the ResCAP could provide no help owing to heavy clouds.

Inbound, Koelsch received a radio briefing on a Marine Corsair that had crashed in a mountain valley. Despite the terrain, approaching darkness, and reduced visibility, Koelsch decided to attempt a rescue.

On the ground, Captain James V. Wilkins heard the chopper's clattering beat. He had been burned in the crash and hardly expected the helo pilot to continue an approach under adverse conditions, as communist troops in the area also were alerted by the noise and began shooting.

The Sikorski emerged from the gloom and made a pass to locate the downed marine. Wilkins later said, "Then, by the lord, he made another turn back into the valley a second time. It was the greatest display of guts I've ever seen." With his man in sight, Koelsch eased into a hover.

While Neal hoisted Wilkins aboard, enemy gunners opened fire again. The engine was hit and the chopper crashed, inverted. All three Americans scrambled from the scene, beginning an incredible nine-day escape and evasion exercise. They remained in the area three days until enemy patrolling became too risky.

The trio reached the coast in seven days by moving only at night. On the ninth day, with no food and little water, they slumped exhausted in a bombed-out farmhouse. That night communist soldiers found them. The fliers were paraded through town with angry villagers shouting threats and throwing objects. Through it all, Koelsch kept drawing attention to Wilkins's injuries. Two guards took Wilkins away; he never saw Koelsch again.

The two Navy men were delivered to a forsaken outpost called Camp Number One near Chiang-Song, North Korea. Subsequently Neal was separated from Koelsch, as officers and noncoms were held in different compounds. Little more was known until after the armistice in July 1953.

On 14 August 1953 the Navy notified his family that Johnny Koelsch had died in captivity. As more former prisoners emerged from communist camps, an inspiring story took shape. John Koelsch, though malnourished and suffering dysentery, consistently refused to cooperate with the camp's extortionists. He set an example that, in the words of his Medal of Honor citation, "inspired his fellow prisoners by his fortitude and consideration for others." Subsequently his insistence on providing only name, rank, and serial number helped establish the American code of conduct for future POWs.

The secretary of the Navy presented the Medal of Honor to Koelsch's family at the Pentagon on 3 August 1955. Koelsch was the first helicopter pilot awarded the Medal of Honor, and in 1965 a Garcia-class frigate (FF-1049) was christened in his name. The ship was operated by the Pakistani Navy as PNS *Siggat* from 1989 to 1993 and was sold for scrap in 1995.

Crew: AMM3c George M. Neal.

6

THE VIETNAM WAR

AIR FORCE: 10
ARMY: 6
NAVY: 2
MARINES: 1

TOTAL: 19

In presenting one of some 240 Medals of Honor awarded for the Vietnam War, President Lyndon Johnson said, "These men are conducting the most careful and the most self-limited air war in history. They are trying to apply the maximum amount of pressure with the minimum amount of danger to our own people."

That was a lie. Hundreds of U.S. airmen died or were condemned to years of prison because of the Johnson administration's treacherous rules of engagement—policies that favored the enemy at nearly every turn. Behind closed doors of the Oval Office, Johnson swaggered, "They can't bomb an outhouse without my say-so." One of those aviators was Commander Jim Stockdale, who later noted, "An entire generation of Americans was left holding the bag."

For accounting purposes the Department of Defense lists the Vietnam era from 1961 to 1975, but most of the major events—and nearly all the American casualties—occurred between August 1964 and January 1973. At the end of that time the nation was bitterly divided along political and cultural fault lines; the armed forces were worn out, embittered, and disillusioned. Billions of dollars and 58,000 lives had been expended to no purpose.

Though undeniably a military and geopolitical defeat, the Vietnam "conflict" also was undeniably a self-inflicted wound. Begun with what now appears hopelessly naïve optimism and surging enthusiasm, the U.S. effort in Southeast Asia was based on the premise that communist expansion had to be contained. When French Indochina was partitioned in 1954, the communist north and the nominally democratic south faced one another across the poorly named "demilitarized zone." Other nations in the region—notably Laos and Cambodia—also were of concern to the nation builders in Washington. President John F. Kennedy's inaugural commitment "to bear any burden" proved ironically apt, especially during the administration of Johnson, his successor, who used two naval incidents in the Tonkin Gulf to increase U.S. presence, though one was fabricated. Not coincidentally, the events occurred three months before the 1964 presidential election, when international communism was a significant issue.

For the next four years Johnson and his defense secretary, Robert Strange McNamara, oversaw a horribly bungled effort—a guns-and-butter, carrot-and-stick effort to entice Hanoi into bargaining in good faith. The North Vietnamese, having outlasted the Chinese, Japanese, and French, correctly assessed their American rivals as dilettantes and settled into a waiting game whose outcome was never in doubt—especially since North Vietnam was immune to invasion. Meanwhile, McNamara told his forces to endure "unlimited losses in pursuit of limited goals."

In 1968 Johnson declined to run for reelection and was succeeded by Richard M. Nixon, who won partly on the basis of a "secret plan" to end the war. Meanwhile, Hanoi maintained its pressure on the South with unimpeded aid from China and the Soviet Union. At length even Nixon's glacial patience eroded and, when Hanoi launched a major offensive in 1972, the gloves finally came off. American airpower, which had been intimately involved but largely restrained from the beginning, finally was unleashed. North Vietnamese ports were mined, bombing of strategic targets resumed, and within months Hanoi agreed to a cease fire after years of "negotiations." The North Vietnamese pledged to halt military operations in the South while the U.S. Congress cut off funding for Saigon, leaving South Vietnam vulnerable when the long-awaited communist offensive resumed in 1975.

Aviation was essential to the conduct of American military operations, both north and south. Vietnam has been called "the helicopter war" and there is much to the claim. Apart from the fact that it was the first major war in which helos played a significant role, ten in-flight and five helicopter-related actions brought Medals of Honor in Southeast Asia. Nearly all were recognized for rescue missions, though the emergence of helicopter gunships was a notable feature of the war.

Though the Air Force became a separate service in 1947, the Korean War award remained the Army version. In 1956 the Air Force was authorized to present its own Medal of Honor, which was struck in 1960. As if compensating for lost time, the USAF medal is half again as large as the Army and Navy versions.

After Captain Ed Freeman's action in 1965 and Major Bernard Fisher's action in 1966, the large majority of aviation medals came over the next two years: six each in 1967 and 1968. The remaining five occurred from 1969 to 1972.

Apart from in-flight awards, others went to downed airmen who resisted communist torture and extortion for periods of months to years. The Vietnam generation of Air Force, Navy, and Marine pilots and aircrews was unlike any previous: thoroughly trained, experienced career professionals were the norm. Many held postgraduate degrees with solid foundations in history, philosophy, and literature. Their strength of character was more severely tested in "the Hanoi Hilton" than in any cockpit, and as a group they emerged with their honor and integrity intact. The same could not be said for their political masters: the U.S. government abandoned unknown numbers of POWs to spend the remainder of their lives in communist captivity.

Of the nineteen in-flight Medals of Honor in Southeast Asia, only one involved aerial combat. Major Leo Thorsness, an F-105 "wild weasel" pilot, received his award for protecting a wingman from MiG interceptors and later earned an awesome reputation as a POW. Of the other medals, the distribution represented most of the combat roles in the war: attack pilots, forward air controllers, gunship crews, and combat support. Ironically, however, the aircraft most identified with the Vietnam air war was not included. The F-4 Phantom was flown by the Air Force, Navy, and Marines, but no in-flight medals went to "Phantom Pflyers," though Captain Lance Sijan received a posthumous award for his exceptional efforts as a prisoner.

Similarly, carrier aviators were underrepresented. Only one Medal of Honor went to an airborne tailhooker—Lieutenant Commander Mike Estocin, an A-4 pilot killed in 1967—but Commander Jim Stockdale ejected from a Skyhawk to become one of the senior prisoners in Hanoi and a pillar of the POW community from 1965 onward.

Anti-SAM pilots—Air Force Wild Weasels and Navy Iron Hands—received three Medals of Honor in a six-week period of March and April 1967. One was captured and one was killed; hunting SAMs was a hard way to make a living.

Whether they rotored into combat at a helicopter's 120 knots or pressed the mach in a Thunderchief, most of the Vietnam airmen shared a common attitude. Whatever they thought of their circumstances and the leaders who sent them on an unachievable quest, their professionalism was summarized in one ironic explanation: "It's the only war we have."

AIR FORCE (10)

MAJOR BERNARD FRANCIS FISHER

11 JANUARY 1927–

BORN: San Bernardino, California

ACTION: Combat rescue; A Shau Valley, Thua Thien Province, South Vietnam; 10 March 1966 (age 29)

UNIT: 1st Air Commando Squadron, 14th Air Commando Wing

AIRCRAFT: Douglas A-1E 52-132649 (2) "Hobo 51"

OTHER DECORATIONS: Silver Star, Distinguished Flying Cross, Air Medal (9)

The first Air Force Medal of Honor went to an erstwhile jet fighter pilot who flew a fourteen-year-old piston attack aircraft on a fireswept runway to save a fellow airman.

The A Shau Valley was scene of a Special Forces outpost held by 360 South Vietnamese troops with seventeen U.S. advisors. The enemy badly wanted the place—badly enough to commit an estimated 2,000 troops to seizing it. The five-to-one disparity was only offset by U.S. airpower, largely owing to the huge facility seventy miles east at Danang. "The Air" was literally oxygen to A Shau, as planes and helicopters provided food, fuel, and ammunition.

Taking advantage of poor weather, the communists pressed hard. The day before they had been held off by some 200 TacAir sorties, but gunners of North Vietnam's 95B Regiment shot down an AC-47 "Puff." Now, under low clouds, they penetrated the perimeter of the triangular base, forcing survivors into the north end. The camp commander, a Green Beret officer engaged in the close-up firefight, was shooting NVA in the head. With word of "Gooks in the wire," more tactical airpower was diverted to A Shau.

Bernard F. Fisher

Despite an 800-foot ceiling among 1,500-foot peaks, a flight of A-1E Skyraiders arrived on scene. They were led by Major Dafford W. Myers, commanding a detachment of the 602nd Air Commandos. The "Spads" bombed and strafed as close to the friendlies as they dared—sometimes within pistol shot. They temporarily stabilized the situation but at a cost. First Myers's wingman was forced to withdraw with battle damage, then Myers's A-1 was hit struck by heavy caliber rounds. He made the call: "This is Surf 41. I've been hit hard."

Overhead, Major Bernie Fisher of the First Air Commandos saw Myers's plane streaming flames past the tail. Myers radioed that he was too low to bail out; he would try a landing despite almost no forward visibility from heavy smoke. With professional cool, Fisher talked Myers onto the runway heading and watched his gear-up landing on the 2,500-foot strip.

Surf 41 erupted in a fireball. An agonizing time passed, perhaps forty seconds, before Myers dashed from the burning wreck and took cover in some brush, his flight suit smoking.

Rescue helicopters were reported inbound but they were twenty minutes out. Enemy troops moved in, determined to kill or capture the downed American.

Fisher deployed his wingman for ordnance runs to keep the VC away from the allied troops inside the perimeter. Two more A-1s arrived, bringing the ResCAP to four; Fisher directed bombing and strafing passes in an attempt to buy Myers and the inbound helos some precious time. It was no use—after ten minutes the airborne controller asked if Fisher could meet the helos on top of the cloud deck and lead them in. They were still "twenty mikes out."

Jump Myers didn't have twenty minutes. After his own pass Fisher dropped gear and flaps and set up for a landing. It was a long way from Kuna, Idaho.

Bernie Fisher was a World War II veteran—a straight-arrow, patriotic Mormon. In 1946 he had returned to the United States as a nineteen-year-old sailor but later stated, "I had always had a yearning to fly as long as I could remember." He entered college, spending three years in the Air National Guard before receiving an ROTC commission in 1951. Subsequently he flew F-102s in Germany and by 1965 he was a major flying fighters in Air Defense Command. He earned an awesome reputation for two successful engine-out landings in Lockheed F-104s. However, Fisher longed for combat and volunteered for Southeast Asia. He had begun his tour eight months before, flying with the First Air Commandos at Pleiku.

On his first landing attempt, Fisher emerged from the smoke and saw that he was "long." The runway was littered with fuel drums, ordnance, shell holes, and parts of Myers's plane, forcing a go-around. He added power to the big Wright R3350. Taking gunfire, with no time for another circuit, Fisher rolled into a 180-degree turn and landed on a reverse heading. As soon as the A-1 touched down, he sucked up his flaps and stood on the toe brakes, slewing to a stop at the end of the runway. Uncertain of Myers's location, he turned around and began a fast taxi through the obstacles, hearing and feeling hits on his airframe.

With his canopy open, Fisher craned his head over the side while S-turning, looking for Myers. He could not see him so he set the parking brake and slid to the right side of the cockpit. At that moment Myers, at once astonished and grateful, dashed from hiding and leapt onto the wing. The A-1E had side-by-side seating, and Fisher pulled Myers in head first. ("He didn't seem to mind," Fisher later quipped.) As Fisher began to taxi, Myers disentangled himself from the precarious situation, got upright, and strapped in.

At the far end of the runway Fisher stood on the right brake, shoved the throttle forward, and spun his plane around, knocking over a fuel drum in the process. Immediately he went to takeoff power, accelerating through increasing gunfire. More hits rang on the Skyraider. Fisher held Hobo 51 nose-low, tucked up the gear, and accelerated through the gunfire.

On the ground at Pleiku, Fisher's men counted nineteen holes in the rugged Douglas airframe. That afternoon they learned that the helicopter evacuation was largely successful, the survivors including thirteen Green Berets. They credited the A-1s with easing the enemy pressure along the east wall, permitting most of the garrison to escape.

Unknown at the time, a Marine Corps Huey was inbound to make the pickup. The pilot was Brigadier General Marion Carl, deputy commander of the First Marine Brigade, who regularly flew combat missions. Carl had heard Myers's mayday and was a few minutes out when Fisher got off the ground. The corps's first fighter ace and record-setting test pilot, Carl had been nominated for the Medal of Honor in 1942 but received a second Navy Cross instead.

Fisher received the Medal of Honor from Lyndon Johnson on 19 January 1967. Following retirement in 1974 the soft-spoken airman settled on a ranch in Idaho but continued flying. With some 14,000 hours, he said in masterful understatement, "I have a great love of flying."

CAPTAIN HILLIARD ALMOND WILBANKS

26 July 1933–24 February 1967

Born: Cornelia, Georgia

Died: Near Dalat, Tuyen Duc Province, South Vietnam

Action: Air support; near Dalat, Tuyen Duc Province, South Vietnam; 24 February 1967 (age 33)

Unit: 21st Tactical Air Support Squadron, 504th Tactical Air Support Group

Aircraft: Cessna O-1G 51-5078 "Walt 51"

Other decorations: Distinguished Flying Cross, Air Medal (18), Purple Heart

Captain Hilliard Wilbanks was a forward air controller, member of an essential aviation community in the Vietnam War. FACs frequently flew low and slow over South Vietnam and Laos, often drawing communist gunfire as

Hilliard A. Wilbanks

a means of spotting the enemy. At that point the FAC pilot used his most lethal weapon—his radio—to call in fighter-bombers. Because Viet Cong and North Vietnamese troops often hid under double or triple-canopy jungle, they were invisible to jets. Consequently, the FACs used smoke rockets to mark the target for the "fast movers."

Various aircraft were used in the FAC role, including twin-engine Cessna O-2s and North American OV-10 Broncos. "Fast FACs" (Mistys) flew F-100 Super Sabres and even F-4 Phantoms, affording the airborne controllers the luxury of a second crewman, excellent performance, and a meaningful ordnance loadout.

Then there were the Bird Dogs. Wilbanks surely flew the least warlike aircraft ever involved in a Medal of Honor combat mission. The O-1 Bird Dog was essentially an "off the shelf" Cessna 170 private plane, acquired as the L-19 beginning in 1950. Some 3,200 had been delivered to the Army (and subsequently to the Air Force) by 1959, redesignated the O-1 with the aircraft standardization system in 1962. Wilbanks's Bird Dog, among the second production batch, was upgraded to O-1G status with extra radios and underwing rocket launchers for marking targets.

Only thirty-three, Wilbanks already had sixteen years of service. Immediately after high school graduation in 1950, he enlisted in the Air Force and became an air policeman during the Korean War. He was accepted for pilot training and received his commission in 1954, subsequently flying F-86s at Nellis AFB, Nevada. Additional duty included aircraft maintenance before completing FAC training at Hurlburt Field, Florida.

On 24 February 1967 Wilbanks was among the most experienced FACs in the 21st Tactical Air Support Squadron at Nha Trang. Over the previous ten months he had logged 487 missions, and in about six weeks he would return home to his wife and four children.

That afternoon Wilbanks was airborne as "Walt 51," working South Vietnam's central highlands near Dalat, some 120 miles northeast of Saigon. He was supporting the 23rd ARVN Ranger Battalion searching a tea plantation for communist units reported in the area. From his perch overhead, Wilbanks noticed prepared positions dug into Hill 955 overlooking Route 20. Though camouflaged, the Viet Cong foxholes were visible from the air, and Wilbanks realized that the South Vietnamese were headed for an ambush.

By 1967 the VC were familiar with the American way of war. Knowing they had been sighted, they opened fire on the rangers sooner than they would have liked. However, the ARVN troops took cover. Wilbanks was in contact with the rangers' American advisor but could do little at the moment other than launch a phosphorous smoke rocket to identify the area. The communists opened fire on his Bird Dog but he remained overhead, exposing himself to 12.7mm gunfire accurate at two kilometers.

Then the Viet Cong moved. From hard experience the guerrillas had learned that where FACs appeared, fighters soon followed. With little time available to them, they broke cover and maneuvered to overrun the South Vietnamese. Later intelligence reports estimated some 400 VC soldiers working to flank two ARVN companies.

It was now a race: either the Viet Cong would overwhelm the rangers or fighter-bombers would arrive to find a lucrative target—most of an enemy battalion out in the open. Wilbanks needed a way to hold up the communists, buying precious time for the ARVN troops.

Wilbanks did not hesitate. He nosed over, drawing a bead on the lead elements of the Viet Cong force, and fired one of his rockets. It exploded among the front ranks and temporarily stopped the charge. Wilbanks added power, pulled around, and prepared to attack again. Twice more he dived his Bird Dog at the VC battalion, drawing heavier return fire each time. Twice more he stopped the enemy attack, buying the ARVN more time.

Now, however, the VC sensed that the persistent gray airplane had shot its bolt. With no fighters in sight, the enemy troops surged forward again, sensing their advantage.

Though flying alone, as O-1 FACs usually did, Wilbanks had a remaining option. He opened his side window and unlimbered the M16 rifle he usually carried as a defensive weapon in case he were forced down. He tugged the charging handle, poked the barrel into the ninety-knot slipstream, and flew low overhead the VC. Dropping as low as 100 feet, he fired short bursts that killed or wounded many VC. More important, he stopped the astonished enemy in their tracks once more.

Wilbanks repeated the process, changing magazines after each "strafing" pass. However, flying that low not even the best evasive maneuvers could prevent damage. Nearly 400 semi- and automatic weapons were available to the VC, who filled the airspace with 7.62mm rounds. Wilbanks ignored the peril, banking around for his third firing run. At that point the communist gunfire took effect, and Walt 51 descended in a long, sloping turn and dived into the ground within 100 meters of the ARVN rangers.

Guided by Lieutenant Colonel Norman Mueller flying as Walt 01, American advisors under Captain Gary Vote sprinted to the O-1. They found the pilot unconscious and pulled him from the Cessna bearing thirty bullet holes. The rangers contacted two U.S. Army Hueys, which tried to pick up Wilbanks, but VC firepower remained too thick. At length, Phantoms screeched overhead, identified the VC, and bombed and strafed while a helo was able to land. Airpower saved the rangers but Wilbanks died en route to a base camp.

USAF Chief of Staff, Gen. J. P. McConnell *(right)*, shows the Medal of Honor to the children of Capt. Hilliard Wilbanks, Paula and Tommy, after the Pentagon ceremony at which Air Force Secretary Harold Brown *(left)* presented the award to Mrs. Rosemary Wilbanks.

Almost a year later, on 25 January 1968, Wilbanks's widow, Rosemary, and two of her four sons received the Medal of Honor from the secretary of the Air Force on behalf of their husband and father.

Wilbanks's feat was memorialized in *Cobra Seven,* a tribute by Phantom pilot Toby Hughes, "the balladeer of the in-country air war."

Hilliard Wilbanks is honored on the FAC Monument at Hurlburt Field, Florida, and on the Vietnam Wall in Washington, D.C. (panel 15E, row 088).

MAJOR MERLYN HANS DETHLEFSEN

29 JUNE 1934–14 DECEMBER 1987

BORN: Greenville, Iowa

DIED: Unknown

ACTION: Strike mission; Thai Nguyen Province, North Vietnam; 10 March 1967 (age 32)

UNIT: 354th Tactical Fighter Squadron, 355th Tactical Fighter Wing

AIRCRAFT: Republic F-105F 63-8341 (also listed as 8354) "Lincoln Three"

OTHER DECORATIONS: Distinguished Flying Cross, Air Medal (10)

At Takhli, Thailand, it was logged as Mission 71: the strike against North Vietnam's major industrial target.

On 10 March 1967 an interval of clear weather permitted visual bombing of the Thai Nguyen steel plant about forty miles north of Hanoi. The North Vietnamese regarded the facility as a symbol of national pride and defended it accordingly: batteries of antiaircraft guns, surface-to-air missiles, and MiG interceptors at bases around the capitol. Thai Nguyen was a Category C (industrial) target that had appeared on the original Joint Chiefs list of ninety-nine targets in 1964. Though it was Hanoi's only steel plant, it had never been struck.

Consequently, the 355th Tactical Fighter Wing launched a strike package of Republic Thunderbolts from Takhli Royal Thai Air Base, 520 miles from Hanoi. The single-seat F-105Ds and two-seat F models formed up, headed northeasterly to the tanker track, and refueled for the ingress to the target area. Every pilot and back-seater knew they were in for a gunfight.

During 1967 the U.S. Air Force lost 302 fixed-wing aircraft in combat, only seven more than 1966 but still the greatest toll for any year of the war. Eighty-three more were lost operationally, for more than a plane a day throughout the year. An increasing proportion of the combat losses were attributable to SA-2s, requiring dedicated units to detect, locate, and destroy the missile sites. It was a high-risk profession but it attracted aggressive, high-quality aircrews flying the fast, rugged F-105F two-seater with a weapon system operator (WSO) or "dancing bear" in the rear cockpit. The SAM hunters called themselves Wild Weasels; their proud motto was "First in, last out."

Merlyn H. Dethlefsen

Merlyn Dethlefsen was a Weasel with seventy-seven previous missions in his logbook. On 10 March he was Lincoln Three, element lead in Major David Everson's defense suppression flight. As usual, the Weasels led the 355th into Thai Nguyen. Dethlefsen's "bear" was Captain Kevin A. Gilroy, known as "Mike."

Dethlefsen entered training as an aviation cadet in 1954 and was commissioned the next year. Initially trained as a navigator, he received his pilot's wings in 1960 and served in Germany the next four years. Upon rotation home he transitioned to F-105s, and newly promoted to major, he deployed to Takhli, Thailand, in October 1966. By March 1967 he had spent all but six months of the previous six years in fighters.

Approaching Thai Nguyen, Major Everson detected a missile battery at Site VN 126. Captain J. D. Luna, his weapon system operator, "locked up" the site and fired a Shrike antiradiation missile. It missed. The defenders did not. They shot down Lincoln Lead and hit "dash two," who was forced to abort. Barely minutes old, the mission had already turned to hash. Everson and Luna were captured; two Phantoms also were bagged though both crews were recovered.

With only his wingman remaining, Dethlefsen assumed responsibility for defense suppression. He and Gilroy targeted a SAM site as two MiG-21s began a classic six o'clock attack. Neatly gauging the timing, he "pickled off" a Shrike and wracked his Thud into a hard turn, avoiding an Atoll air-air missile. He coolly reckoned that the Vietnamese pilots (or whomever they were) would not follow him into the flak zone, so he kept his bombs rather than hitting the jettison button. Another Takhli pilot, Captain Max Brestel of the 354th Squadron, gunned two MiG-17s—the only U.S. kills claimed on the mission.

Bottoming out of his diving break turn, Dethlefsen lit his afterburner and regained altitude. He had barely reached a roll-in position when another pair of MiGs appeared. He evaded them but was hit by a 57mm shell, as was his wingman, Major Kenneth Bell, whose controls were damaged. The awesome Republic airframe shook off the damage, as neither the engine nor flight controls were hurt.

Dethlefsen heard the strikers pulling off target and knew that his job was largely accomplished. However, he also knew that Thai Nguyen was too tough a nut to crack in one mission. With good weather forecast over the next few days, the Thuds and Phantoms would return tomorrow and the day after. (In fact, strikes lasted into August.) Therefore, the dedicated Weasel elected to take another shot at the SAMs.

Evaluating the flak pattern, Dethlefsen again descended into the bursting, rippling air below. Gilroy found another site electronically and the crew fired a Shrike. Then Dethlefsen led Bell back to the original area where Lincoln One had gone down. Spotting Site 126 through the smoke, he rolled into a dive bombing attack and laid his bombs across the missile battery. As insurance he horsed the damaged Thud into a reverse, flipped his armament switch to "gun," and hosed down the site with 20mm shells.

By then it was definitely time to go.

Dethlefsen and Gilroy nursed their stricken bird back to the airborne tankers and on to Takhli. It was a Medal of Honor performance, but to Merlyn Dethlefsen, "It was a case of doing my job to the best of my ability. I think that's what we mean when we call ourselves professional airmen in the Air Force."

In June 1967 Dethlefsen was assigned as an instructor at Vance Air Force Base near Enid, Oklahoma. He received the Medal of Honor at the White House on 1 February 1968; his "bear," Mike Gilroy, received the Air Force Cross.

Merlyn Dethlefsen died in 1987, only age fifty-three, and was buried at Arlington National Cemetery. He is memorialized at the Air Force Museum with a display that includes the Bible he carried on 10 March 1967.

Crew: Capt. Kevin A. Gilroy (WSO).

MAJOR LEO KEITH THORSNESS

14 FEBRUARY 1932–

BORN: Walnut Grove, Minnesota

ACTION: Air combat; North Vietnam; 19 April 1967 (age 35)

UNIT: 357th Tactical Fighter Squadron, 355th Tactical Fighter Wing

AIRCRAFT: Republic F-105G 63-8301 "Kingfish One"

OTHER DECORATIONS: Silver Star, Legion of Merit, Distinguished Flying Cross (6), Air Medal (10), Purple Heart (2)

It was one of the epic missions of the Vietnam War. Amid broken cloud layers with turbulence and thunderstorms, in darkening skies, Major Leo Thorsness fought MiGs, dodged SAMs, hit two missile sites, covered a downed wingman, and declined an aerial tanker in favor of a comrade while running low on fuel himself. In a world where five minutes could lead to eternity, Thorsness and his back-seater prevailed for nearly an hour.

Leo Thorsness had enlisted in the Air Force in 1951 and earned his commission three years later. His first assignment was F-84 Thunderstreaks with the 31st Fighter Wing at Albany, Georgia. Later he flew F-100 Super Sabres in Germany before transitioning to the F-105 Thunderchief. He became a '105 instructor at Nellis AFB in 1964, remaining for the next two years. He reported to Takhli, Thailand, in October 1966, with the Wild Weasel SAM hunters of the 357th Tactical Fighter Squadron.

The 19 April target for the Takhli Thuds was Xuan Mai Army Base southwest of Hanoi. Leading the Weasel flight as Kingfish One, Thorsness directed his second section to hunt SAMs to the north. Almost immediately Thorsness's backseater, Captain Harold E. Johnson, detected radar emissions of a nearby SA-2 site. Thorsness turned into the threat, got a lock, and fired a Shrike. Seconds later the site went off the air, possibly a "soft kill" Hobson's choice to shut down or eat the missile.

However, the Vietnamese had no shortage of SAM batteries. Thorsness led Kingfish Two, Major Thomas W. Madison and Captain Thomas J. Sterling, back northward to engage another site. Thorsness got a visual, dived on the position, and dropped cluster bombs from 8,000 feet. To ensure a kill, he pressed to 3,000 and released more CBUs. The submunitions erupted across the star-shaped site in a rippling, churning sensation that ignited missiles on their launchers and trailers: a definite hard kill.

Bandit calls punctured the routine chatter as Kingfish Three and Four reported MiGs to the north. But one Thud's afterburner had failed—a "no go" item in combat. The element departed for home, leaving the Weasels at 50 percent strength.

Thorsness led Madison in a low-level sweep of the area, hunting visually. Then heavy AA fire burst around the Thunderchiefs and tagged Kingfish Two. Madison called that his plane was badly damaged; Thorsness directed him to turn toward the nearest high ground in event of a bailout.

Leo K. Thorsness

Long moments dragged past; Thorsness and Johnson heard the distinctive electronic whip-whip-whipping sound; Madison and Sterling had just ejected deep in "Indian country."

Thorsness padlocked the parachutes and turned to cover them while assessing rescue prospects. At that moment a MiG-17 popped up to his left. Vietnamese often fired at chutes, and the Chief Weasel took no chances. He hauled around to engage when Johnson hollered a bone-chilling warning: more MiGs at six o'clock. Coolly assessing the situation, Thorsness reckoned he had time for a shot. Overtaking at 550 knots, he pressed the trigger, hosing 20mm rounds at the MiG, which spun and crashed. Then he shoved his throttle into afterburner. The huge J75 responded with 24,500 pounds of thrust, outrunning the trailing MiGs.

After prolonged maneuvering at low level, kicking in and out of afterburner, Thorsness needed fuel. He exited the area, raced to the tanker track over Laos, and sucked in JP-4 while a rescue effort was assembled for Kingfish Two. Thorsness knew his wingman's exact position and, though low on ammunition, felt he could cover the shootdown site.

Conducting a radio briefing for the rescuers, Thorsness glimpsed three more MiGs in the gathering dark. Johnson chipped in with four more astern. A highspeed tailchase ensued, in and out of darkened valleys, bottoming out at fifty feet. The Thud responded as only a '105 could down low. Thorsness pulled deflection on one of the MiGs and triggered his last 500 rounds. He was too busy to watch the results, but that bandit was out of the fight.

With no 20mm remaining, Thorsness turned back to attract the other MiGs while the rescue package ingressed. But things turned for the worse: more MiG-17s jumped the A-1E "Sandys" and shot one down and Major J. S. Hamilton of the 602nd Air Commandos was lost. Though other '105s arrived and Nitro Three claimed a kill, there was no longer an option. The operation was called off; Madison and Sterling were captured.

Thorsness finally was able to turn for home, again needing fuel, but the long day was not done. Approaching the tanker, he heard an emergency call from another fighter, also critically low on fuel. Kingfish One unselfishly coached the other pilot to the KC-135 and coaxed his Thunderchief toward Udorn, 200 miles closer than Takhli. Seventy miles out, Thorsness retarded the throttle to idle: it was going to be *very* close. The gauge read empty when his tires streaked the runway.

Between Merlyn Dethlefsen and Leo Thorsness the Takhli Thuds had earned two Medals of Honor in less than six weeks. Harold Johnson received the Air Force Cross.

Richard Nixon with Leo K. Thorsness, his mother, and his wife, Gaylee

It seemed that Thorsness had done it all: gunned two MiGs and survived fifty-plus SAM launches while hunting their sites to destruction. He was eight missions from rotating home.

Throughout the war Thuds outfought MiG-17s three to one, but supersonic MiG-21s were another matter. They bagged three Takhli planes on 30 April; one was flown by Thorsness and Johnson. Ejecting at 600 knots, Thorsness was badly hurt. Owing to his "uncooperative attitude" his captors denied him medical attention and inflicted severe injuries during torture. But on 4 March 1973 the Chief Weasel and his "bear" walked away from prison, Thorsness on crutches.

Seven months later Leo Thorsness received the Medal of Honor. He retired shortly thereafter and moved to South Dakota, where he contested the U.S. Senate seat held by George McGovern. Many POWs felt that the defeatist policies advocated by the Democratic presidential candidate had prolonged the war, but the electorate that made Joe Foss a two-term governor retained McGovern, a B-24 pilot in World War II. Subsequently Leo and Gaylee Thorsness settled in Arizona.

Crew: Capt. Harold E. Johnson (WSO).

CAPTAIN GERALD ORREN YOUNG

9 MAY 1930–6 JUNE 1990

BORN: Chicago, Illinois

DIED: Unknown

ACTION: Combat rescue; Salavan Province, Laos; 9 November 1967 (age 37)

UNIT: 37th Aerospace Rescue and Recovery Squadron, 3rd Aerospace Rescue and Recovery Group

AIRCRAFT: Sikorski HH-3E 66-13279 "Jolly Green 26"

OTHER DECORATIONS: Distinguished Flying Cross, Air Medal (2), Purple Heart

Six in-flight Medal of Honor actions occurred in 1967—as many as during the entire Korean War. Two medals also were awarded for POW events that year, which remained the aviation record for the Vietnam War. The final action for the "class of '67" occurred on a cloudy night in November.

Like Major Bernie Fisher, Captain Gerald Young had been a sailor before entering the Air Force and winning his silver wings in 1958. Nine years later Young was a helicopter aircraft commander and instructor pilot with the 37th Aerospace Rescue and Recovery Squadron at Danang Air Base, South Vietnam. It was a high-risk profession: of fifty HH-3Es built, ten were lost in combat and four more operationally. Fourteen pilots and aircrew were killed while pursuing the Rescue Service motto, "That others may live."

Young's sixtieth mission was a full-blown rescue operation involving two

Gerald O. Young

HH-3 "Jolly Green Giants," a C-130 to drop flares, and three Army helicopter gunships. Their mission was a covert one: an allied reconnaissance team had been ambushed in the Samuoy District of Laos, and two helos were shot down trying to get in. The soldiers on the ground were live bait in a well-plotted flak trap. Knowing the odds, Young and his crew accepted the challenge. They had been to bad places before.

As if the tactical situation weren't bad enough, the weather and terrain conspired to complicate things that night. The rescue package departed Danang after midnight, bound for a mountainous area with 5,000-foot peaks stuffed inside the clouds.

Approaching the ambush site some 120 miles north-northwest of Danang, Young moved into a holding position as the other Jolly Green searched beneath the garish orange-white parachute flares dropped by the C-130. Harsh shadows along the ridge lines concealed enemy positions including automatic weapons that soon opened up. Under heavy fire the primary helo managed to snatch three men off a rocky slope, then turned for Khe Sanh, hemorrhaging fuel and hydraulic fluid. The aircraft commander radioed Young, saying the gunfire was too heavy to attempt another approach, despite support of the gunships.

After repeated passes the Army helos were getting low on fuel and ammunition. Young realized that he faced a now-or-never situation—the survivors on the ground could not hold out until daylight. He turned in to attempt the rescue.

The Jolly Green flew directly toward the hill, pivoted, and entered a precarious hover. Young finessed the controls, keeping one of his main mount wheels on the ground while his rotor blades slashed within a few feet of the upward slope.

In the left seat Captain Ralph Brower directed the gunships in their final runs, trying to suppress the awesome volume of fire from the ground. Meanwhile, Sergeant Larry Mansey jumped onto the hillside to help push five wounded soldiers aboard, covered by Staff Sergeant Gene Clay's machine gun.

At the word from Mansey, Young added power, pulled on the collective, and lifted the big Sikorski off the hill.

Then an engine exploded. Punctured by automatic weapon fire, the T-58-GE turbine tore itself to shreds. Jolly 26 rolled inverted, impacted the mountain, and tumbled downhill.

When the wreckage came to rest, Young was hanging inverted in his shoulder harness, his flight suit ablaze from fuel-fed flames. He beat his way out through the broken windscreen and remembered to roll on the ground to smother the fire. At that moment he did not know it but he had sustained second and third-degree burns over 20 percent of his body.

Scrambling uphill, Young found one of the soldiers he had just picked up. The man was unconscious, his clothes afire, but Young beat out the flames with his bare hands. Then he climbed back toward the blazing hulk of JG-26, looking for other survivors. He saw none.

Young took the wounded soldier into the brush and applied first aid, wrapping some of his own burns in charts from his flight suit pockets. Reckoning their chances would improve at daylight, he was proven right—Skyraiders sighted him and "capped" the site. However, large numbers of Vietnamese were returning to the area and a gunfight developed. Young witnessed a ResCAP nightmare—Sandys dueling with automatic weapons. There were casualties on both sides; Young knew that a Jolly Green would be hovering nearby, willing to repeat his own effort.

Gerald Young made a hard decision: he led the enemy away from the rescue site. Despite serious burns to his back, legs, arms, and hands, Young ignored the pain. He placed the soldier, still unconscious, in a safe place and headed for the boondocks, knowing that capture meant death. Through the agonizing pain of his burns he realized that he would never survive captivity.

For hours Young picked his way across the rugged, forested hills, keeping ahead of the pursuing NVA. At length his strength faded and he had to crawl but he kept moving. By late afternoon he had covered an incredible six miles, then heard a helicopter searching for survivors. Young pulled his emergency radio, contacted the helo, and providentially was rescued. He had been on the run for seventeen hours.

On return to Danang, Young learned that other Jollys had landed at the crash scene, picked up one survivor and the bodies of the dead, including the soldier Young had succored. His crew received posthumous Air Force Crosses.

Gerald Young spent the next six months undergoing a series of painful skin grafts. At the end of that time, on 14 May 1968, he received the Medal of Honor from President Johnson at a ceremony dedicating the Pentagon's Hall of Heroes. Owing to political concerns, for years Young's attempted rescue was stated as "southwest of Khe Sahn." Actually it was twenty-five miles south-southwest, six miles inside Laos.

Subsequently Young became an instructor at Sheppard Air Force Base, Texas. Later he served at the Air Force Academy, flew with the presidential transport squadron at Andrews Air Force Base, and was appointed air attaché to Colombia. He retired as a lieutenant colonel in 1980.

In 1985 Young told *Air Force* magazine, "The air rescue mission was one of the best in the war. There is no greater compensation than to participate in saving lives."

Gerald Young died in 1990, just past his sixtieth birthday.

Crew: Capt. Ralph W. Brower (CP); SSgt. Eugene Clay (FE); Sgt. Larry W. Mansey (PR).

LIEUTENANT COLONEL JOE MADISON JACKSON

14 March 1923–

Born: Newman, Georgia

Action: Combat rescue; Kham Duc, Quang Tin Province, South Vietnam; 12 May 1968 (age 45)

Unit: 311th Air Commando Squadron, 315th Special Operations Wing

Aircraft: C-123K 55-4542 (WV 542) "Bookie 771"

Other decorations: Legion of Merit, Distinguished Flying Cross (2), Air Medal (7)

It was Joe Jackson's third war.

The eighteen-year-old Georgian had enlisted in the Army in March 1941 and served as a B-25 crew chief. Commissioned in April 1943, he saw no combat but flew fighters in Germany during 1946–47. He flew 107 F-84 missions in Korea and later commanded a fighter squadron at Turner AFB in his native state. Most notably, in 1957 he became deputy commander of the 4080th Strategic Reconnaissance Squadron, placing him among the earliest U-2 pilots.

Joe M. Jackson

Now, at age forty-five, Jackson possessed a wealth of military aviation experience. The fact that he was flying a decidedly unglamorous C-123 cargo plane in Southeast Asia made no difference to him. Much of South Vietnam was still aflame following the Tet offensive three months before, and the enemy maintained the pressure in some areas.

One of them was Kham Duc.

Barely ten miles from the Laotian border, Kham Duc assumed greater importance than before. After the loss of Lang Vei, Kham Duc remained the only U.S. and ARVN observation base in I Corps. However, its remote position precluded an adequate defense. When enemy mortar rounds began falling on 10 May, the U.S. military command ordered the 1,700 American and South Vietnamese personnel to be evacuated.

The camp was fogged in at dawn on the twelfth, and an air evacuation was attempted. With a combat control team (CCT) on the ground to direct incoming aircraft, landings were attempted on the 6,000-foot-long strip. However, enemy gunners in the surrounding hills had the field zeroed; an Army CH-47 and two Air Force C-130s landed safely but were almost immediately hit by mortar and rocket rounds. One of the Hercules transports exploded, killing more than 150 people. Another "Herc" got in and out, but the crew radioed a warning to other planes circling nearby: "For God's sake stay out of Kham Duc. It belongs to Charlie."

Major General Burl McLaughlin, commanding the 834th Air Division, was the overall airborne commander at Kham Duc. Subsequently he wrote, "The battle scene was awesome—almost beyond description—as the destructive power of countless air strikes merged with the relentless onslaught of enemy mortar, rocket, and machinegun fire."

Jackson's Provider with his three-man crew arrived in the area about 3:30 that afternoon, diverted from a periodic check ride from his right-seater, Major Jesse Campbell. As the last C-130 took off amid the explosions of mortar shells, Jackson heard the FAC commander direct waiting fighter-bombers to bomb the place and deny its facilities to the enemy. However, the Hercules pilot immediately interrupted. His crew had seen three men of the combat control team near the runway, evidently unaware that "the last stage out of Dodge" had just departed.

Still circling overhead, Major General McLaughlin requested the next available aircraft to try a pickup. Bookie 750, another C-123, made the approach and touched down on the runway. However, communist gunfire increased, forcing a "waveoff." As the Provider lifted off, the CCT leapt from a ditch and was seen by Bookie 750 and other fliers overhead. It would take too long for 750 to make a circuit of the pattern; McLaughlin asked for "the next transport in the stack" to make the pickup.

Bookie 771 was next up. As a C-123 instructor pilot, Campbell began an assault landing: full flaps and near redline airspeed. Through cloudy skies Jackson and Campbell could see the strip with burning fires, exploding ordnance, and a riot of wreckage.

From 9,000 feet the Provider plummeted at more than 3,500 feet per minute, affording the least exposure time to enemy gunners. Nevertheless, the final 4,000 feet were made under increasingly heavy gunfire. At about 500 feet Jackson resumed control from Campbell.

In his twenty-seven years of service Jackson had flown jet fighters and U-2s, but Kham Duc presented a serious problem. The normal procedure for a short-field landing was to reverse the propellers, but that would cut out the small jets beneath each wing. Instead, he trod on the brakes. The Provider lurched to a stop and the CCT airmen dashed from cover, almost immediately taken under fire. Jackson was unable to taxi to them because of helicopter wreckage on the runway. A wrecked O-2 and damaged C-130 also impeded one side of the strip. Nevertheless, Jackson turned around while the

Americans sprinted toward his plane. As soon as they leapt through the cargo door the loadmaster hollered, "All aboard!"

Jackson was shoving up the power to take off the way he had come when Campbell shouted a warning. A 122mm rocket skipped off the runway ahead of them, broke in two, and rolled to a stop barely thirty feet away. Providentially, it did not detonate. Jackson wasted no time taxiing around the rocket and, with props in low pitch and mixture rich, he accelerated off Kham Duc's tortured runway. He had probably been on the ground no more than sixty seconds, but every one of them was under fire—each with a separate beginning, middle, and end. Within seconds of starting its roll, a string of mortar shells exploded behind the Fairchild while tracer rounds scythed ahead of it. The Provider shuddered down the strip, lifted off, and banked for home.

After landing at Danang, the two pilots looked over Number 542, expecting to count bullet holes. Incredibly, like Nathan Gordon's PBY at Kavieng twenty-three years before, a large, slow aircraft had escaped untouched from repeated high-volume gunfire and mortar rounds.

That evening Jackson wrote his wife, Rosie: "I had an extremely exciting mission today." In all, 1,500 people had been evacuated from Kham Duc at cost of 259 lives and eight aircraft.

One of the CCT members, Technical Sergeant Morton Freedman, said it best: "We were dead and all of a sudden we were alive. I don't remember what I said to the crew, but they were magnificent."

The squadron and wing commanders recommended Jackson and Campbell for the Medal of Honor, noting that both pilots shared responsibility and flying chores. On 16 January 1969, Jackson received the Medal of Honor in the same ceremony as Navy Lieutenant Clyde Lassen and Marine Captain Steve Pless. Though sixteen years older, Jackson already knew of the leatherneck helo pilot—they both hailed from Newman, Georgia. Jesse Campbell received the Air Force Cross; Sergeants Ed Trejo and Manson Grubbs, the Silver Star.

Years later, Jackson reflected on his Air Force career and said, "Remember, people are never a failure until they quit trying." Three combat control men were extremely glad that Joe Jackson lived by that creed.

Crew: Maj. Jesse Campbell (CP); TSgt. Edward Trejo (CC); SSgt. Manson Grubbs (LM).

LIEUTENANT COLONEL WILLIAM ATKINSON JONES III

31 MAY 1922–15 NOVEMBER 1969

BORN: Norfolk, Virginia

DIED: Woodbridge, Virginia

ACTION: Rescue support; Quang Binh Province, North Vietnam; 1 September 1968 (age 46)

UNIT: 602nd Special Operations Squadron, 56th Special Operations Wing

AIRCRAFT: Douglas A-1H 52-139738? (TT 738?) "Sandy One"

OTHER DECORATIONS: Distinguished Flying Cross, Air Medal (4), Purple Heart

Another fast mover was down.

For the pilots of the 602nd Special Operations Squadron, the increasing number of American jets shot down in Indochina provided a sort of job security. In the previous month the U.S. Air Force, Navy, and Marines had lost twenty-three fighters or reconnaissance jets, plus piston planes and helicopters. The aging Douglas A-1 Skyraiders at Nakhom Phanom were irreplaceable for the dangerously esoteric job of combat search and rescue (C-SAR). Though designed as a naval attack aircraft during World War II, it proved invaluable to the Air Force in Vietnam. Known generically as "Sandys"—the call sign for ResCAP aircraft—A-1s had exceptional loiter time and an awesome ordnance loadout. Their ability to remain on station far longer than unrefueled jets, flying down in the weeds while looking for downed fliers or rooting out AA guns, was an asset that the fast movers just did not possess.

Early that September morning the CO of the 602nd departed Nakhom Phanom with three other A-1Hs escorting two helicopters. An F-4D from Udorn, Thailand, had been bagged during the night, and despite marginal weather, Lieutenant Colonel Bill Jones was determined to find the crew. "NKP" or "Naked Fanny" had a reputation to uphold. Tucked away in eastern Thailand, hard on the Cambodian border, it was reputedly the holdout of assorted spooks and commandos—cloak-and-dagger types who had a way of fetching good men from bad places.

Like C-123 pilot Joe Jackson, who earned a Medal of Honor in May, Jones was a senior airman, wearing silver wings since 1945. At age forty-six he had previously flown transports and bombers, including six years at Pease AFB,

New Hampshire. Though new to the single-engine, low-level world of the Sandys, he quickly adjusted. As commanding officer of the 602nd he was Sandy Lead, with ninety-seven previous missions.

William A. Jones III

It was monsoon season, with typical cruddy weather: low clouds, rain, and reduced visibility. Flying 100 miles east from the Thai-Laotian border, Jones kept his second section orbiting above the cloud deck while he and his wingman, Captain Paul Meeks, began searching the valleys. Their goal was known only as Carter Two Alpha, the front-seater of the missing Udorn Phantom.

The Sandys spent a frustrating hour searching the briefed shootdown site, near the coast. Eventually an F-100 Super Sabre established radio contact with the downed pilot, Captain J. R. Wilson of the 432nd Tactical Fighter Wing. The site was well eastward, twenty-two miles northwest of Dong Hoi in a rugged area defended by 37mm antiaircraft guns and automatic weapons. Repeatedly flying low among 1,200-foot peaks to establish visual contact, Jones's Skyraider was exposed to Vietnamese gunners who proved to be accurate. Jones felt his A-1 shudder from a near-miss; an explosive shell had detonated just below him. He tested his controls, determined that the rugged Douglas airframe was still intact, and continued his search. Shortly Wilson came up on the rescue frequency: Jones had just overflown him.

Noting the location, Jones was taken under fire again—from above! A gun with a commanding view of the area was sited on a hilltop within lethal range of Wilson. Consequently, the fast movers could not attack the AA gun. Jones, however, had a ResCAP ordnance loadout, including 20mm cannon and rockets. He decided to attack.

On the run-in, an automatic weapon opened up, scoring multiple hits.

One round ignited the rocket motor that would propel his seat out of the aircraft if he pulled the handle. Searing flames erupted in the cockpit, but Jones remained seated. He was the only pilot who knew Wilson's position and needed to relay that information before he abandoned ship. Enduring the flames, he made the call.

Accounts vary: either the frequency was jammed with calls urging Jones to bail out or his transmitter went dead. In either case, time was running out; he felt searing heat on his neck, arms, and hands. He felt no option but to join Carter Two Alpha on the ground.

Grasping the handle for the Yankee extraction system, Jones pulled hard. The canopy disappeared in the swirling slipstream but the seat did not budge. It would have to be a manual bailout.

He began unstrapping when he noticed the flames abating somewhat. Thinking of the lone F-4 pilot down on the ground, Jones realized that he needed to get word to Nakhom Phanom. He tucked in tight formation on Meeks and endured an agonizing forty-minute flight home. Badly burned with his instruments useless, windscreen shattered, and weather deteriorating, Jones pressed on. Crossing the Thai border, ignoring the blistered pain of his hands, he manually dropped the landing gear and, without flaps, flew a precision ground-controlled approach despite clouds and turbulence.

Once on the ground the CO had to be lifted from his charred cockpit. However, he refused medication until he pinpointed Two Alpha's position on a map. Captain Wilson was picked up later that day; his back-seater was captured.

Jones returned home, and following a four-month recovery, he assumed command of the First Flying Training Squadron at Andrews AFB, Maryland. He was promoted to full colonel on 1 November 1969 and later that month a self-published book was released. Entitled *Maxims for Men at Arms,* it featured Jones's drawings.

One day after the book was printed, Bill Jones was killed in the crash of a private aircraft. His widow received his Medal of Honor from President Nixon at the White House on 6 August 1970.

FIRST LIEUTENANT JAMES PHILLIP FLEMING

12 MARCH 1943–

BORN: Sedalia, Missouri

ACTION: Combat rescue; near Duc Co, Pleiku Province, South Vietnam; 26 November 1968 (age 25)

UNIT: 20th Special Operations Squadron, 14th Special Operations Wing

AIRCRAFT: Bell UH-1F 64-15492?

OTHER DECORATIONS: Silver Star, Distinguished Flying Cross, Air Medal (8)

Jim Fleming made an implied contract; he considered it binding.

The son of a World War II AAF officer, Fleming wanted to fly from childhood. After receiving a degree in criminal investigation from Washington State, he was commissioned in 1966 and trained as a fixed-wing and helo pilot. He flew SAC bombers before arriving in Vietnam in July 1968, assigned to the 20th Special Operations Squadron.

The 20th SOS called itself the Green Hornets, presumably because their green helicopters buzzed all over Southeast Asia at treetop level. Headquartered at Nha Trang Air Base, they flew the UH-1F, the Air Force version of the ubiquitous B model Huey. With a more powerful engine and larger rotor for greater lift capability, 119 were acquired, mainly for air-sea rescue.

The Hornets often supported the "Studies and Observation Group," the innocuous title for covert operations throughout Southeast Asia. On 26 November 1968 Fleming inserted the six-man Recon Team Chisel under Staff Sergeant Ancil Franks, accompanied by Captain Randolf Harrison, who commanded the company. Chisel's mission was support of Operation Daniel Boone by observing enemy boat traffic in the Central Highlands about 270 miles north of Saigon. Before liftoff Fleming had indulged in the ritual hugs; the tacit pledge: "If I put you off, I'll pick you up."

After return to the 20th's base at Duc Co, the helos refueled and flew another insertion that afternoon. Meanwhile, RT Chisel was in "deep serious." Surprised by North Vietnamese troops, Franks's men were pinned down near the river the team was to observe. Surrounded on three sides with the river at their back, the SOG men fought for their lives. Fortunately, their

James P. Fleming

distress calls were heard by an Air Force forward air controller. The Cessna O-2 contacted the helo team, which diverted from its second insertion mission to answer the emergency.

Opposition increased alarmingly. Both Green Hornet gunships rolled in to suppress NVA gunfire and silenced two heavy machine guns. But Captain Dave Miller's helo was fatally hit; he force landed and his crew was picked up by Major Dale Eppinger, flying the lead transport helo. Low on fuel, Eppinger headed directly for base. Almost immediately a second "slick" transport reached "bingo" fuel and turned for home.

The only helos remaining on scene were flown by Jim Fleming and Major Leonard Gonzales, whose gunship took battle damage. The Covey FAC circled overhead, coordinating rescue efforts, but Fleming called soon thereafter. He also was dangerously low on fuel: the pickup attempt became a now-or-never affair.

The FAC, Major Charles Anonsen, used his altitude to direct Fleming via the safest route into the Vietnamese flak trap. Using terrain masking, Fleming followed Anonsen's directions to the spot the SOG men had described and settled his skids into the shallow river, expecting the team to appear momentarily.

By this time the NVA sensed their growing advantage. With U.S. air support diminished, the communists closed in. Chisel's six troopers were too hard pressed to run for the pickup spot; firing madly, their radio operator called, "They've got us!" He urged Fleming to pull out. Then the team detonated its last claymore mines.

Hurried radio calls from the FAC and the team clarified the situation. The SOG men were nearly out of ammunition, daylight was fading, and the other Hornets were more than an hour away. Fleming and Major Gonzales hastily agreed to try once more with the gunship making a suppressive pass while the slick crossed the river. Gonzales led the way, expending his remaining ammo, followed by Fleming. The chopper crews scanned anxiously, seeking the SOG team, which had become invisible in the foliage.

There they were.

A gunner saw one of the Montagnard team splash into the water and dash toward the Huey; four others followed. NVA gunfire increased as AK-47 rounds ricocheted off rocks and the water. Ignoring the threat, Fleming slowed his Huey into a steady hover. His gunners returned NVA gunfire until the left M60 jammed. The other gunner continued firing, one-handing exhausted SOG men aboard. By then Captain Harrison was missing but time, pressure, and fuel demanded they leave.

While backing away from the riverbank, Fleming's crew saw Harrison emerge from the brush. The captain sprinted into the river, almost close enough to touch the Huey as Fleming lifted off. The crew chief tossed down a rope ladder that Harrison grasped, and as Fleming hauled up on the collective, Harrison was dragged across the water. The SOG men reached out and grasped their leader's hands and hauled him aboard to safety.

Fleming landed at Duc Co with his fuel warning light illuminated; evening sunlight filtered through 7.62mm holes in the windscreen.

Jim Fleming received the Medal of Honor for one of the most dramatic combat rescues in history. The other pilots and aircrew received an Air Force Cross, a Silver Star, eleven Distinguished Flying Crosses, and two Air Medals. The fliers also received something even greater: the profound respect and gratitude of six SOG men.

In turn, the flier paid tribute to the "grunts." He said, "An American soldier, when he's under fire, running to a helicopter that's his lifeline out of there . . . he always turns to help his buddy behind him. That's who we are."

On 14 May 1970 Fleming received the medal in the same ceremony with Sergeant John Levitow. Later Fleming transitioned to C-141 transports. He and former POW Colonel Bud Day were among the pallbearers for the unknown soldier of the Vietnam War.

In summarizing his career, Fleming wrote, "I did what every other helicopter pilot did: no more, no less. What is different about me is that I was awarded the Medal of Honor. Therefore, it's my honor, privilege and duty to represent those who served as helicopter pilots during the Vietnam War."

Crew: Maj. Paul E. McClellan (P); SSgt. Fred Cook (CC); and Sgt. Paul R. Johnson (G).

AIRMAN FIRST CLASS JOHN LEE LEVITOW

1 November 1945–8 November 2000

Born: Hartford, Connecticut

Action: Gunship mission; Bien Hoa Province, South Vietnam; 24 February 1969 (age 23)

Unit: 3rd Special Operations Squadron, 14th Special Ops Wing

Died: Rocky Hill, Connecticut

Aircraft: Douglas AC-47B 43-49770 (EL 770) "Spooky 71"

Other decorations: Air Medal (8), Purple Heart

Airman John Levitow was returning a favor. Ordinarily he flew with his assigned crew, but Major Ken Carpenter's loadmaster had filled in during a previous mission when Levitow was ill. As he boarded the AC-47 on the night of 24 February 1969, the Connecticut native had no way of knowing that he had volunteered for a bitter experience. The Third Special Operations Squadron flew Douglas AC-47 gunships, twenty-five-year-old transports armed with an awesome array of firepower: 21,000 rounds of ammunition for three 7.62mm miniguns plus dozens of Mk24 parachute flares to illuminate targets on the ground. The eight-man crew included two gunners and a loadmaster to feed the voracious miniguns and drop flares. Flares were a crucial part of the mission, producing two million candlepower. The eye-watering light show of flares and tracers was responsible for the 3rd SOS call sign: "Spooky."

Standard nightly procedure called for two gunships airborne from Bien Hoa Air Base, and at 2000 hours Major Ken Carpenter's Spooky 71 launched with Spooky 73. Levitow was thoroughly familiar with the procedure: in seven months he had flown 180 missions. It was Levitow's first flight with Carpenter, who was completing his aircraft commander upgrade.

John L. Levitow

Levitow's action: 10-second exposure of AC-47 gunship near Long Binh, 24 February 1969 (Photograph by Larry Hinson)

The gunships had been airborne several hours, suppressing enemy forces around Bien Hoa, when an urgent call was received for an illumination mission near Long Binh, just north of Saigon. American units reported communist mortar fire of increasing intensity; if they could not be detected at least the threat implied by parachute flares might deter them. The VC and NVA had enormous respect for Spookys.

Taking a heading from the navigator, Major William Platt, Carpenter soon had Spooky 71 over the contact area. Two enemy mortar positions were identified as Levitow, Sergeant Tom Baer, and Airman Ellis Owen set fuse settings and dropped flares through the cargo door. Flying the gunship's typical pylon turn, Carpenter used the brilliant illumination to place his side-mounted sight on the targets; the miniguns spewed thousands of rounds and silenced both mortar batteries. When a third target was identified, Carpenter wheeled Spooky 71 into another approach as Levitow, Baer, and Owen prepared more flares.

Depending on fuse setting, the twenty-seven-pound flare ignited after being thrown overboard. A ten-foot lanyard secured to the aircraft was abruptly jerked taut, pulling the safety pin, beginning a countdown to extract the parachute and ignite the magnesium, which burned at 3,000 degrees Fahrenheit.

The crew just pulled a flare from the rack when the airframe lurched violently and rolled right. An incredible coincidence had brought Spooky 71, barely 1,000 feet off the ground, into the same airspace as an 82mm mortar shell. The explosion in the right wing tore a gaping hole outboard of the tank, puncturing a fuel line and staggering the C-47 and all aboard.

The four men in the cargo compartment were knocked over by the force of the explosion; all were wounded. The flare was wrenched from Owen's hand but he kept his grasp on the lanyard, unconsciously pulling the safety pin.

As Carpenter and copilot Frank Slocumb fought to regain control of the crippled gunship, they had little idea of the damage behind them. Levitow had sustained 135 fragmentation wounds to his right side, legs, and back. He compared the sensation to "somebody breaking a two-by-four against my side." Though bleeding heavily, he retained his senses. His immediate concern was for Owen, who had collapsed near the open cargo door. Levitow forced himself to ignore his pain and sapping strength, brought himself upright, and grasped the wounded airman's clothes, pulling him away from the door.

Then Levitow saw smoke. He saw something rolling across the cabin floor. It was the Mk24 flare; its twenty-second fuse counting down to ignite the magnesium that would destroy Spooky 71. However, before that happened, the crew would collapse from inhaling the noxious fumes in a matter of seconds.

Levitow reached for the rolling cylinder but missed; the aircraft's erratic flight tossed men and equipment back and forth. He tried again, missed again. With time running out, he dived onto the flare and pinned it to the floor.

No one knew how long the fuse had to burn, but it began to smoke. Unable to regain his feet, Levitow began an "uphill" crawl against the plane's descending left turn. The other crewmen, themselves wounded, watched in horror as he inched toward the door, leaving blood trails behind him.

As Levitow neared the cargo door, the aircraft bucked unpredictably. He realized that he might be tossed into the night with the flare. Though at the point of exhaustion, he willed himself to crawl a little farther, then shoved the lethal cylinder away from him. It disappeared overboard and seconds later ignited in the dark sky with a garish white blast.

About ten eternal minutes after the explosion, Carpenter and Slocumb managed a safe landing at Bien Hoa, not bothering to clear the runway. Ambulances swept the wounded away to Long Binh. Levitow was then evacuated to Japan for treatment of forty significant puncture wounds.

Despite his own injuries (a detached left bicep, detached retinas, and damaged eardrums), Carpenter remained to inspect his airplane before retiring to the Spooky Hootch. He could hardly believe the damage: a three-foot hole in the right wing near the fuel tank and 3,500 shrapnel holes in the airframe. Looking at the bloody compartment, he was convinced that John Levitow deserved the Medal of Honor, and he pursued the case tirelessly.

The wounded loadmaster made a full recovery and logged twenty more missions before completing his tour. He was discharged as a sergeant in July 1969 and spent the next twenty-two years with the Connecticut Veterans' Administration. He became a role model for many wounded vets, overcoming the serious injuries to his legs and demonstrating his recovery by one-foot water skiing.

Levitow also was devoted to the stature of the Medal of Honor. In 1999 he wrote the secretary of the Air Force, supporting Airman William Pitsenbarger's posthumous award. Levitow felt so strongly that he offered to give up his own medal to enable an even more deserving enlisted man to receive the award.

John Levitow succumbed to lymphatic cancer on 8 November 2000. Pitsenbarger's medal was awarded four weeks later; in the audience was John Lee Levitow Jr.

Crew: Maj. Kenneth B. Carpenter (P); Capt. Frank S. Slocumb (CP); Maj. William Platt (N); SSgt. Edward Fuzie (FE); Sgt. Thomas Baer (G); A1C Ellis C. Owen (G); South Vietnamese observer.

CAPTAIN STEVEN LOGAN BENNETT

22 April 1946–29 June 1972

Born: Palestine, Texas

Died: Offshore, Quang Tri Province, South Vietnam

Action: Lifesaving; Quang Tri, South Vietnam; 29 June 1972 (age 26)

Unit: 20th Tactical Air Support Squadron

Aircraft: North American OV-10A 68-3804 "Covey 87"

Other decorations: Air Medal (4), Purple Heart

The long guerrilla war was over. When the People's Army of Vietnam launched its Spring Offensive of 1972, it was a combined-arms asssault based on nearly four years of preparation. Hanoi had outwitted and outwaited Washington—though Lyndon Johnson was gone, Richard Nixon's "secret plan" to end the war remained well hidden. Not so General Giap's intent. His divisions bulldozed their way southward with armor, artillery, and state of the art antiaircraft weapons.

The man-portable SA-7, called Grail by NATO forces, featured prominently in the North Vietnamese lineup. Supplied by the Soviets in large numbers, it began taking a toll of U.S. and South Vietnamese aircraft. American airmen soon learned to respect it, and the area around Quang Tri became known as "SA-7 Alley."

North Vietnamese troops had forced a crossing of the My Chanh River, putting serious pressure on ARVN units. One of the many forward air controllers working the area was Captain Steve Bennett, call sign Covey 87, of the 20th Tactical Air Support Squadron. He flew the North American OV-10A Bronco, a twin-engine type with impressive performance, armed with machine guns, marker rockets, and—most important—five radios. In his back seat was a Marine Corps observer, First Lieutenant Michael B. Brown, whose radio was linked to warships capable of providing gunfire support.

Bennett entered the Air Force in 1968 and received his wings in 1970 but had only been in Vietnam for three months. Like helicopter Medal of Honor pilot Jim Fleming, he qualified in B-52s before completing FAC and fighter courses leading to Southeast Asia duty.

As evening set in, Bennett's resources were stretched to the limit. The

Steven L. Bennett

South Vietnamese platoon he was supporting had been in "hot contact" for a prolonged period, and though Bennett had stymied the NVA with four passes, he needed help. Therefore, the direct air support center diverted another Bronco to the scene, flown by First Lieutenant Darrel Whitcomb of the 20th's sister squadron, the 23rd TASS. Whitcomb, "Nail 70," also was low on ordnance, having directed three air strikes along the Demilitarized Zone. With only machine gun ammo remaining, he headed south to rendezvous with Covey 87, whose identity was unknown to him.

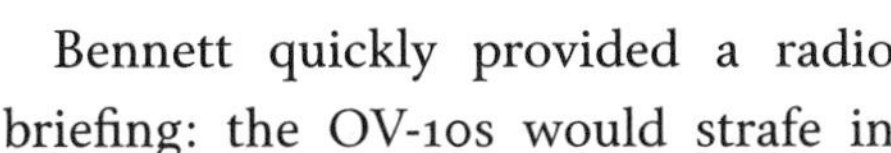

Bennett quickly provided a radio briefing: the OV-10s would strafe in opposite directions to split the ground fire. However, in order to be effective they had to descend well into the SA-7 envelope. Whitcomb had already dodged flak and SAMs that afternoon but the need was urgent. He agreed with Covey's assessment.

On his second pass at the communist troops, Whitcomb saw an airburst to the north at about 6,500 feet. He called on UHF and got no reply so he switched to VHF and heard Bennett exclaim that an SA-7 had struck his plane. The crippled Bronco was proceeding easterly, toward the shoreline for a bailout. Whitcomb quickly joined and was astonished at what he saw: "The missile had hit the exhaust port on the left engine and destroyed it. The left gear was hanging and flames were visible in the engine bay."

Nail 70 made the emergency call for Covey 87, asking the controller to scramble a rescue force. Crossing the coast, the pair was joined by another Nail OV-10. However, moments later Bennett radioed dire news: his observer's parachute had been damaged by the missile hit. For a pilot to eject and leave his observer was unthinkable—Bennett said he intended to land at Danang if possible. Running the time-distance equation, Whitcomb advised diverting to Hue, only twenty miles west. Bennett accepted the advice but immediately an unknown operator called, "You'd better ditch, Covey!"

As far as anyone knew, an OV-10 had never been ditched successfully; Whitcomb himself had seen a failed attempt. Nevertheless, Bennett elected to make the effort, evidently because the engine fire was spreading. Whitcomb and the other Nail continued orbiting the area, coordinating rescue efforts of A-1 Skyraiders, F-4 Phantoms, and a helicopter.

Bennett set his crippled Bronco down about 200 yards offshore, and though the air support center advised that the area was considered friendly, the Nails took no chances. When a sampan came out from shore, First Lieutenant Robert Tempko strafed ahead of the craft, forcing its return.

Whitcomb made a low pass and saw one man in a raft as the OV-10 sank. The survivor radioed to identify himself as Wolfman 45, the observer, who was rescued within minutes. Now critically low on fuel, the two Nails turned over rescue control to the A-1 "Sandys" and headed for Danang.

That evening Whitcomb held a two-hour debriefing with Mike Brown. The marine said that he was badly jarred by the explosion and force of the landing, and he nearly drowned. However, the fuselage buckled between the cockpits, allowing him to escape. He surfaced, gulped in some air, looked for his pilot, and realized that Bennett was still in the sinking aircraft. Brown had time for one shallow dive before the wreckage sank, but he had ingested seawater and aviation fuel. He could do no more.

It had been a dreary day for the 20th TASS, which lost another Bronco to gunfire. Moreover, it was a bad month for the Air Force generally: eleven Phantoms, four O-2s, a pair of A-1s, and a C-130.

More than two years passed. Then Darrel Whitcomb read that on 8 August 1974, Linda Bennett accepted her husband's Medal of Honor from Vice President Ford. Much later, in 1990, Whitcomb replied to a magazine request from Steve Bennett's daughter, seeking contact with anyone who had known him. Whitcomb later wrote, "I only wish that I could have known him. . . . But his final act has always remained with me. I watched him die—you can't know a man any better than that."

Bennett was among the last of 219 forward air controllers killed in Vietnam. He is remembered on the FAC Monument at Hurlburt Field, Florida, and at the Vietnam Memorial in Washington, D.C. (panel 01W, row 051).

Additionally, in 1999 the *Captain Steven L. Bennett* (T-AK 4296) joined the Military Sealift Command.

Crew: 1Lt. Michael B. Brown, USMC (O).

Air Force Aviation Related (3)

Airman First Class William H. Pitsenbarger, 38th Air Rescue Squadron, South Vietnam, 11–12 April 1966. An exceptionally experienced paramedic, Pitsenbarger left his Kaman HH-43 helicopter to treat critically wounded GIs surrounded by communist forces. He elected to remain on the ground that night and was killed while protecting soldiers in his care. He was awarded one of the early Air Force Crosses, but in December 2000 his family received the Medal of Honor in his name.

Major George E. Day, 4th Allied POW Wing, North Vietnam, 1967–73. As a "Fast FAC," Day was an airborne forward air controller whose F-100F was shot down in the southern part of North Vietnam on 26 August 1967. He was captured, but despite serious injuries, he escaped and attempted to reach the Demilitarized Zone. After wandering ten days without sufficient food or water, often delirious, he was shot by communist forces and moved to Hanoi. There, he resisted torture and extortion for more than five years. After retiring as a colonel, he wrote a memoir titled *Return with Honor*.

Captain Lance P. Sijan, 4th Allied POW Wing, North Vietnam, 1967–68. An F-4 pilot of the 366th Fighter Wing, Sijan was downed by premature detonation of his own ordnance on 9 November 1967. His back-seater died in the explosion, but Sijan survived forty-five days in the jungle before being captured. Despite physical debilitation, he briefly escaped but was recaptured and taken to Hanoi. There he waged a tireless campaign against his captors until he died 21 January 1968, age twenty-five. His family received his Medal of Honor in March 1976.

ARMY AVIATION (6)

CAPTAIN ED W. FREEMAN

20 NOVEMBER 1927–

BORN: Neely, Mississippi

ACTION: Combat supply and MedEvac; Pleiku Province, South Vietnam; 14 November 1965 (age 37)

UNIT: Company A, 229th Assault Helicopter Battalion, 1st Cavalry Division.

AIRCRAFT: Bell UH-1H "Serpin 26"

OTHER DECORATIONS: Distinguished Flying Cross, Air Medal

Landing Zone X-Ray was deep in "Indian country." Situated in the Ia Drang Valley, close to the Cambodian border, it became the center of one of the bitterest battles of the young "conflict" in South Vietnam. At X-Ray the under-strength First Battalion, Seventh Cavalry, was in constant contact with an enemy "main force" unit, the North Vietnamese 66th Regiment. Ammunition, water, and medical supplies were going fast with the nearest resupply base fourteen miles east at Plei Me.

Rather than risk additional helicopters, the battalion CO went on the air, closing the LZ. However, Captain Ed Freeman, a transport helo platoon leader, would have none of it. At six feet six inches, Freeman needed a waiver for flight training and became known as "Too Tall to Fly." A veteran of Pork Chop Hill in Korea, he realized how hard-pressed the grunts were, down in the tall grass that concealed a determined, aggressive enemy. Repeatedly throughout the day he voluntarily flew in the face of heavy fire, landing his unarmed "slick" Huey to provide critically needed supplies.

Despite Freeman's example, senior officers still refused authorization for medical evacuation flights. The reasoning was based on experience and logic, as X-Ray lay within 200 yards of the thinly held defensive perimeter. Consequently, Freeman launched a series of fourteen sorties in and out of the fireswept landing zone, evacuating nearly thirty wounded GIs. Witnesses testified that many of the soldiers would have died without timely evacuation to rear area hospitals. As it was, Lieutenant Colonel Harold G. Moore's skytroopers sustained 25 percent casualties that day.

Originally, Freeman was awarded the Distinguished Flying Cross, as was Major Bruce Crandall, commanding "A/229th." Though Freeman's superiors felt he deserved far more, little action was taken for decades. He retired as a major in 1967 and flew helicopters for the Forest Service in Idaho until 1991. He retired with nearly 26,000 hours flight time, including more than 18,000 in helicopters.

The award situation finally was redressed when Ed Freeman received the Medal of Honor on 16 July 2001 in the presence of fifty other recipients. Retroactively he became the first Army helicopter pilot awarded the Medal of Honor, nearly thirty-six years after the firefight at LZ X-Ray.

Ed "Too Tall" Freeman was portrayed by Mark McCracken in the 2002 film *We Were Soldiers.*

Crew: CWO2 Frank Marino (CP); SP.4s Angel Cumba (G) and Michael Raph (CC).

MAJOR PATRICK HENRY BRADY

1 October 1936–

Born: Philip, South Dakota

Action: MedEvac near Chu Lai, Quang Tin Province, South Vietnam; 6 January 1968 (age 31)

Unit: 54th Detachment, 67th Medical Group, 44th Medical Brigade

Aircraft: Three Bell UH-1D?/H "Dustoff 55"

Other decorations: Distinguished Service Cross, Legion of Merit, Distinguished Flying Cross (6), Bronze Star Medal (2), Purple Heart, Air Medal (53)

It was another Saturday in Vietnam. Thick fog covered much of Quang Tin Province, but MedEvac helos kept flying regardless of weekends, weather, or war. Major Patrick Henry Brady became the first of two Huey pilots awarded the Medal of Honor during the communist Tet Offensive in January 1968.

Following graduation from Seattle University in 1959, Brady entered active duty as an Army officer. He served in Germany, then applied for flight

Patrick H. Brady

school, received his wings in 1963, and almost immediately was sent to South Vietnam.

Brady was among the early "Dustoff" pilots of the 57th Medical Detachment, which had been in-country since 1962. He led the Pleiku detachment in January 1964 and finished his tour as commander of the 57th.

Brady's second tour began in 1967, by which time MedEvac equipment and tactics were well developed. His new unit, the 54th Medical Detachment, lifted five times the number of casualties of his first tour. It was a huge job, especially with an average daily availability of only three Hueys. One in every three Dustoff crews became casualties themselves. However, Brady conducted on-the-job training for his nineteen or twenty-year-old pilots, who arrived in-country with barely 200 hours flight time. "Those young warrants were wonderful," he says. "They would fly down a gun barrel to get wounded."

However, most pilots were lacking in night navigation and instrument flight time so Brady often filled the gap. He flew a terrifying mission in October 1967: with other helos grounded in a drenching monsoon, he made the first extraction with help of Air Force flare planes. Throughout the night he used two helos and three crews and received the Distinguished Service Cross.

Three months later the 54th received an urgent call for MedEvac of wounded South Vietnamese soldiers in enemy territory. It was a nightmare scenario: the men were surrounded in mountainous area blanketed by thick fog. With the skill and experience to risk the flight, Brady volunteered, manned up with his crew, and launched into an epic Dustoff mission.

Navigating to the extraction site in darkness and fog posed a huge problem; visibility was essentially zero. Yet Brady let down through the fog and smoke to a narrow valley trail. There he used a technique he had developed previously: hovering sideways, he allowed his rotor wash to disperse the fog enough to see the ground. Using his rotor tips and tree branches for depth perception, Brady hovered uphill sideways, an incredible feat of flying. Having found the tiny LZ, he ignored close-range gunfire, landed, and evacuated two wounded ARVN soldiers.

That was the beginning of a long day.

Next Brady was informed of a U.S. infantry unit in another area also shrouded in fog. The wounded were within fifty meters of communist forces: two helos already had been shot down attempting a pickup and others had been driven off by heavy gunfire. Yet Brady made four flights into the besieged landing zone and lifted out all the wounded.

The day's last evolution was the toughest yet. Another rifle unit was pinned down by enemy fire and unable to secure the landing zone. But as before, Brady was willing to try a rescue and approached the area, making an initial pickup. Then heavy gunfire struck his Huey and damaged his flight controls. He pulled off to evaluate the damage but returned within minutes and rescued the remaining GIs.

But other Americans remained in peril. Learning of a platoon trapped in a minefield with no clear way out, Brady switched Hueys and landed where the mines were exploding. One detonation wounded two of his crew and damaged his helo, but still Brady extracted six severely injured men.

Throughout the day Brady used three Hueys to evacuate fifty-two wounded men. Yet to Brady, it was merely "an average day." In two tours he flew more than 2,000 MedEvac sorties.

Brady retired as a major general after a thirty-four-year career, including Army chief of public affairs and secretary to the Military Armistice Commission in Korea. He earned an MBA from Notre Dame and has been chairman of the Citizens Flag Alliance and president of the Congressional Medal of Honor Society. He was inducted into the Army Aviation Hall of Fame in 1990 and the Dustoff Hall of Fame in 2001.

Brady has written, "We are not born equal in terms of ability or opportunity. There is only one way we are equal and can compete equally in life: courage!"

Crew: two separate crews, identities unknown.

CHIEF WARRANT OFFICER 2 FREDERICK EDGAR FERGUSON

18 AUGUST 1939–

BORN: Pilot Point, Texas

ACTION: Combat rescue; Hue, Thua Thien Province, South Vietnam; 31 January 1968 (age 28)

UNIT: Company C, 227th Aviation Battalion, 1st Cavalry Division

AIRCRAFT: Bell UH-1H 66-16923 "Piranha One-One"

OTHER DECORATIONS: Silver Star (2), Distinguished Flying Cross, Bronze Star Medal, Air Medal (38)

The 1968 lunar new year brought a traditional holiday to Vietnam and with it a countrywide communist assault. As a North Vietnamese officer later observed, the Tet Offensive was a military defeat for Hanoi and the Viet Cong but a geopolitical victory that led to the conquest of Saigon seven years later.

Among the U.S. and South Vietnamese forces pinned down by the massive enemy assault was a Huey helicopter crew near Hue, on the coast. It had been shot down with the battalion commander and commander of C Company, 227th Aviation Battalion. Though temporarily safe with ARVN troops, heavy North Vietnamese pressure threatened to overwhelm the position. Ground fire was so intense in the area that five helos had aborted rescue attempts and others were waved off by the regional command.

Flying his UH-1H on a resupply mission was Warrant Officer Fred Ferguson of the 227th, "opconned" to the Third Brigade, First Cavalry Division. He quickly organized an impromptu relief force with three gunships and conducted a radio briefing, then informed his company commander of his intentions. Mindful of the threat, Ferguson's CO advised him against the attempt but declined outright refusal. Another bonus was the fact that Ferguson's copilot was also his platoon leader, Lieutenant William H. Anderson, though with nearly 600 hours "in-country," Ferguson was the more experienced flier.

Actually, Ferguson did not have to be in Vietnam. He had served four years in the Navy, and upon discharge in 1962, the former sailor could have remained home in Phoenix, Arizona. But he was already a commercial pilot interested in helicopters. When the Navy said he lacked aviation aptitude, the Army warrant officer program allowed him to scratch his flying itch. He became an Army aviator in May 1967, and with 210 hours military flight time, he arrived in Vietnam three weeks later.

Frederick E. Ferguson

Arriving over Hue, Ferguson surveyed the situation. It was chaos: heavy automatic weapons fire, mortar shells impacting within the perimeter, and at least two wounded Americans. The ARVN compound was nearly surrounded at the south end of a bridge just west of the old Imperial Palace. Ferguson advised the three gunships that he was beginning the approach in his "slick," flying up the Perfume River. The gunships nosed down, hosing suppressive fire at the likeliest threat zones.

It did little good. Communist gunners maintained their volume of fire, hitting the Huey repeatedly: the airframe was gouged with holes while cockpit glass shattered from bullet impacts. Ferguson flew so low that his crew observed NVA troops firing downward from roofs and horizontally from both river banks. Behind him, Spec. 4s Jim Coles and John Etzle returned fire with their M60s. They passed the Imperial Palace, flying a Viet Cong flag from the parapet, and headed for a rail cut at the south end of the bridge.

Approaching the perimeter, Ferguson cleared the wall, pushed down on his collective, eased the cyclic back, and dropped into the compound for a "quick stop" landing with two feet clearance for his rotor. No sooner had he touched down than ARVN soldiers began loading casualties: four Americans and a South Vietnamese.

A mortar round exploded to the left rear of the Huey; the enemy had the range. Ferguson added power, churning up the dust, and lifted off. Almost immediately two more rounds impacted between his skid marks. The helo lurched from the concussion, spun left, and Ferguson compensated on the rudder pedals. Continuing leftward, he accelerated back toward the rail line he had followed inbound.

During the egress upriver the battered Huey took more hits. If anything, NVA fire increased; a gunship was hit and radioed that it was setting down.

Ferguson nursed his UH-1 to Hue Phu Bai and eased it into a final landing. Ferguson heaved a sigh of relief but shrugged off the episode: "It was just one day in a long war." His Huey was so shot up that it was lifted out beneath a Chinook.

A week later a major appeared, taking depositions for a Distinguished Flying Cross; Ferguson gave it little thought. Much later he was ordered to see his battalion commander, and the suspicious CWO2 immediately wondered, "What'd I do *now*?" Then he learned that the division commander had recommended him for the Medal of Honor. Lieutenant Anderson received the Silver Star; Specialists Coles and Etzle the Distinguished Flying Cross.

In May 1969 President Nixon presented the Medal of Honor with the Joint Chiefs of Staff in attendance. Ferguson could not resist informing the chief of naval operations that the U.S. Navy had declared him "lacking in aviation aptitude"—an ironic assessment for a pilot who also received forty-two U.S. combat decorations and the Vietnamese Cross of Gallantry.

After the Vietnam War, Ferguson remained in aviation, rising to major in the Arizona National Guard, where he commanded an assault helicopter company. He loved flying so much that in 1982 he accepted a reduction to chief warrant officer to stay in the cockpit, and he remained a helicopter instructor until 1997. Subsequently he accepted a position with the Arizona Department of Veterans' Services. His other honors include Military Aviator of the Year, the Kitty Hawk Award, the Order of Saint Michael, and induction into the Army Aviation and Arizona Aviation Hall of Fame.

"We worked together to do our job," Ferguson reflects on his combat days. "We were lucky and were just glad to be around at the end of the day."

So were five men who owed their lives to Fred Ferguson and the Air Cav.

Crew: 1Lt. William H. Anderson (CP); Sp.4s James Y. Coles and John J. Etzle Jr.

STAFF SERGEANT RODNEY JAMES TADASHI YANO

13 December 1943–1 January 1969

Born: Kealakekua Kona, Hawaii

Died: Bien Hoa, South Vietnam

Action: Lifesaving; Bien Hoa Province, South Vietnam; 1 January 1969 (age 25)

Unit: Air Troop, 11th Armored Cavalry Regiment

Aircraft: UH-1C 66-00528 "Thunderhorse Six"

Other decorations: Air Medal, Purple Heart

Rodney Yano was devoted to his job, his aircraft, and his unit. As the helicopter technical inspector of the Air Cavalry Troop of the Eleventh Armored Cavalry Regiment, the native Hawaiian—son of a fisherman—was universally respected for the dedication he brought to his position. He had enlisted in 1961, barely age seventeen, and served in Germany from 1962 to 1966. Contemporaries in the Black Horse regiment insisted that nobody knew helicopters more intimately and that no one was more conscientious about maintaining them. Though responsible for keeping the troop's twenty-six choppers in "up" status, he also volunteered to relieve a crew chief once a week for some badly needed rest. Those who flew with him described Yano as "a wild man" in combat, often standing on the skid while firing an M60 machine gun supported by bungee cords rather than a pillar mount to obtain the best field of fire. Yet he was so calm and unobtrusive on the ground that he did not even apply for flight pay. One of his officers took note and corrected that "oversight."

Yano also was a morale builder. When faced with yet another of the inevitable problems with materiel, command, or environment, he would give an ironic smile and say, "Ya gotta love this place." It became the unofficial motto of the Black Horse air troop.

On New Year's Day 1969, Yano had been in Vietnam nearly two years. He was not obliged to fly but volunteered to take the place of a crew chief who had celebrated the night before. The Huey pilot was Major John C. Bahnsen, commander of the regiment's air troop, who launched in response to a contact in War Zone D to the north. A scout helicopter already was calling artillery fire when Bahnsen arrived to coordinate Air Force fighter-bombers.

Rodney J. T. Yano

"It was necessary for us to fly low level to mark the area with white phosphorous grenades," Bahnsen recalled. "It required several passes to get the target marked for the fighters."

In the process, Yano gripped his M60, firing out the open door to help suppress enemy gunfire from thick foliage. He also dropped smoke and phosphorous grenades to help the inbound "fast movers" identify the "hot" areas. One of his white phosphorous grenades exploded prematurely, with appalling results. Part of Yano's left hand was blown off and he sustained agonizing burns to the face. The explosion also set off ammunition aboard the chopper while thick smoke blocked Bahnsen's view. The Huey started a slow descent, partially out of control with reduced visibility for the pilots.

Yano was immediately incapacitated by partial blindness and paralysis of one arm. However, he groped in the acrid white smoke and found ammunition that was "cooking off." He flung burning material and the boxes overboard even while rounds were detonating. Bahnsen and the copilot regained control of the aircraft only twenty feet off the trees. "I was finally able to see and leveled the helicopter and realized that it could fly," Bahnsen explained. "I then made a beeline to the hospital pad in Bien Hoa and landed about ten minutes later."

Everyone aboard sustained painful burns but Yano's wounds were mortal. Bahnsen visited his bedside, and though Yano was unable to speak, "he acknowledged my presence."

When word passed that Rod Yano had died that night, a hushed silence fell over the troops' screening of the John Wayne movie *The Green Berets*.

Yano received a posthumous promotion to sergeant first class and was buried at the National Memorial Cemetery of the Pacific near Honolulu.

Meanwhile, every member of his crew signed the Medal of Honor recommendation, which was endorsed by Colonel George S. Patton III, the regimental commander. President Richard Nixon presented the medal to Yano's family at the White House on 7 April 1970. He was inducted into the Army Aviation Hall of Fame in December 1986.

In January 1997 the U.S. Military Sealift Command christened the USNS *Yano* (AKR-297), a maritime prepositioning ship of 54,000 tons full displacement. Additionally, Rodney Yano is remembered by a library in Hawaii, a hangar at Fort Rucker, Alabama, and a range at Fort Knox, Kentucky. However, his most enduring tribute comes from his fellow fliers. As "Doc" Bahnsen said in 2001, "He gave me, and the other crew members, another thirty-one great years of life by his heroic actions."

Yano's name is etched on the Vietnam Memorial (panel 35W, row 018).

Crew: Maj. John C. Bahnsen (P); unknown CP; Spec.5 Carmine Conti (G).

CWO MICHAEL JOSEPH NOVOSEL

3 SEPTEMBER 1922–

BORN: Etna, Pennsylvania

ACTION: Combat rescue; Kien Tuong Province, South Vietnam; 2 October 1969 (age 47)

UNIT: 82nd Detachment, 45th Medical Company, 68th Medical Group

AIRCRAFT: Bell UH-1H "Dustoff 88"

OTHER DECORATIONS: Distinguished Flying Cross, Air Medal, Purple Heart

It was another busy day in South Vietnam. "Dustoff" Hueys of the 82nd Detachment, 45th Medical Company, flew continuously in response to medical evacuation calls from U.S. and ARVN infantry units along the Cambodian border. MedEvac was what Dustoff was all about—their UH-1s were flying ambulances.

Chief Warrant Officer Mike Novosel already had logged nearly eight hours by that afternoon. Operation Python was targeted against communist training areas in the "Parrot's Beak" area, but the offensive had bogged down. Poor weather hampered air and artillery support, but the Dustoffs kept flying, hot refueling without bothering to shut down their engines.

Michael J. Novosel

About 1600 Novosel learned of a crucial situation developing. The command-and-control helo, in contact with an Air Force FAC, learned of a South Vietnamese unit trapped near the border. The ARVN were out of ammunition, surrounded, and being pounded by mortars. There were many, many wounded.

Though no fighters or armed helos were available to suppress enemy fire, Novosel decided to try a rescue. To do otherwise was unthinkable: he had been a military pilot for twenty-seven of his forty-seven years. He found the combat area and rolled in from 2,000 feet.

Mike Novosel was an extremely unusual helicopter pilot in more ways than one. At five feet five inches, he had nearly missed his first war and barely got to combat, flying B-29s in 1945. He had been retained as an instructor on Superfortresses, but eventually he logged three combat missions before VJ-Day. Subsequently he commanded the 99th Squadron of the Ninth Bomb Group.

After the war Novosel was active with the Air Force reserve and flew as an airline pilot. He was a lieutenant colonel when the Vietnam War brewed up in 1964, but the Air Force was unable to find a position that satisfied him. Consequently, he resigned from the Air Force and became an Army warrant officer qualified on helicopters. The contrast between the Superfortress and the Huey could hardly be greater—to say nothing of their respective wars—but Novosel flourished as a Dustoff pilot.

Novosel joined the 283rd Medical Detachment in January 1966 and remained throughout the entire year. Expecting to return to the left seat of a Southern Airways liner, he found a stumbling block in the form of glaucoma. The FAA would not renew his commercial license so he requested a waiver from the army. With a growing need for MedEvac pilots, he returned to Hueys.

Novosel was well into his second Vietnam tour on 2 October 1969. He had logged almost eight hours in the cockpit when he received directions to a rescue along the Cambodian border.

Arriving on scene, Dustoff 88 found the ARVN troops pinned down by surrounding communist forces in an area overgrown with tall grass. In reduced visibility some of the South Vietnamese had become separated from their unit. Finding the casualties would not be easy.

Novosel made two passes over the area but his crew saw no one in the high grass. The Huey took small arms fire both times but the Dustoff creed was taken seriously: "That others may live." On the next two passes the crew chief and medic glimpsed isolated ARVN soldiers and scooped them up. Under almost constant fire from unseen VC, the Huey took more hits. Novosel pulled off, checked systems with Warrant Officer Tyrone Chamberlain, and returned for another effort. Finally with ten casualties aboard, Novosel turned for the Special Forces camp at Moc Hoa. The wounded were offloaded and fuel brought up to half capacity—a concession to time and the weight expected of additional casualties.

On the next trip into the area, the crew repeated the previous procedure. Novosel knew that Chamberlain was flying his first serious MedEvac mission but the copilot kept a running commentary on engine and rotor systems.

Novosel realized that the tall grass could be a help as well as a hindrance. He lowered the Huey into the tops of the stalks, reducing the chopper's profile to the persistent gunfire. Hopscotching around the area, with Spec. 4 Herbert Heinhold treating more South Vietnamese as they were pulled aboard, Novosel was temporarily satisfied with nine more saves. He returned to Moc Hoa, unloaded, and set out again.

The Dustoff had been operating without suppressing fire for two hours—several eternities in combat. When two F-100s arrived, they bombed and strafed ahead of the Huey, but the VC gunfire hardly abated. Finally two AH-1 Cobras provided close-in support, and Novosel entered the cauldron for the third time.

Hovering for another pickup, Novosel was appalled to see a Viet Cong emerge from the grass thirty meters ahead. The VC lifted his AK-47 and fired a long, scything burst. Novosel's left boot was struck; bullet fragments bloodied his right leg and hand. Chamberlain saved the Huey from a nose-high, right-hand pitchup, then Novosel regained control. The crew picked up ten more ARVN, then headed for the SF camp. They landed the shot-up Huey after dark, having saved twenty-nine South Vietnamese in an epic three-and-a-half-hour mission.

As soon as his wounds were treated, Novosel recommended his crew for Silver Stars. He had no way of knowing that he was on the way to becoming the oldest pilot ever to receive the Medal of Honor, awarded in June 1971. During his two Vietnam tours, Novosel evacuated 5,589 casualties in 2,543 sorties totaling some 2,000 hours combat time. Even more remarkable, late that year he was joined by his son, also Michael, and they flew together in the 82nd.

When Novosel retired in 1985, he was the last active duty U.S. airman who had logged combat missions in World War II. He had been a military pilot for an incredible forty-two years, with 12,400 hours of flight time, including 4,000 hours in Hueys. As a master Army aviator and an Air Force command pilot, Novosel held the top pilot ratings of both service branches. He retired as a CWO4 and wrote *Dustoff: The Memoir of an Army Aviator.* He declared, "The Medal of Honor recipient carries within himself a fear, the possibility that he did not deserve the medal." It is not recorded that anyone ever said that of Mike Novosel. He was inducted into the Army Aviation Hall of Fame in May 1975, one month after the fall of Saigon.

Crew: WO Tyrone Chamberlain (CP); Spec. 4s Herbert Heinold and Joseph Horvath.

MAJOR WILLIAM EDWARD ADAMS

16 June 1939–25 May 1971

Born: Casper, Wyoming

Died: Kontum Province, South Vietnam

Action: MedEvac; Kontum Province, South Vietnam; 25 May 1971 (age 31)

Unit: 227th Assault Helicopter Co., 52nd Aviation Battalion, 1st Aviation Brigade

Aircraft: Bell UH-1H 69-15704 (715?) *Little Annie's Fannie*? "Chickenman Six"

Other decorations: Air Medal, Purple Heart

Bill Adams was getting "short" on his second tour. He had commanded the 411th Transportation Detachment of the 176th Assault Helicopter Company in 1967–68, and he returned to Vietnam on 6 July 1970. By the following May, as commanding officer of the 227th Assault Helicopter Company, "Chickenman Six" was within six weeks of rotating home.

Based at Phieu-Hiep, the 227th supported U.S. Army and South Vietnamese forces throughout Kontum Province. On 25 May, Adams received word of three soldiers seriously wounded at Firebase Five, a small outpost besieged by a superior communist force. Hard information was sketchy, but Adams knew that clear skies meant serious trouble for helicopters flying within range of the inevitable automatic weapons surrounding an allied base. Owing to the terrain, it would be nearly impossible to surprise the opposition, which commanded excellent fields of fire.

Nevertheless, Chickenman Six manned up and launched with a gunship escort. As events proved, it was an ironic call sign.

Approaching Firebase Five, the Huey flew into a hailstorm of gunfire: small arms, heavy machine guns, and even rocket-propelled grenades. During the run-in, Adams coolly assigned targets to his gunships, identifying the most serious threats. Nevertheless, opposition increased. There were simply too many gunners for the available escorts.

Adams was absolutely determined to extract the casualties and managed a landing inside the base perimeter. The men were loaded on board while the helo crew could only sit tight and try to ignore the maelstrom of gunfire from the hills overlooking the compound.

William E. Adams

With the wounded soldiers secured, Adams lifted off. Almost immediately the Huey sustained more hits. Losing airspeed, the UH-1 dropped in a sickening plunge. Adams and Captain John Curran regained control and picked a spot for a forced landing. Apparently struck by RPGs, the chopper rolled inverted and smashed into the ground, exploding on impact. The casualties included Spec.4 John W. Littleton, the eighteen-year-old crew chief of a downed helo who had made his way to the firebase, as well as some South Vietnamese.

Captain Curran, crew chief Melvin Robinson, and gunner Dennis Durand received posthumous Distinguished Service Crosses. Adams's widow received his Medal of Honor from Vice President Gerald Ford on 8 August 1974.

Adams was inducted into the Army Aviation Hall of Fame in May 1990, at the same time as Pat Brady and Gary Wetzel. He is buried at Fort Logan National Cemetery in Denver, and his name is inscribed on the Vietnam Memorial (panel 03W, row 054).

Crew: Capt. John D. Curran (CP); Spec.4s Melvin Robinson (CC) and Dennis C. Durand (G).

Army Aviation Related (3)

Private First Class Gary G. Wetzel; 173rd Assault Helicopter Company; near Ap Dong, South Vietnam; 8 January 1968. As door gunner on a UH-1D in a "hot LZ," Wetzel was blown out of the grounded helo, losing his left arm and sustaining other serious wounds. Nevertheless, he returned effective fire, and after collapsing in shock, Wetzel regained consciousness. He then helped the crew chief drag the pilot to safety. He was inducted into the Army Aviation Hall of Fame in 1990.

Sergeant First Class Louis R. Rocco; U.S. Military Assistance Command; near Katum, South Vietnam; 24 May 1970. Flying with a heliborne medical evacuation team, Rocco was injured when the chopper crash-landed near enemy forces. Despite his injuries he pulled three unconscious airmen from the flaming wreck, sustaining severe burns, but risked communist gunfire to carry each man to cover. He then provided first aid until he fainted from shock and pain.

Lieutenant Colonel Andre C. Lucas; 2nd Battalion, 506th Infantry, 101st Airborne Division; South Vietnam; 1–23 July 1970. In separate actions over a three-week period, Lucas provided command and control that saved one of his companies from destruction, conducted resupply efforts, and personally attempted to rescue a crewman from a burning helicopter. Lucas was killed while directing the successful evacuation of a besieged fire base.

MARINE CORPS (1)

CAPTAIN STEPHEN WESLEY PLESS

6 SEPTEMBER 1939–20 JULY 1969

BORN: Newman, Georgia

DIED: Near Pensacola, Florida

ACTION: Combat rescue; Quang Nai Province, South Vietnam; 19 August 1967 (age 27)

UNIT: VMO-6, Marine Air Group 36, 1st Marine Aircraft Wing

AIRCRAFT: Bell UH-1E BuNo 154760 (WB 15)

OTHER AWARDS: Silver Star, Distinguished Flying Cross, Bronze Star Medal, Air Medal (38), Purple Heart

Marine Corps aviation accounted for one Medal of Honor in the Vietnam War. The award went to an aggressive young aviator who quickly adapted to a tactical situation for which there was little precedent.

It started as a gunship escort for a medical evacuation flight out of Ky Ha, near Chu Lai, South Vietnam. Captain Steve Pless of Marine Observation Squadron Six was returning to base, monitoring the guard frequency, when an Army CH-47 pilot screamed for help. The big Chinook had force-landed

Stephen W. Pless

in hostile territory, hoping to effect repairs, when Viet Cong troops began firing. The Army pilot "pulled pitch" and lifted off, but in the confusion four of his passengers remained on the ground. They were stranded on a beach near the mouth of the Song Tra Khuc River, about eighty miles south of Danang. With VC closing in, heavy ground fire kept other helos either offshore or making gun runs on defense. Recognizing the danger, Pless asked his crew, "You all with me?" All three men agreed.

Pless accelerated his Huey gunship toward the site, running a precombat check list. Arriving overhead, the marines saw perhaps forty VC surrounding the GIs, who were being clubbed and bayoneted. With Americans and Vietnamese intermingled, opening fire was likely to cause friendly casualties, but Pless knew the GIs would be killed regardless. He told his right-door gunner to begin shooting. Gunnery Sergeant Leroy Poulson opened up with his M60, and the first burst prompted the VC to scramble for cover.

Keeping up the pressure, Pless rolled in hot, firing white phosphorous rockets and machine guns. He pressed his attacks so low that the airframe was spattered with dirt and debris from the rocket explosions. The Viet Cong now scattered, affording the UH-1E a chance to land. Pless's crew chief, Lance Corporal John Phelps, later said, "I couldn't believe what he was making that helo do, but when the smoke started to clear we saw bodies lying everywhere."

Pless maneuvered his helo, landing between the soldiers and the VC. With the engine idling, the crew scrambled onto the sandbar and began dragging the wounded men aboard, returning close-range gunfire with enemy troops, who repeatedly attempted to prevent a liftoff. Copilot Rupert Fairfield killed three VC with the right-side M60, merely ten feet from the aircraft. Phelps shot another with his pistol. Meanwhile, the marines determined that one GI was dead and left him for an inbound H-34.

With three extra men on board, Pless and Fairfield eased the laden Huey off the ground. At least 500 pounds overweight, the gunship barely lifted off, but Pless coaxed the chopper to relative safety offshore. Flying in ground effect, the pilots narrowly averted disaster as the Huey's skids settled into the water; Pless jettisoned the empty rocket pods before regaining sufficient airspeed to continue a climb. He did not know that his tail rotor drive shaft and an oil line had been struck by gunfire; the Huey should have crashed. After return to base, the fliers learned that two of the men they rescued had died of serious wounds, but one survived.

An Army UH-1 pilot wrote, "This was the most heroic action I have witnessed. . . . The marine crew did their utmost to save four Americans while under fire from the enemy nearly all the time. I highly recommended that this crew be properly rewarded for their unselfish act of heroism." The Navy agreed: Pless was nominated for the Medal of Honor; his crew was recommended for Navy Crosses.

During two Vietnam tours Pless logged 750 missions for 1,000 combat hours. His aircraft were struck by gunfire ninety-seven times and he was shot down twice.

Pless and Air Force Major Joe Jackson received the Medal of Honor on 16 January 1969. The marine was the first of eight helicopter pilots awarded the medal for the Vietnam War, though Army pilot Ed Freeman's 1965 action was recognized in 2001.

Less than two years later Pless was killed at age twenty-nine while riding his motorcycle near Pensacola, Florida. According to police reports, he attempted to jump a drawbridge as it was raising and smashed into the abutment on the far side of the river. He is buried at Barrancas National Cemetery near Pensacola.

After the Vietnam War, maritime prepositioning ships were named for Medal of Honor recipients, including the SS *Stephen W. Pless* (T-AK 3007) in 1985. In 2000 Marine Corps Air Station Miramar dedicated Pless Avenue with his mother in attendance.

Crew: Capt. Rupert E. Fairfield Jr. (CP); Lance Corp. John G. Phelps (CC); Gunnery Sgt. Leroy N. Poulson (G).

Marine Corps Aviation Related (1)

Private Raymond M. Clausen; Marine Medium Helicopter Squadron 263; South Vietnam; 31 January 1970. During a medical evacuation mission, Clausen defied orders and left his CH-46D to assist wounded marines into the helicopter despite the threat of mines and gunfire. He made six trips out and back, including one in which a mine exploded, killing one marine and wounding three. After discharge, Clausen was recalled to duty for three days to receive his medal from President Nixon, who also awarded a meritorious promotion to private first class!

NAVY (2)

LIEUTENANT COMMANDER MICHAEL JOHN ESTOCIN

27 APRIL 1931–26 APRIL 1967

BORN: Turtle Creek, Pennsylvania

DIED: Haiphong Province, North Vietnam

ACTION: SAM suppression; near Haiphong, North Vietnam; 20 and 26 April 1967 (age 35)

UNIT: Attack Squadron 192, USS *Ticonderoga* (CVA-14)

AIRCRAFT: Douglas A-4E BuNo 150033 (NM-208) "Jury 208"

OTHER DECORATIONS: Distinguished Flying Cross, Air Medal (12), Purple Heart

Lieutenant Commander Mike Estocin was an Iron Hand, one of the few A-4 Skyhawk pilots qualified for the Shrike antiradar missile. By 1967 the air war over North Vietnam required constant use of Iron Hands to suppress the surface-to-air missile threat against American aircraft. Seventh Fleet carriers operating from "Yankee Station" in the Tonkin Gulf had taken heavy losses from the Soviet SA-2 that was guided to its target by ground radar. When things worked right, the AGM-45B Shrike could hit a radar control van from about eight miles away, allowing the "strikers" to penetrate Hanoi's defenses.

When they didn't work right, suppressors or strikers died.

Estocin was one of the most experienced pilots in Air Wing 19 aboard the USS *Ticonderoga* (CVA-14), a modified Essex-class carrier. Brisk and business-like, Estocin was a veteran of ten years in carrier aviation. Widely known for his professionalism, he was captivated with his work. "Mike didn't just want to suppress SAMs," said a shipmate. "He wanted to kill them."

Michael J. Estocin

On 20 April, Estocin led a flight of three A-4E Skyhawks against Haiphong Harbor. He identified the active SAM sites, assigned targets to his wingmen, and pressed through missile and antiaircraft gunfire. Estocin's division destroyed two sites but in the process drew heavy SAM launches. One SA-2 detonated near his jet, inflicting blast damage. Estocin pulled off to check his aircraft's systems, and momentarily satisfied, he returned to the combat area, launched his last Shrike, and struck the third site.

Headed east for the gulf, Estocin noticed his fuel state dropping alarmingly. The SAM's warhead had punctured his fuel cells, which streamed a cloud of JP-5. Estimating that he had five minutes of fuel remaining, he called a KA-3 tanker that arrived with moments to spare. Estocin plugged in and trailed the "Whale" back to the USS *Ticonderoga,* linked by the refueling umbilical. The Skywarrior was pumping more fuel than the stricken Skyhawk was using, as the JP hemorrhage increased.

The two Douglas jets made a long straight-in to "Tico," with Estocin passing instructions to the tanker pilot: "You're half a ball low, take it up."

Less than three miles from the ship, the tanker reeled in the drogue and turned away. Estocin had enough fuel for one try at the deck. With his A-4 now afire from the trailing edge aft, he flew a "roger" pass, snagged a wire, and waited for the fire fighters to soak his jet in foam. When he tossed his helmet down to the plane captain, the A-4's aluminum skin was charred and blackened. Estocin strolled away without looking back.

Six days later, 26 April, Estocin was back at work, supporting an "alpha" strike against oil storage tanks near Haiphong. With his F-8 Crusader escort he "coasted in" at 21,000 feet under clear skies. The strikers ingressed with only moderate opposition, as the missile batteries had learned to respect U.S. Navy Iron Hands. While the attack divisions withdrew, Estocin orbited, trolling for SAMs. His wingman, Lieutenant Commander John Nichols of VF-191, felt that Estocin was elated when the radar warning receivers came alive. Estocin called, "The site is up!" The section turned toward Site 109, north of the city.

The "Red Crown" radar controller offshore had lost the lone pair as the attack planes safely egressed. "The strike is feet wet," called the controller. "What is your position?"

Estocin did not reply. Instead, he was intently leaning forward, scanning visually for the missile shot he knew would come. Both pilots saw the SA-2's booster ignite about eight miles ahead. Estocin called as the SAM lifted off, arcing toward the A-4 and F-8. Rocketing upward, the missile's booster separated and the sustainer motor cut in. The mindless killer was tracking one of the two planes, approaching head on.

Nichols expected Estocin to turn one way or another, reducing the closure rate and permitting a better assessment of the SAM's aspect. But the devoted Iron Hand pressed on, apparently hoping for a high-percentage shot at the launch site.

Estocin had waited too long. The SAM arced downward, homing on the A-4, and detonated close aboard. Rocked by the concussion, the little jet rolled right, stopping almost inverted. It shed debris in a nose-down, diving turn. A fire burned in the belly.

Slowly, Estocin recovered, returning to level flight at 2,000 feet. Nichols slowed dangerously, dropping to about 160 knots airspeed but unwilling to leave the doomed Skyhawk. He heard the high warble of another SAM's radar guidance, even felt the slipstream of its passing, but kept his eyes locked on the A-4. Estocin was slumped forward, not moving. There was no reply to Nichols's urgent calls.

Crossing to port, Nichols was appalled at the damage to the Skyhawk's nose. The intake was smashed, the skin perforated from nose to wing. Nichols called for a Rescue CAP, but he knew the A-4 couldn't last. Within three miles of the coast, down to 1,000 feet, the little bomber began an uncommanded roll to inverted. It hung momentarily, then both Shrikes fired as the flames burned through the electrical circuits.

Nichols saw the nose fall through the horizon and the A-4 impacted the ground. There was no parachute. Mike Estocin died the day before his thirty-sixth birthday.

The air wing recommended Estocin for a posthumous Navy Cross but CinCPacFleet replied, "Resubmit. Will support an upgrade." In February 1978 Estocin's Medal of Honor was presented to his widow, Marie, who for decades wondered at the contradictions in the citation. Among other things, it said that Estocin fired his Shrikes "and exited the area." Other sources said he crashed offshore; one covert POW report even hinted that he was alive in Hanoi. The family—and John Nichols—agonized over the prospects for years. Its bungling of the Estocin case, with many others, remains an eternal blot on the record of the United States Navy.

However, Estocin's memory was perpetuated in the annual award for the Navy's outstanding strike-fighter squadron and in a guided missile frigate (FFG-15) commissioned in 1981.

Estocin's name on the Vietnam Memorial is found at panel 18E, row 092.

LIEUTENANT (JG) CLYDE EVERETT LASSEN

14 MARCH 1942–1 APRIL 1994

BORN: Ft. Myers, Florida

DIED: Pensacola, Florida

ACTION: Combat rescue; Nghe An Province, North Vietnam; 19 June 1968 (age 26)

UNIT: Detachment 104, Helicopter Support Squadron 7

AIRCRAFT: UH-2A BuNo 149764 (VH 15) "Clementine 2"

OTHER DECORATIONS: Bronze Star Medal, Air Medal

It was a moonless, overcast night in the Tonkin Gulf, but that was insufficient reason to keep the carrier aviators on deck. Cruising "Yankee Station" was the USS *America* (CVA-66), which launched interdiction sorties over North Vietnam. One of her Phantoms of Fighter Squadron 33 was shot down by a surface-to-air missile and the F-4J crew ejected from "Rootbeer 214."

Clyde E. Lassen

The pilot was Lieutenant Commander John W. "Claw" Holtzclaw; his radar intercept officer, Lieutenant Commander John A. "Zeke" Burns, broke a leg on ejection eighteen miles north of Vinh.

Aboard the destroyer USS *Prebble* (DLG-15) the duty helo crew was awakened shortly past midnight. Hardly had the four men laced up their boots when they launched with a "sick bird": inoperative or malfunctioning compass, ADF, and gyro. Lieutenants (jg) Clyde Lassen and copilot Leroy Cook nevertheless pressed on with PO2 Bruce Dallas and PO3 Don West as their crewmen.

The crash site was seventy nautical miles off as "Clementine Two" checked in with the controller aboard the frigate USS *Jouett* (DLG-29). Two SAMs were fired on ingress, but the rescue combat air patrol (ResCAP) coached "Clem Two" onto the scene, where Rootbeer 214 still burned on the ground. The helo established radio contact with the downed Phantom crew and confirmed ID from record card (Holtzclaw's favorite dessert was ice cream.) The VF-33 crew started for a limestone hill but was impeded by Burns's broken leg. Even with radio contact, effecting a join-up was difficult in the black night, so the tailhookers fired tracers from their pistols.

When Clem Two arrived, "Claw" and "Zeke" were partway up a wooded hill whose trees prevented a helicopter approach. Therefore, Lassen landed in a rice paddy about seventy yards away. It was frustrating: dense foliage prevented the F-4 crew from reaching the helo, and small arms fire erupted from a nearby village. In the rush through the vegetation the crew lost its best emergency radio.

Following Dallas's and West's directions, Lassen edged the Seasprite up the gradient of the hill. The ResCAP dropped flares, permitting the helo crew a better view, but the Rootbeers were still beneath thick jungle canopy.

Lassen maneuvered fifty feet over the men, holding a hover between two large trees.

Clem Two's crewmen lowered a hoist with a jungle penetrator that came within inches of Burns's hands. After four or five attempts it was apparent that there was not enough cable to descend farther.

Then the flares burned out.

Down low, out of ground effect, Lassen lost his visual horizon. Adding power, he began climbing out of danger when the helo struck a tree on its starboard side. The little Seasprite nosed down, spiralling right, headed for the trees. In a superb display of flying skill, Lassen instantly recovered control and climbed away.

Twice Lassen landed in North Vietnam, conserving fuel and waiting for the situation to improve before the threat forced him to take off. Said copilot Leroy Cook, "That whole evening, there were two large hands around that helicopter, holding it."

It was time to regroup, but time was critical. Lassen pulled off and orbited nearby—an agonizing fifteen minutes while another ResCAP flight arrived with more flares. Meanwhile, the F-4 crew pushed through the underbrush, knowing the only chance for rescue was to reach the paddy at the base of the hill. All the while, North Vietnamese troops were closing in—it was a race.

Gunfire began cracking around the UH-2. As if that weren't bad enough, fuel now was a factor. Clem Two had been "feet dry" over for three-quarters of an hour, with thirty minutes of fuel remaining. But the crew decided on first things first. The door-mounted M60 machine guns opened fire, shooting at enemy muzzle flashes. Cook, unoccupied for the moment, unlimbered his M16 and joined in. His expended brass ricocheted off the interior of the windscreen, bouncing into Lassen's face. The pilot exclaimed, "I'm hit!" For a horrible moment Cook thought he would have to take the controls. Then Lassen recovered.

At length Zeke and Claw groped their way to the bottom of the hill and radioed their position. Then the new flares burned out, returning the area to darkness except for Vietnamese tracers. With no option, Lassen turned on the searchlight.

Burns and Holtzclaw could hear movement around them. Burns lit a strobe light on his torso harness. Holtzclaw looked back and saw a Vietnamese about twenty feet behind. They dashed into the paddy, bullets kicking up dirt and water. Cook and Dallas kept up a sustained fire, trying to beat down the pursuers.

Burns, with his broken leg, beat Holtzclaw to the helo. Dallas reached out, pulled the RIO aboard, then grabbed the pilot. Burns tapped Lassen on the shoulder, "Sir, we need to go!"

Lassen picked up Clem Two, pedal-turned about, and bent the throttle. The Seasprite accelerated to 140 knots (redline was 130), dodging automatic weapons and bursting flak in its dash for the coast. The instrument panel flashed red-orange warning lights but both pilots ignored them.

With less than ten minutes fuel remaining, Lassen put down on the USS *Jouett,* barely five miles offshore. Once Clem Two was tied down, the immensely grateful crew checked the aircraft. Incredibly, despite prolonged minutes of illumination, no shell fragments or bullets had struck the UH-2. It was a testament to courage, skill, judgment—and luck.

Someone produced a bottle of scotch, and in complete disregard of regulations, the aircrewmen settled down to enjoy it. Lassen received the Medal of Honor in January 1969; Cook received the Navy Cross and the Dallas and West Silver Stars.

Clyde Lassen died of cancer in 1994. He is buried in Barrancas National Cemetery, Pensacola, Florida, as is fellow helicopter pilot Steve Pless. A destroyer, DDG-82, was named for Lassen in November 1999.

Crew: Lt. (jg) Leroy Cook (CP); PO2 Bruce Dallas; PO3 Don West.

Navy Aviation Related (1)

Captain James B. Stockdale; 4th Allied POW Wing; Hanoi, North Vietnam; 1965–73. As commanding officer of Carrier Air Wing 16 in the USS *Oriskany* (CVA-34), Stockdale ejected from his stricken A-4E in September 1965. Over the next seven years he was confined and tortured in an effort to limit his effectiveness as the senior Navy POW in Hanoi. At one point he attempted suicide to prevent the Vietnamese from exploiting him for propaganda purposes. He retired as a vice admiral and has written extensively, including a memoir with his wife, Sybil: *In Love and War.*

7

THE AVIATION MEDALS OF HONOR IN PERSPECTIVE

The ninety-one in-flight citations represent just under ten percent of all Medal of Honor awards since World War I. The greatest portion of aviation medals for a specific period was the six (28 percent) of twenty-one awards during the interwar period from 1919 to 1940, only one of which was for combat action. However, from barely 5 percent in World War I the in-flight ratio more than doubled to 12 percent in World War II before declining to roughly 5 and 8 percent for Korea and Vietnam.

Demographics

Medal of Honor airmen were born in thirty-six states and four nations (Britain, the Philippines, China, and India). Texas had the most with nine, followed by Illinois with six, New York with four, and Alabama, Michigan, Missouri, Oklahoma, Pennsylvania, Washington, and Wisconsin with three each. However, several men born in one state grew up in another, so too much should not be made of the geographic component. Jimmy Doolittle, for instance, was born in California but felt himself an Alaskan. Tommy McGuire spent his youth in New Jersey and Florida, but during the war he was claimed by Texas because his wife lived in San Antonio.

For most of the twentieth century, aviation was considered "a young man's

Table 1 In-Flight Medal of Honor Distribution

Era	*Total*	*In-flight*	*Percentage*
WW I	119	7	5.8
Interim	21	6	28.5
WW II	463	53	11.4
Korea	131	6	4.5
Vietnam	43	19	7.8
Total	977[a]	91	9.3

[a]As of 2001; waivers and delayed awards continue adding to the total.

game" (to quote Canadian ace Raymond Collishaw). However, the median age of Medal of Honor airmen steadily increased from World War I through Vietnam, and five fliers in that period were over forty; twenty-two more were over thirty. Greater education requirements and increased professionalism were the dominant factors rather than simply age and experience.

The oldest of the Great War recipients was Harold Goettler at twenty-eight; the median was twenty-three. In World War II the median age rose to twenty-six; the Army Air Force figure was twenty-five. The median for the Navy and Marines was twenty-eight. Five of the golden wingers were older than thirty, with Henry Elrod (a prewar captain) being the eldest at thirty-six. In contrast, an AAF brigadier general and two colonels also were thirty-six.

The six Korean War recipients were between twenty-six and thirty-four. Four were over thirty, the median being thirty-one.

Nineteen in-flight medals were awarded for the Vietnam War, with ten Air Force recipients ranging from twenty-three to forty-six (Bill Jones); Army men were twenty to forty-seven (Mike Novosel); the three naval recipients were twenty-two to thirty-five. It is instructive of the greater professionalism in military aviation that the median for both Korea and Vietnam was thirty-one years, though in Southeast Asia four recipients were in their mid-to-late forties.

The typical Medal of Honor airman was a twenty-seven-year-old captain (Navy lieutenant) on his thirtieth combat mission. If he was a fighter pilot, he had logged about 1,000 hours at the time of his action; Joe Foss fits the profile almost exactly.

Mortality

Across the board, the wartime aviation Medal of Honor recipients sustained 45 percent mortality in commission of their actions. That figure does not include those lost after the action, regardless of whether they had already received the award. O'Hare and Kearby were subsequently killed in action; Pease and Wilkins survived their shootdowns but died at the hands of their captors. Hammann, Talbot, Vance, and Bong died in aircraft accidents.

In at least a dozen cases the recipient's only other decoration was the Purple Heart.

The Medal of Honor mortality rate was more than 40 percent for both world wars but doubled in Korea. It was lowest in Vietnam but was still a substantial one in four.

For all eras the Air Force and its antecedents sustained the highest rate of fatal actions: a staggering 53 percent. Navy pilots were next at 40 percent. Ironically, considering its "first to fight" reputation, the Marine Corps was by far the lowest at 27 percent. The combined Navy-Marine figure is 33 percent.

Combat Experience

Combat experience was no indicator of Medal of Honor potential. Two Army Air Forces fliers—Jimmy Doolittle and Maynard Smith—received the award for their first missions; four others for their second. Where figures are known, the median mission count for AAF medals was twenty; the highs were more than 200 (Bong and McGuire).

In the AAF, bomber crews were far more likely to receive medals than fighters (twenty-five to five) with the Fifth Air Force accounting for three of

Table 2 Posthumous In-Flight Awards

Era	*Service (total and percentage)*
WW I	3 of 4 USAS; 0 of 2 USMC; 0 of 1 USN (3 of 7–43%)
Interim	0 of 1 USAS; 2 of 4 USN; 0 of 1 USMC (2 of 6–33%)
WW II	20 of 36 AAF; 2 of 6 USN; 4 of 11 USMC (26 of 53–49%)
Korea	1 of 2 USN; 4 of 4 USAF (5 of 6–83%)
Vietnam	2 of 6 USA; 2 of 10 USAF;1 of 2 USN; 0 of 1 USMC (5 of 19–26%)
Total	41 of 91 (45%)

Note: Excludes those killed after their Medal of Honor action.

the "pursuit" pilots. However, Marine Corps fighter pilots dominated the field with ten of eleven; in the Navy, two fighter pilots and four others received Medals of Honor.

Throughout World War II, seventeen fighter pilots and thirty-six other fliers received in-flight Medals of Honor. Among the naval aviators, Henry Elrod, Richard Fleming, and Butch O'Hare all were decorated in whole or in part for their initial combats. However, many received the medal for successive missions that often included their entire combat careers, notably most of the marines.

Among the Korean War recipients, three of the four Air Force pilots had World War II combat experience (55 to 266 missions.) The Korean War decorations occurred between the twenty-fifth and sixtieth missions.

Mission counts in Vietnam often were meaningless, especially for helicopter pilots. It was not unusual to sit in the chopper twelve hours a day with a dozen takeoffs, any one of which could involve combat—or none. Jim Fleming, for instance, made 810 flights "in-country."

Forward air controllers also logged enormous numbers: Hilliard Wilbanks was killed on his 487th sortie. In contrast, Air Force "fast movers" usually flew a fixed number of North Vietnam missions during a tour, generally pegged at one hundred. Leo Thorsness was shot down and captured on his ninety-third mission.

Career Influence

Presumably the Medal of Honor would boost a military career, but the evidence indicates otherwise. Not all recipients remained in the armed forces, and even those recalled in later wars seldom chose to remain. The natural leadership evidenced by a Jimmy Doolittle or a Leon Johnson probably would have led to general's rank in any case, though often combat results do not translate to peacetime success. Among other capable airmen, careers peaked at lieutenant colonel or colonel, frequently in staff or administrative positions. One officer retired as director of a motor pool.

Two flying generals received posthumous medals: Ken Walker and Fred Castle. Of the eleven AAF officer recipients who survived the war, three (27 percent) became generals: Doolittle, Johnson, and Howard. Among the ten surviving naval aviators (seven marines and three navy), Bob Galer was honored with a retirement promotion to brigadier, and Joe Foss achieved his star in the Air Force Reserve. From the interim era, Christian Schilt became a Marine Corps general in the 1950s.

The only Korean War Medal of Honor airman to survive was Tom Hudner, who retired as a Navy captain.

Five Air Force and three Army officers survived Vietnam, but among in-flight recipients only helicopter pilot Pat Brady attained general officer rank. (POW Jim Stockdale retired as a vice admiral.) However, for many pilots—perhaps most—rank by itself meant little. For some it meant absolutely nothing; after the war two Army pilots gladly dropped commissioned officer status for warrant officer rank so they could remain flying.

Overall, from World War II through Vietnam, six of thirty-two surviving officers (19 percent) awarded in-flight awards eventually achieved regular or reserve flag rank. The majority of the others retired as lieutenant colonels or colonels, or the Navy rank of captain, though not all recipients pursued military careers. An excellent example was Marine Private Raymond Clausen, who was recalled to active duty to receive his medal, and was given a meritorious promotion to private first class.

The Medal of Honor has provided a starting point in postwar careers, most notably Joe Foss as governor of South Dakota and Nathan Gordon as lieutenant governor of Arkansas. Bob Galer was active in the Dallas Cowboys organization following retirement from the Marine Corps and the aerospace industry. Others chose to contribute to their fellow soldiers: Fred Ferguson, Tom Hudner, and John Levitow all worked for their respective states' veterans administrations.

Eighty-three of the ninety-one in-flight recipients were commissioned officers, but warrant officers and noncoms featured throughout. In fact, the first was Landsman for Quartermaster Charles Hammann in August 1918. He is usually cited as an ensign but he was not commissioned until after his action. His quartermaster rating was approximately a warrant rank, whereas Ralph Talbot's gunner, Robert Robinson, was a corporal. Smith, Mathies, and Erwin were NCO aircrew during World War II, as were Yano and Levitow in Vietnam. Typical of most Army helicopter pilots in Vietnam, Ferguson and Novosel were warrant officers. They enjoyed vastly longer careers than their warrant or NCO counterparts—and longer than many commissioned officers.

Aviation-Related Actions

Most of the eighteen "aviation related" Medal of Honor actions are not difficult to categorize because they occurred entirely on land or sea in an aviation context, such as nonfliers aboard aircraft carriers; others involved airmen in prison camps or ground combat. However, a few tread close to the border of in-flight action established as the criterion for full treatment in this volume. Incidents in which the recipient arrived at the scene by aircraft but conducted himself heroically on the ground are considered aviation related, with one exception: Tom Hudner's attempted rescue of his squadronmate in Korea occurred because he made the decision to crash land and executed the landing in a single-seat aircraft.

Three more men deserve acknowledgment, as they achieved aviation ratings after their Medal of Honor actions. Commander William A. Moffett and Ensign Edward O. McDonnell were among the fifty-eight recipients in the two-day punitive expedition to Vera Cruz, Mexico, in April 1914. Moffett's later career was particularly significant: he was designated an aerial observer and became one of the chief architects of U.S. naval aviation. As a rear admiral he died in the crash of the airship *Akron* in 1933.

McDonnell made technical and operational contributions to naval aviation during and after World War I, including the first U.S. launch (in a Sopwith Camel) from a battleship turret in 1919.

A Korean War marine, Second Lieutenant Henry A. Commiskey, received the Medal of Honor for a 1950 action in which he took a pistol to a machine gun fight—and won. Subsequently he earned wings of gold and followed an aviation career.

Yet another Vera Cruz veteran achieved aviation acclaim. Though never a pilot, Vice Admiral Frank Jack Fletcher (whose uncle commanded the Mexican expedition) successfully led U.S. carriers in the Battles of the Coral Sea, Midway, and Eastern Solomons. No other American commanded in three carrier battles.

Table 3 Aviation-Related Medals of Honor

Era	*Navy*	*USMC*	*AAF/USAF*	*Army*
WW I	2	0	0	0
WW II	5	1	2	0
Vietnam	1	1	3	3
Total	8	2	5	3

Medal of Honor Aircraft

The ninety-one in-flight Medals of Honor were presented for actions aboard thirty-one fixed-wing aircraft types and four variety of helicopters. By a wide margin the Boeing B-17 produced the most Medals of Honor, with seventeen awards from 1942 through 1944. General Curtis E. LeMay said of the classic bomber, "The Air Force kind of grew up with the B-17. It was as tough an aeroplane as was ever built. It did everything we asked it to do, and did it well."

Next in line were nine Consolidated B-24 awards (including one Navy PB4Y), followed by eight for Grumman F4F Wildcats. The helicopter and "jointness" records are held by the ubiquitous Bell UH-1 "Huey," which featured in six Army, one Air Force, and one Marine in-flight actions.

Five Douglas aircraft types produced seven medals, followed by four North Americans (eight medals) and three Voughts (six awards). Seventeen other manufacturers were represented, including four foreign: DeHavilland, Fokker, Macchi, and SPAD.

Though the large majority of medal actions involved one aircraft (two crew members of the same plane were decorated on seven occasions), some citations acknowledged outstanding service over a prolonged period. Frank Luke reportedly used five SPAD XIIIs in his spectacular eighteen-day spree on the Western Front, but most serial numbers are unknown. The plane in which he flew his last mission was brand new, having only arrived at the 27th Aero Squadron the day before Luke's death.

At Guadalcanal during World War II, Joe Foss flew thirty-four Wildcats and claimed victories in ten. On his best day, 25 October 1942, he flew two F4Fs to score five kills. Thus, it is impossible to identify him with a personal aircraft. Similar situations exist for other marines, such as Smith, Galer, Walsh, Boyington, and Hanson, who flew multiple fighters in a succession of Medal of Honor missions.

In other instances a pilot's assigned aircraft was not flown during his action. A case in point is Jim Howard's P-51B named *Ding Hao!* Though repeatedly used to illustrate his one-handed combat in January 1944, Howard's personal Mustang, coded AJ-A, was replaced by AJ-X on the Oschersleben mission. Likewise, Greg Boyington was identified with a Corsair named *Lulubelle,* when in fact he never flew that F4U in combat. The name and twenty victory flags were applied once only for publicity photos.

The Corsair and Mustang are the only two-war Medal of Honor aircraft, with multiple awards in World War II and one each in Korea. Three very different U.S. aircraft also were involved in Victoria Cross actions: the Catalina of Flying Officer J. A. Cruickshank over the Atlantic in July 1944; the Douglas Dakota (C-47) of Flight Lieutenant David Lord during the Arnhem operation of September 1944; and the Corsair of Flight Sub-Lieutenant Robert H. Gray in August 1945. Lord's and Gray's Victoria Crosses were posthumous.

Obviously, very few Medal of Honor aircraft remain. The best known is Lindbergh's Ryan, preserved at the National Air and Space Museum in Washington, D.C. Byrd's Fokker Trimotor is retained by the Ford Museum in Dearborn, Michigan. Fisher's A-1E Skyraider is displayed at the Air Force Museum near Dayton, Ohio. Yano's and Pless's Hueys are held by the National Warplane Museum in Elmira, New York, and the Marine Corps Air-Ground Museum at Quantico, Virginia, respectively. As of 2001, Clausen's CH-46D was still flying in the Marine Corps—more than thirty years after his Medal of Honor event! Sadly, in the mid-1990s Jackson's C-123 was scrapped after use by the Thai armed forces.

Though unrelated to his wartime citation, Bob Galer's prewar Grumman F3F was recovered from the ocean off San Diego and fully restored for exhibit at Pensacola, Florida.

Table 4 Aircraft Medal of Honor Citations

Aircraft	*Number and Service*
In-Flight	
Bell UH-1	8 (6 Army, 1 USAF, 1 USMC)
Boeing B-17	17
Boeing B-29	1
Cessna O-1	1
Consolidated B-24/PB4Y	9 (1 Navy)
Consolidated PBY	2
Curtiss JN-4	1
DeHavilland Model 4	4 (2 Army, 2 USMC)
Douglas A-1	2
Douglas A-4	1
Douglas A-26	1
Douglas AC-47	1
Douglas SBD	2
Fokker Trimotor	2
Fairchild C-123	1
Grumman F4F	8
Grumman F6F	1
Kaman UH-2	1
Lockheed P-38	2
Lockheed F-80	1
Macchi M-5	1
Martin B-26	1
North American B-25	3
North American F-86	1
North American OV-10	1
North American P-51/F-6	3 (2 WW II, 1 Korea)
Republic P-47	2
Republic F-105	2
Ryan NY-P	1
Sikorski Ho3S	1
Sikorski HH-3	1
SPAD XIII	2
Vought O2U	1
Vought SB2U	1
Vought F4U	4 (3 WW II, 1 Korea)
Total	91

Continued on next page

Table 4 *(continued)*

Aircraft	*Number and Service*
Aviation Related	
Bell UH-1	3
Boeing CH-46	1
Burgess N-9	1
Kaman HH-43	1
McDonnell Douglas A-4	1
McDonnell Douglas F-4	1
North American F-100	1
Kite balloon	1
Total	10 (8 did not involve aircraft)

BIBLIOGRAPHY

Allmon, William B. "Ensign Charles H. Hammann." *Aviation History,* May 2001.

Anderson, Carroll R. "Mission to Kavieng." *Journal of the American Aviation Historical Society,* summer 1965.

Avery, Norman L. *B-25 Mitchell: The Magnificent Medium.* St. Paul: Phalanx Publishing, 1992.

Bennett, William J. "Research Project 6910: Medal of Honor Aircraft." *Journal of the American Aviation Historical Society,* winter 1997.

Bong, Carl, and Mike O'Connor. *Ace of Aces: The Dick Bong Story.* Mesa, Ariz.: Champlin Museum Press, 1985.

Byrd, Martha. *Kenneth N. Walker: Airpower's Untempered Crusader.* Maxwell Air Force Base, Ala.: Air University Press, 1997.

Carter, Kit C., and Robert Mueller. *Combat Chronology, 1941–1945.* Washington, D.C.: Center for Air Force History, 1991.

Chinnery, Philip. *Vietnam: The Helicopter War.* Annapolis, Md.: Naval Institute Press, 1991.

Cole, Sam. *The Last Flight of the Lady Jeanette.* Kirkland, Wash.: Battery Willis S. Cole Military Museum, 1998.

Cressman, Robert C., et al. *A Glorious Page in Our History.* Missoula, Mont.: Pictorial Histories, 1990.

Dugan, James, and Carroll Stewart. *Ploesti: The Great Ground-Air Battle.* New York: Random House, 1962.

Durkota, Alan E. *Medal of Honor Aviators of WW I.* Stratford, Conn.: Flying Machines Press, 1998.

Emmons, Roger M. "The First Marine Aviation Force." *Cross and Cockade Journal,* autumn 1965.

Ewing, Steve, and John B. Lundstrom. *Fateful Rendezvous: The Life of Butch O'Hare.* Annapolis, Md.: Naval Institute Press, 1997.

Frank, Pat, and Joseph D. Harrington. *Rendezvous at Midway.* New York: Paperback Library, 1967.

Freeman, Roger. *The Mighty Eighth.* New York: Doubleday, 1970.

Frisbee, John L. "Valor" series in *Air Force* magazine, 1983–94.

Futrell, Robert Frank. *The United States Air Force in Korea, 1950–1953.* Washington, D.C.: Center for Air Force History, 1983.

Gamble, Bruce. *Black Sheep One: The Life of Gregory "Pappy" Boyington.* Novato, Calif.: Presidio Press, 2000.

———. "Time Flies: Clyde Lassen." *Foundation,* spring 1994.

Glines, C. V. *Chennault's Forgotten Warriors: The Saga of the 308th Bomb Group in China.* Atglen, Pa.: Schiffer, 1995.

———. *The Doolittle Raid.* Atglen, Pa.: Schiffer, 1999.

Haiber, William P. *Frank Luke: The September Rampage.* LaGrangeville, N.Y.: Info Devel Press, 1999.

Hardy, Gordon, et al. *Above and Beyond.* Boston: Boston Publishing, 1985.

Hess, William N. *America's Aces in a Day.* North Branch, Minn.: Specialty Press, 1996.

Howard, James H. *Roar of the Tiger.* New York: Orion Books, 1991.

Jordan, Kenneth N. *Men of Honor.* Atglen, Pa.: Schiffer Books, 2000.

Lemon, Peter C. *Beyond the Medal.* Golden, Colo.: Fulcrum Publishing, 1997.

Lundstrom, John B. *The First Team and the Guadalcanal Campaign.* Annapolis, Md.: Naval Institute Press, 1994.

McAulay, Lex. *Into the Dragon's Jaws: The Fifth Air Force over Rabaul.* Mesa, Ariz.: Champlin Museum Press, 1986.

Martin, Charles A. *The Last Great Ace: The Life of Major Thomas B. McGuire, Jr.* Fruit Cove, Fla.: Fruit Cove Publishing, 1998.

Mersky, Peter B. *U.S. Marine Corps Aviation: 1912 to the Present.* Annapolis, Md.: Nautical & Aviation Publishing, 1987.

Mitchell, John H. *On Wings We Conquer: The 19th and 7th Bomb Groups in the Southwest Pacific.* Springfield, Mo.: GEM Distributors, 1990.

Nichols, John B., and Barrett Tillman. *On Yankee Station: The Naval Air War over Vietnam.* Annapolis, Md.: Naval Institute Press, 1987.

Novosel, Michael J. *Dustoff: The Memoir of an Army Aviator.* Novato, Calif.: Presidio Press, 1999.

Olynyk, Frank J. *Stars & Bars: A Tribute to the American Fighter Ace, 1920–1973.* London: Grub Street, 1995.

Proft, R. J., ed. *United States of America's Congressional Medal of Honor Recipients.* Second edition. Columbia Heights, Minn.: Highland House II, 1998.

Rickenbacker, Edward V. *Rickenbacker: An Autobiography.* New York: Prentice Hall, 1967.

Schneider, Donald K. *Air Force Heroes in Vietnam.* Maxwell Air Force Base, Ala.: Air War College, 1979.

Tillman, Barrett. *Corsair: The F4U in World War II and Korea.* Annapolis, Md.: Naval Institute Press, 1979.

———. *Wildcat: The F4F in World War II.* Annapolis, Md.: Naval Institute Press, 1990.

Tooker, D. K. *The Second-Luckiest Pilot.* Annapolis, Md.: Naval Institute Press, 2000.

U.S. Navy. *Dictionary of American Naval Fighting Ships.* Multiple volumes. Washington, D.C., 1959–91. (Online edition maintained by Andrew Toppan.)

Whitcomb, Darrel. *The Last Flight of Covey 87.* OV-10bronco.net.

PHOTOGRAPHY CREDITS

Collection of the author: pp. 28, 37, 56, 150, 153, 156, 162, 168, 171, 174, 180, 183, 193, 245 (*right*).

Air Force Magazine, Arlington, Virginia: pp. 112, 222, 224, 229, 230, 235, 239, 242, 245 (*left*), 249.

Army Aviation Museum, Fort Rucker, Alabama: pp. 254, 257, 260, 262, 266.

National Air and Space Museum Archives, Washington, D.C.: pp. 15, 33, 42 (*top*), 126, 132.

National Archives, College Park, Maryland: pp. 23, 51, 62, 64, 67, 73, 77, 79, 81, 83, 86, 89, 92, 94, 97, 100, 103, 106, 109, 115, 118, 121, 123, 129, 135, 138, 141.

Naval Aviation Museum Library, Pensacola, Florida: pp. 25, 39, 41, 42 (*inset*), 45, 145, 147, 159, 165, 177, 187, 190, 209, 212, 268, 271, 274.

United States Air Force Museum, Wright-Patterson Air Force Base, Ohio: pp. 19, 71, 198, 201, 204, 207, 219, 226, 232.

Douglas Walker, courtesy of the United States Air Force: p. 59.

INDEX

Boldface page numbers indicate illustrations